Conversations with
Dave Eggers

Literary Conversations Series
Monika Gehlawat
General Editor

Conversations with Dave Eggers

Edited by Scott F. Parker

University Press of Mississippi / Jackson

The University Press of Mississippi is the scholarly publishing agency of
the Mississippi Institutions of Higher Learning: Alcorn State University,
Delta State University, Jackson State University, Mississippi State University,
Mississippi University for Women, Mississippi Valley State University,
University of Mississippi, and University of Southern Mississippi.

www.upress.state.ms.us

The University Press of Mississippi is a member
of the Association of University Presses.

First printing 2022
∞

Library of Congress Cataloging-in-Publication Data

Names: Eggers, Dave, interviewee. | Parker, Scott F., editor.
Title: Conversations with Dave Eggers / Scott F. Parker.
Other titles: Literary conversations series.
Description: Jackson : University Press of Mississippi, 2022. |
   Series: Literary conversations series | Includes bibliographical
   references and index.
Identifiers: LCCN 2021040973 (print) | LCCN 2021040974 (ebook) |
   ISBN 9781496837851 (hardback) | ISBN 9781496837868 (trade paperback) |
   ISBN 9781496837875 (epub) | ISBN 9781496837882 (epub) |
   ISBN 9781496837899 (pdf) | ISBN 9781496837905 (pdf)
Subjects: LCSH: Eggers, Dave—Interviews. | Authors, American—
   21st century—Interviews. | Authors, American—United States—Interviews.
Classification: LCC PS3605.G48 Z46 2022 (print) | LCC PS3605.G48 (ebook) |
   DDC 818/.609—dc23/eng/20211012
LC record available at https://lccn.loc.gov/2021040973
LC ebook record available at https://lccn.loc.gov/2021040974

British Library Cataloging-in-Publication Data available

Works by Dave Eggers

Nonfiction

A Heartbreaking Work of Staggering Genius (2000)
Teachers Have It Easy: The Big Sacrifices and Small Salaries of America's Teachers
    (with Daniel Moulthrop and Nínive Clements Calegari, 2005)
Zeitoun (2009)
Understanding the Sky (2016)
The Monk of Mokha (2018)
Phoenix (2019)

Fiction

You Shall Know Our Velocity! (2002)
Sacrament (2003)
Jokes Told in Heaven About Babies (as Lucy Thomas, 2003)
The Unforbidden Is Compulsory; or, Optimism (2004)
How We Are Hungry (2004)
Short Short Stories (2005)
What Is the What: The Autobiography of Valentino Achak Deng (2006)
How the Water Feels to the Fishes (2007)
A Hologram for the King (2012)
The Circle (2013)
Your Fathers, Where Are They? And the Prophets, Do They Live Forever? (2014)
Heroes of the Frontier (2016)
The Parade (2019)
The Captain and the Glory (2019)
The Museum of Rain (2021)
The Every (2021)

Screenplays

Away We Go (with Vendela Vida, 2009)

Where the Wild Things Are (with Spike Jonze, 2009)
Promised Land (story by Eggers; screenplay by Matt Damon and John Krasinski, 2012)
A Hologram for the King (with Tom Tykwer, 2016)
The Circle (with James Ponsoldt, 2017)

For Young Readers

The Wild Things (2009)
When Marlana Pulled a Thread (2011)
This Bridge Will Not Be Gray (2015)
The Story of Captain Nemo (2016)
Her Right Foot (2017)
The Lifters (2018)
What Can a Citizen Do? (2018)
Tomorrow Most Likely (2019)
Abner & Ian Get Right-Side Up (2019)
Most of the Better Natural Things in the World (2019)
The Lights and Types of Ships at Night (2020)
We Became Jaguars (2021)
Faraway Things (2021)

Humor

Giraffes? Giraffes! (with Christopher Eggers, as Dr. and Mr. Doris Haggis-On-Whey, 2003)
Your Disgusting Head (with Christopher Eggers, as Dr. and Mr. Doris Haggis-On-Whey, 2004)
Animals of the Ocean, in Particular the Giant Squid (with Christopher Eggers,
    as Dr. and Mr. Doris Haggis-On-Whey, 2006)
Cold Fusion (with Christopher Eggers, as Dr. and Mr. Doris Haggis-On-Whey, 2009)
Children and the Tundra (with Christopher Eggers, as Dr. and Mr. Doris Haggis-On-
    Whey, 2016)

Art

It Is Right to Draw Their Fur: Animal Renderings (2010)
Ungrateful Mammals (2017)

As Editor

The Best American Nonrequired Reading series (2002–2013)

The Future Dictionary of America (with Jonathan Safran Foer, Nicole Krauss, and Eli
    Horowitz, 2004)
Created in Darkness by Troubled Americans: The Best of McSweeney's, Humor Category
    (with Kevin Shay, Lee Epstein, John Warner, and Suzanne Kleid, 2004)
Surviving Justice: America's Wrongfully Convicted and Exonerated (with Lola Vollen, 2005)
The Best of McSweeney's (with Jordan Bass, 2013)
The Voice of Witness Reader: Ten Years of Amplifying Unheard Voices (2015)

Notable Introductions

The Autobiographer's Handbook: The 826 National Guide to Writing Your Memoir,
    edited by Jennifer Traig (2008)
*Some Recollections of a Busy Life: The Forgotten Story of the Real Town of Hollister,
    California*, T. S. Hawkins (2016)
*Unnecessarily Beautiful Spaces for Young Minds on Fire: How 826 Valencia, and Dozens
    of Centers Like It, Got Built—and Why* (with Amanda Uhle), International Alliance
    of Youth Writing Centers (2020)

Contents

Introduction

The goal is to have fun and push forward, no?
—Dave Eggers

When it came time to write this introduction, I was tempted, reader, to offer you thousands upon thousands of words of analysis-cum-appreciation detailing the various phases of Dave Eggers's career, scrutinizing the cultural force he's been since founding *Might* magazine in 1994, evaluating his writing with every gasp of my critical wherewithal, and getting fairly deep into Eggers arcana.

Instead, I will make haste for the interviews themselves. Two reasons. First, it allows me to largely skirt the question of persona. As much as any writer of his generation, Eggers sees his reputation precede discussions of his work. He is the kind of literary figure about whom people have *opinions*. Indeed, I have my own. But when someone's standing is as overwrought as Eggers's is in the literary world, giving his interviews as much room as possible to speak for themselves seems not only fair but also the most fruitful way to proceed among the various ready-made reactions that pepper the discourse. Second, jumping right in aligns much better than any commentary could with my motivation for collecting these interviews in the first place. A book like this one has a simple conception: *I'd like to read a volume of Dave Eggers's interviews, and I bet others would too.* You're here, I figure, for the same reason I am. So instead of anything like literary scholarship, just this brief introduction to provide some context and background to the interviews.

Most of the early interviews in this volume were tracked down via links on Gary Baum's *FoE!* [Friend of Eggers] *Log* (accessed through the Internet Archive's Wayback Machine). Eggers belonging to the first generation of authors whose career has taken place entirely in the internet era (and, in his case, to a significant degree actually taken place online) means that exploring the trenches of the web reveals a veritable treasure chest of Eggers ephemera. It makes for a deep dive into an essentially bottomless pool.

I'm very pleased with what I have been able to bring to the surface, beginning with Eggers's 1993 interview with the *Daily Illini,* his alma mater's student newspaper. Eggers is only recently removed from the University of Illinois in Champaign-Urbana here, returning to discuss his first magazine, *Might,* with what will become his signature ethos already taking form: "If I could have a goal," he tells Adam Wolfe, "it would be to get people motivated and give up complaining about what we don't have and come together and work our asses off for what we want."

The next interview included here, from the *Village Voice,* catches Eggers in the brief but crucial period during which he has launched his second magazine, *Timothy McSweeney's Quarterly Concern,* but has not yet become a household name.

Beginning in 2000, around the publication of *A Heartbreaking Work of Staggering Genius,* the interviews proliferate. Eggers finds himself suddenly a literary celebrity forced to grapple with the effects of fame in real time. And because his grappling takes an unorthodox form (see his public appearances discussed in the early interviews of this book), almost no one in this period, perhaps not even Eggers himself, seems capable of discerning what is performance art and what isn't.

But as great an interest as the media takes in him, its reductive tendencies are real to Eggers and acutely felt. After his iconic manifesto that concludes his frustrating (to him) email interview with the *Harvard Advocate* and his very public dustup with David D. Kirkpatrick over Kirkpatrick's portrayal of him in the *New York Times,*[1] Eggers distances himself from interviewers through the middle part of the decade. Responding to a question from a reader in an interview published at *McSweeney's Internet Tendency* around the release of his second book, *You Shall Know Our Velocity!,* but not included here, Eggers explains,

> Last time around, Geoff Kloske, my editor at Simon & Schuster, made me promise to help do publicity for the book. He gave me an advance that allowed me to quit my job, and he did that based on a few pages of notes I'd sent him. I was really grateful to him because he took a huge chance on me based on his instincts and courage, and the trade-off was that I'd do interviews to help them sell the books and make their money back. So I did a lot of interviews. I honestly didn't know I was allowed to say no to people. But this time I have to. It's just too much pressure to deal with while trying to concentrate on everything at 826 [the nonprofit writing and tutoring center Eggers founded in San Francisco]. If it turns weird

like it did last time around, and we all get distracted trying to correct the record all the time, we won't have time to run the center well, so we're just gonna bow out quietly this time around.

When Eggers takes interviews up again in earnest around the publication of *Zeitoun* in 2009, time has passed, celebrity has settled, and the occasional antipathy between interviewer and subject has dissipated. Eggers has metamorphosed rather dramatically in the public eye from something of an *enfant terrible* to an established and respected statesman of the literary community. He comes across in the interviews of the 2010s as optimistic and generous, just as he did in the 2000s, but now he's wiser and mellower too. This mellow wisdom reaches perhaps its zenith in Eggers's 2019 appearance on *The Ezra Klein Show*, which culminates in something like an impromptu dharma talk on the nature of attention.

The podcast with Klein is well worth listening to, but a transcript is not included here. A surfeit of material on the Eggers scale and the practical constraints of a book make it easy for an editor to respect a divide between one medium and another. I encourage the reader to read the text interviews and listen to the recordings that are readily available online.

In the decade following *Zeitoun*, as Eggers has written for children as well as for adults, and as his educational and philanthropic ventures have continued to expand, his interviews have followed apace. In addition to coming from traditional literary venues, the interviews collected here are drawn from blogs, various trade publications, international magazines, and student newspapers, and focus on subjects ranging across philanthropy, education, oral history, art, international and domestic politics, as well as his books. In selecting interviews for this book, I have done my best to reflect the range of Eggers's projects, even, inevitably, as some of them (including books like *Your Fathers, Where Are They? And the Prophets, Do They Live Forever?* and *Heroes of the Frontier*) largely fall through the cracks.

While protective of his time and privacy, Eggers has effectively determined his response to the dilemma he described to Kirkpatrick early in his career: "I endlessly see-saw between wanting to publish and tell stories because why the hell not, and then thinking maybe I should just go somewhere and dig ditches and have a quiet life." He's still on the see-saw, but he's seemingly balanced the thing. He's a public figure, to be sure, but on his own terms. Many of his interviews are still conducted over email with his approval needed for edits, a practice he adopted early in his career.

Which brings us just about to the present. At the time of this writing, in mid-2020, Eggers is fifty. This book will almost certainly need updating in the future. Three interviews in this book are from the first half of this year alone. And by the time you are reading it, I expect there will have been more. Nevertheless, now is a good time to gather and read Eggers's interviews from the past quarter century. His career has been a living, growing, changing, surprising thing to witness, and to take stock of it *in medias res* is to take some pleasure in the luxury of a limited perspective. A retrospective such as this one is necessarily also prospective of the unknown.

And if by the end of the book you should find your appetite not yet sated, there are plenty of notable interviews with Eggers that are not included here. Among the best of these are the following:

Bookworm, Michael Silverblatt, KCRW
  "David Eggers" (April 6, 2000)
  "Dave Eggers" (June 22, 2000)
  "Dave Eggers" (September 19, 2002)
  "Dave Eggers" (February 10, 2005)
  "Dave Eggers" (February 1, 2007)
  "Dave Eggers: A Hologram for the King" (July 5, 2012)
  "Mokhtar Alkhanshali and Dave Eggers: The Monk of Mokha" (March 8, 2018)
  "Dave Eggers: The Parade" (May 30, 2019)
"Some Complaining about Complaining," Jonathan Lethem, *McSweeney's Internet Tendency* (2000)
"3 Things You Should Know Before Reading This," Sam Jemielity, *Chicago Tribune* (March 1, 2000)
"The Agony and the Irony," Stephanie Merritt, *The Guardian* (May 13, 2000)
"Around the World in a Week," Andy Borowitz, *New Yorker* (August 12, 2002)
"Readers Interview Dave Eggers," *McSweeney's Internet Tendency* (2002)
"Dave Eggers," Tasha Robinson, *Onion A.V. Club* (February 23, 2005)
"The Believer," David Amsden, *Salon* (March 10, 2005)
"A Muslim American Hero: A Conversation with Dave Eggers," Ali Wajahat, *Huffington Post* (September 7, 2009)
"Dave Eggers on His Favorite Things about Newspapers," Scott Gordon, *Onion A.V. Club* (January 5, 2010)
"Talking with Dave Eggers about 'A Hologram for the King,'" Cressida Leyshon, *New Yorker* (June 19, 2012)
"Dave Eggers: The Art Believer," Evan Pricco, *Juxtapoz* (August 2, 2016)
"Dave Eggers Author of the American Conscience," *52 Insights* (August 20, 2016)
"Writer Dave Eggers Assembles Youth Summit to Keep Lifting Up Student Voices After Parkland," Max Larkin, WBUR (June 1, 2018)

"Dave Eggers: 'I Always Picture Trump Hiding under a Table,'" Paul Laity, *The Guardian* (June 22, 2018)
"Author Dave Eggers in Conversation with President Barack Obama," Obama Foundation Summit 2018 (November 19, 2018)
"Dave Eggers: 'Being around Young People Is the Balm to All Psychic Wounds,'" Lisa O'Kelly, *The Guardian* (March 16, 2019)
"Having a Bad Day? Dave Eggers Can Help," Ezra Klein, *The Ezra Klein Show* (November 18, 2019)

■ ■ ■

The only edits I have made to the original interviews are silent corrections of book titles, typographical inconsistencies, clear solecisms, and obvious mistakes of fact. To limit redundancy, I have excluded some of the introductions that attended the original publications of these interviews.

I would like to thank all the copyright holders who granted the necessary permissions to make this book possible. Special thanks to Abbey Gaterud for her help in the archives. Amanda Uhle was a consultant, an ally, and a delight to work with. Thank you, Amanda. Thanks also to Dave Eggers for his cooperation with the project and his willingness to be interviewed for it. Finally, thanks to Mary Heath and the rest of the University Press of Mississippi staff for giving me the opportunity to take on this project.

SFP

Note

1. To include the Kirkpatrick interview would have necessitated including the fallout of the Kirkpatrick interview, which would have accounted for too great a share of the book. Interested readers may wish to begin with Eliza Truitt's recap of the exchange at https://slate.com/culture/2001/02/culturebox-rules-dave-eggers-vs-david-kirk patrick.html.

Chronology

1970   Born March 12 in Boston, Massachusetts, to John K. Eggers and Heidi McSweeney Eggers.

1973   Moves to Lake Forest, Illinois.

1991   John dies of brain and lung cancer.

1992   Heidi dies of stomach cancer; Eggers leaves the University of Illinois at Urbana–Champaign to help care for eight-year-old brother, Christopher. Moves with Christopher to Berkeley, California, where their sister, Beth, attends law school.

1994–97   Edits *Might*, a satirical magazine cofounded with David Moodie and Marny Requa.

1998   Founds the publishing company McSweeney's and literary journal *Timothy McSweeney's Quarterly Concern*.

2001   Receives Addison M. Metcalf Award in Literature from the American Academy of Arts and Letters; Beth commits suicide.

2002   Opens 826 Valencia, a nonprofit writing and tutoring center in San Francisco, with Nínive Calegari.

2003   Marries Vendela Vida; named Story Teller of the Year at the Independent Publisher Book Awards for *You Shall Know Our Velocity!* and for founding McSweeney's Books.

2005   With Lola Vollen, launches the Voice of Witness (VOW) oral history book series.

2006   With Valentino Achak Deng, founds VAD Foundation, an organization that provides educational opportunities and supports sustainable development initiatives in South Sudan; receives *Salon* Book Award for *What Is the What*.

2007   Receives Heinz Award for contributions to the arts and humanities; receives gold medal for General Fiction at the Independent Publisher Book Awards for *What Is the What*.

2008   Receives TED Prize. Helps found 826 National to coordinate the growth the 826 centers across the country.

2009   Cofounds Zeitoun Foundation, a nonprofit dedicated to rebuilding New Orleans after Hurricane Katrina; receives National Book Award's Literarian Award; receives Prix Médicis award for *What Is the What*; receives *Los Angeles Times* Book Prize for Current Interest (*Zeitoun*) and the *Los Angeles Times* Book Prize Innovator's Award.

2010   Founds ScholarMatch, an organization that supports first-generation college students; receives the American Book Award and the Dayton Literary Peace Prize for *Zeitoun*.

2011   Receives PEN Center USA Award of Honor.

2012   Receives Inforum's 21st Century Visionary Award from the Commonwealth Club.

2013   With Mimi Lok, receives the *Smithsonian* magazine's American Ingenuity Award for Social Progress.

2015   Inducted into the American Academy of Arts and Letters.

2018   With Amanda Uhle, cofounds the International Congress of Youth Voices; receives Muhammad Ali Humanitarian Award for Education.

Conversations with
Dave Eggers

Might Be Interesting: Former UI Student Dave Eggers Serves Up a Magazine for a New Breed of Readers

Adam Wolfe / 1993

"To CHANGE the things you want to, you have to get out of bed.
To BE where you want to be, you have to get off the train.
To SKI through a revolving door, you need great timing.
To HAVE it your way you have to know how you want it."

These are only some of the powerful ideals that drive *Might*, a new magazine for post–high school adults. If you just read this and had any of the following reactions to it, you may as well go on and read the next article:

1. "Yeah! I want to read about Axl Rose's latest narrow
   escape from the St. Louis police!"
2. "I hope they talk about Luke Perry for at least fifty
   pages. He's so HOT! (Immature squeal)"
3. "All right! What I really need is some overpaid
   airhead to tell me how to dress!"

Might is a shockingly new breed of magazine. It combines important issues, fiction, satire, dreams, new perspectives, and a large dose of humor to form a reading experience unlike anything anyone's ever known.

David Eggers, the dreamer who conceived and published *Might*, feels that *Might* will provide a much-needed alternative to those "music rags" and "make-up magazines" that plague our generation's popular culture today.

"There's a certain insult to our intelligence," said Eggers. "[Other publishers] feel that the only way to get to [our generation] is to tell us what to wear or what celebrities are doing. We felt that there was a different story to tell, apart from the usual baloney."

Might is about a different look at the world. "It's a word we've always kicked around," Eggers said. He chose it because of both of its meanings. "Might means that the possibilities are open to you"—all we can say for sure is what might happen. The other meaning Eggers cited is "might" as strength and power. Combining the uncertainty and the power of "might," Eggers feels, brings out the whole point of the magazine.

Eggers, a university alumnus, has been learning the value of making dreams come true ever since high school, where he worked on a literary magazine called *Young Idea*. While at YI, he developed skills in computer design.

Moving on to the university, Eggers gained experience in virtually every aspect of newspaper production from the *Daily Illini*, working as a photographer, writer, graphic artist, and "The Directory" entertainment section editor. His work on the paper fascinated him so much that he changed his major from art to journalism.

During the second semester of senior year in college, tragedy struck Eggers. His parents had both been afflicted with cancer for some time, and he had spent every weekend going home to visit with them and take care of the family in general.

Within six months of each other, both of his parents died, leaving Eggers, his sister (a law student at University of California–Berkeley), and his eight-year-old brother to watch out for each other. As soon as he graduated in May 1992, Eggers took his brother to live with their sister in San Francisco, where they live today.

Eggers described his response to the tragedy by saying, "With homework, most of us don't do the assignment until the day before, because we can see the deadline looming before us. . . . Watching my parents die, I saw my deadline. I saw what space I had to live in." Eggers believes that it takes an event as shocking as the one he suffered through to wake people up to living and being.

"From where I stood, I could see both the beginning and the end," Eggers said. This event motivated him to turn his near decade of dreams into a reality.

Eggers had noticed ever since high school that popular young-adult magazines were "ignoring the soul of our generation." He envisioned a magazine that explored the future, getting to the core of making things happen.

"We'll teach you how to get from working in a coffee shop to standing on a Greenpeace ship," Eggers said of *Might*. For him the project is a dream come true, and he wants to see everyone fulfill personal goals as he did.

However, before he could build his dream Eggers needed a starting point. In San Francisco he landed a job, thanks to his computer experience, on various newspapers, such as the *San Francisco Chronicle* and *San Francisco Weekly*. He eventually became an editorial cartoonist.

Establishing his career, Eggers estimates that he was working an average of one hundred hours a week. He made those hours pay off, though.

Together with a friend from Chicago and the freelance client base he had built up, Eggers rented an office, and *Might*, a mere fantasy that he and his friends had batted around in high school, began to really take shape. Their starting capital came from the surplus profit in their design business, and *Might* started recruiting writers and artists.

"The main thing is hard work," Eggers said. "I tell people you can do what you want to do and live life on your own terms, but getting started on your own is at least four times harder." Eggers is now balancing his work in his design business and his work on *Might*, along with taking care of his brother, now ten. Although he works late into the night, he is thankful for doing the work he loves.

Eggers's story is a perfect example of his goals for *Might*. "If I could have a goal," he said, "it would be to get people motivated and give up complaining about what we don't have and come together and work our asses off for what we want."

"It's not about 'self-help,'" Eggers said. "We don't pity ourselves." He doesn't want to see people dwell on their problems. "I abhor introspection to the point of apathy," he said.

While these sentiments may sound like material for an underground publication, *Might* is not intended as such. While many publishers of current magazines may consider it to be an alternative magazine, Eggers wants to see *Might* become a bit more widespread. "The more people we reach, the better," Eggers said.

Although his goals may seem lofty, Eggers believes that too many people are satisfied doing things they really don't like to do, just for the sake of making other people happy or making money.

"I did some calculations. You only need about $18,000 to live for a year. What do you do with the other money? How much money do you need to be happy? If you have to make that money by doing a job you hate, then fuck it." According to Eggers, dollars are motivating people today more than dreams.

He noted that our "standard of living is still high, despite crime, drugs, and disease. . . . Because the media has been barreling us with bad news, we think that the future is bleak."

While he could not comment definitively on the personal future of each of his readers, Eggers's outlook is bright for himself and for *Might*. He wants to see people make something of themselves and is trying to help. Eggers said of the future of *Might*, "As long as we're fresh and have different things to say, we'll do it. I'm just hoping this will be something we can live off of."

These are the reasons for *Might*: to provide an alternative to fad, fashion, and music rags that insult our intelligence. "It's all drivel . . . there's such a chasm where our generation is concerned," said Eggers. "It's easy to get lulled into a sense of . . . huh. It's easy not to feel."

"*Might* looks unlike anything else, ever." It uses humor to show the writers' new perspective on life. Eggers intends to attack and satirize everything, from the "exploitation of Generation X" to the traditions of wearing suits and shaving legs. "We want to redefine the 'American Dream' in a way," Eggers said.

Eggers feels that his main point is that right now, while we have no lifetime ties or responsibilities, is the time to do what we've always wanted to do.

Might makes use of a fresh, humorous perspective of the world, but is about waking up to life. The outrageous graphics and stories are just parts of someone else's dream, there to stimulate our own into action.

Eggers hopes that readers will ask themselves, "Why wait? Why not pursue what I want most right now?" Of his work, Eggers explained, "I don't own a suit. I wear anything I want every day to work. I have no pension, no health plan, and no security, but at least I'm happy."

If you are interested in ordering a subscription to *Might*, orders should be sent to *Might* magazine, 544 Second St., San Francisco, CA 94107. The premiere issue costs $3.50, and a six-issue (one-year) subscription costs $20. Make checks payable to *Might*. The expected launch date for the magazine is January 17, so hurry up and subscribe. Also, if you want to contribute any work to the magazine or make comments, send mail to the above address.

Mighty *McSweeney's*

Matt Goldberg / 1999

It's common in the magazine business to see talented editorial folks get jobs at glossy corporate pubs once their underfunded labors of love finally go down the drain. But even the most jaded media observers were surprised when David Eggers became an editor at *Esquire* in the wake of the much bemoaned demise of *Might* magazine a few years back. With Eggers and friends at the helm, *Might* had taken on every brand of poseur and pretender that American culture has to offer.

So it came as less of a shock when Eggers resigned in September. As he prepared to jump ship, Eggers scored a book deal from Simon & Schuster, so, as he puts it, he'd have "a way to pay rent." Collecting a book advance, it seems, prompted Eggers to conceive of a new publication, one that wouldn't be nearly as contemporary as *Might* and wouldn't even be, technically, a magazine, lacking as it would regular departments, features, and columns (not to mention pictures and artwork).

The result is *McSweeney's Quarterly Concern*, a journal that comprises killed articles and odd, obliquely humorous experiments culled from Eggers's circle of former *Might* cronies, as well as from a few A-list scribes like Rick Moody and David Foster Wallace (none of whom get paid). Some of *Might's* more devout followers report being disappointed at the lack of current, media-centric editorial in *McSweeney's*—especially in its just published second issue—but Eggers says they'll have to get over it. Or at least go to the website.

Because there's obviously a website, as there always is these days. Even if you're Eggers, alone in a Brooklyn apartment in your underwear, producing the site on a six-year-old computer with one free megabyte of memory (which is either very refreshing or unfortunately reminiscent of 1995). Eggers originally saw the web as a cheap and timely way to publish sarcastic, ephemeral rants about pop culture and the media. Indeed, one of the site's biggest draws is a serialized feature called "The Service Industry," in which the editor and other unnamed guest authors eviscerate just the sort of people that Eggers worked for at *Esquire*.

But just as "The Service Industry" started winning over readers and attracting more site traffic—and subscriptions to the journal—Eggers's interest waned. Barely any new episodes have been posted in recent weeks, a situation the editor is loath to remedy (though he admits a few more are in the works). "People were livid when we stopped doing as much of that," Eggers says. "But my worst fear of all is that it become repetitive." Instead, he posted the first installment of a three-part, five-thousand-word interview with an epidemiologist specializing in viruses transmitted by bugs. Visit the site (McSweeneys.net) while you can, because it's hard to know what you'll find the next time you look. Which for Eggers is precisely the point.

Village Voice: You've just published the second issue of *McSweeney's*. How does it compare with the first issue?

David Eggers: The quarterly is a weird, esoteric thing. I wanted the new issue to have a lot of hard-core science stuff. There's a fascinating interview with a mathematician that I modeled after the *Paris Review* interviews—it looks exactly the same. There's also a piece positing that Supreme Court decisions are actually decided on the basketball court. It runs about fourteen pages, with diagrams. It takes a certain kind of reader to invest that much time in a lengthy piece of comic fiction or satire.

VV: How is *McSweeney's* different from *Might*?

DE: *McSweeney's* has less edge. At *Might* we were sneering, and everything had this gnashing tone—because we were angry. *McSweeney's* is more banal. It's the same reason I can only read *Suck* once every few weeks, because it's like having someone shouting in your ear.

VV: How many subscribers do you have?

DE: Over five hundred, which to me is an unbelievable number. It took five people three and a half hours to get the mailing together. And it's taken me four days to mail them out. We filled up the blue mailboxes in front of the pizza place to the point where you couldn't get them open, and this woman came up behind us and couldn't get her letter in. And she was just livid.

VV: You also put up a website. Why?

DE: I get really itchy if I don't have somewhere to publish things. I have all these friends with no forum for their weird satire and exercises, so we use the web to put up reactive things in a timely way. The beauty of the website is that we're not answering to anybody. Early on, some people who hook up alterna websites with advertising came calling, but I'm not interested in any of that. There will never be any money exchanged in connection with the *McSweeney's* website.

VV: Do you have any interest in making the site more interactive?

DE: I've never found chat groups that interesting. I'm not even a huge web reader, though I think *The Onion* is the best use of the English language in my lifetime. But my computer is from 1990, and I have a really slow web connection. I might do all that stuff if it didn't take any time. But the idea is not to spend too much time on this stuff.

VV: But don't the quarterly and the site take up a good deal of your time?

DE: Oh God, no. Not even remotely. With the quarterly, it's three weeks of intense work. With the web—and I don't mean this to sound glib—it's about a half hour a day, unless I'm writing something. I don't do much editing. If people send me stuff and it's good, I just put it up. If it isn't, I just send it back.

VV: If *McSweeney's* doesn't take up that much time, what have you been doing since quitting *Esquire*?

DE: Well, I quit to write a book. A semiautobiographical nonfiction novel. I'm designing the book and have total control over all the packaging. I'm even inputting the corrections.

VV: Are you reluctant to do the publicity that Simon & Schuster will ask of you?

DE: I don't mind going out and meeting people who buy it. At *Might* we had parties every month or so and invited the local subscribers. But if I have to read, I'm not sure that would work out. I'm not such a great reader. Maybe we could have pool parties instead of readings.

VV: Would you have bailed on *Esquire* even if you didn't get a book deal? It was clearly not your cup of tea.

DE: I'm not sure how long I could've lasted there. Obviously, I think there are a lot of things wrong with most glossy magazines. It's an unfortunate clash between a crass, commercial enterprise and some wonderfully creative people who want to create art, or the closest thing to it under the circumstances. It's so rare for someone who writes passionately about something late at night in their apartment to ever really find the right reader.

VV: Didn't the web help those people out?

DE: For so many years I was such a skeptic about the web. But it's a truly beautiful medium. You can retain a level of purity that you can't achieve almost anywhere else. No distributors, no people to pay off, no grocery stores, or all the other stuff that goes on with large-circulation magazines—all of which is so depressing that I can't even think about it.

VV: Isn't the web in danger of getting too commercial itself?

DE: Maybe. *Salon* is trying to make it as a commercial enterprise. People criticize them for having too [many articles about] sex, and [for] the whole Henry Hyde thing. But I don't think there's a move they've made that I wouldn't have made in the same situation. They just have so many people to answer to, so many people have pumped money into it, so many employees—that sort of thing doesn't intrigue me as much anymore.

VV: Do you ever wish *Might* were still around?

DE: I don't think things like that are supposed to last. If it were still around, I think I'd be really depressed and bored and lifeless. In my heart, I knew it would never be a way to pay the rent. Back in San Francisco, once Dave Moodie and I had done the mind-numbing graphic design work that paid the bills, we'd work until two or three in the morning on *Might*—even if we didn't have to. It was like an endurance contest, and whoever left first was a kind of traitor. There was a lot of peer pressure. A few people dropped out. They said, "You guys are morons." And they were right.

VV: How are things different now?

DE: I do as much as I can do well. I've tried to lower people's expectations. We might not put something new up on the site every day; it might not always be humor. But this is why I'm home in my underwear. So I don't have to answer to this feeling of obligation, to deadlines or what the audience expects. I don't think that has any place in the artistic process. I try not to be contemptuous of readers, who I very much appreciate. But I have no interest in meeting expectations. I'd much rather confound them.

Email from a Staggering Genius

Caryn B. Brooks / 2000

From *Willamette Week*, February 23, 2000. © 2000 by *Willamette Week*. Reprinted by permission.

When Dave Eggers was orphaned at age twenty-one, he took custody of his eight-year-old brother, Toph, and lived to write about it. He wouldn't talk to us on the phone. We didn't really care.

WEDNESDAY, FEBRUARY 9, 2000 9:30:10 AM
FROM: CBROOKS@WWEEK.COM
SUBJECT: FYI, DAVE EGGERS
TO: MZUSMAN@WWEEK.COM

Mark,

FYI, I'm thinking of running a story on Dave Eggers. Remember *Might* magazine in the early 1990s? They nailed the media to the wall and sifted the zeitgeist of those insanely disaffected Gen-Xers. They ran cover stories about whether Black people are cooler than white people, started this hilarious column rating people's gayness, and in one memorable issue colluded with Adam Rich, of *Eight Is Enough* fame, to fake his death and write an over-the-top memorial that was picked up by many, many news sources as fact.

Might fell victim to the thing that claims most energetic projects started by people in their twenties (lack of funds), and Eggers went to work at *Esquire* magazine. Of course he didn't like it there. Too much T & A and Q & A and R & D etc. He then started a website and literary mag called *McSweeney's* (bookmark this baby: www.mcsweeneys.net) that takes on some of the same issues as *Might*, but in a more composed, literary, and altogether mature and interesting way (he gets people like Rick Moody and David Foster Wallace to contribute to the quarterly, but even the letters on the website are compelling). One of my favorite features on the site is this series they did called "The Service Industry" that is just a recounting of dialogue and scenarios from various jobs, mostly media-related. There's also the series called "The Top 10 Most Censored Press Releases" and, of course, "Interviews with Drivers of Lunch Trucks."

Now he's just released a book called *A Heartbreaking Work of Staggering Genius*. It's a memoir of sorts. When Eggers was twenty-one, both of his parents died of unrelated cancers within a five-week period, and he took over custody of his eight-year-old brother, Toph. But wait, there's more. Yes, you've got your loss, your love, your hope, your career, your family, as most of these tell-all books do. But Eggers is able to zoom in on the orphan in us all. He uses a lot of unconventional writing styles to engage you (he offers "rules and suggestions for enjoyment of this book" and often breaks out of a scene to speak directly to the reader). I know it sounds gimmicky, but it's effective in drawing you in. I haven't been this seduced by a book in quite a while. He's coming to Powell's. I am trying to get an interview, but apparently he's no longer doing phoners. I can get an email interview, though; I'll let you know how it goes.

Caryn

FRIDAY, FEBRUARY 18, 2000 11:53:30 AM
FROM: CBROOKS@WWEEK.COM
SUBJECT: CALLING DAVE EGGERS
TO: MCSWEENEYS@EARTHLINK.NET

Hello Dave Eggers,

I was set up for a phone interview with you, but then I was told by your harried publicist that "Dave doesn't do phone interviews anymore," and that our only way to communicate was via email.

I am pushing aside my fears that

1. I am not really communicating with Dave but most likely a stand-in, and the result of this media "experiment" might run on the *McSweeney's* site. Ha ha, hee hee.

2. You will not respond to my email by the God-demanded time of 5:00 p.m. Pacific Standard Time this Saturday, February 19, and I will be left with a huge, gaping hole in the paper where the interview was supposed to go.

3. Your refusal to answer my questions will make me not like you. I really want to like you because I think your book is fucking amazing.

Attached are the questions:

Thanks for your time, Dave.

Caryn

SUNDAY, FEBRUARY 20, 2000 6:51:12 AM
MESSAGE FROM:
MCSWEENEYS@EARTHLINK.NET
SUBJECT: RE: CALLING DAVE EGGERS
TO: CBROOKS@WWEEK.COM

Caryn,

A few questions I skipped. Hope this is all okay.

DE

Caryn Brooks: In AHWOSG you do a lot of *McSweeney's*-style antics. You include a list of "rules and suggestions" for reading the book (for example, you tell readers they might want to skip a chunk of the middle of the book because it concerns "the lives of people in their early twenties, and those lives are very difficult to make interesting"). On the copyright page you list your physical attributes and rate your gayness. But the meat of the book is not really antic-filled; it's as if the antics were a moat to keep certain kinds of people away. Because really, most anyone could grab on to your book. This could be an Oprah Book Club selection. Maybe you didn't want that. Your thoughts?

Dave Eggers: You pretty well got it. Obviously, the preface and acknowledgments sections are a sort of stalling. That sort of thing, where you inhabit some safe, even if unusual, context—like a copyright page or whatever—is easier than writing a straight-ahead linear narrative about your mother's slow death. So I stall with the gimmickry until I can't stall anymore. But everything I do is about or as a result of stalling. *McSweeney's* came about as I was stalling on the book proposal (which I never actually completed). While I stall on *McSweeney's* I draw a lot. While I stall on the drawing I write silly things under pseudonyms. While I'm stalling on these things, usually very very late at night, I call friends in San Francisco and LA; anyone who's still awake. I pity my friends on your coast.

CB: *Might* magazine tried to invert the media machine, often by using media celebs to make fun of themselves. I get a sense from your book that you now kind of regret some of those things, that eviscerating these people was the result of envy and bitterness. What made you change your mind? Has your own little bit of fame given you some clarity on the proceedings?

DE: That's exactly it. The world of journalism is inhabited by both the good-hearted sort, who feel no need to bring down anyone simply because they're enjoying some success, and the bitter sort, who wish *they* were acting in movies or running for Senate or whatever, and thus sublimate their bitterness through cheap shots and sniping. We were definitely the latter type. We tore into famous people simply because they were famous and we were not. And that's what a lot of journalists do: they seek to even the playing field between themselves and whatever famous person du jour with little jabs and supposedly telling observations meant to embarrass their subject. No one wants to be an acolyte, or part of the chorus, so the writer who has something to prove must stand apart and say mean or speculative things, to make clear that they are apart from the pack, that they think independently.

For example, a while back, an interviewer from a daily newspaper talked to me, and we got along, and she very much liked my book, and all seemed well with the world. Well, she then talked to her editor there, and that editor, in the wake of some of the publicity the book had gotten, wanted to slant the piece in a new way; he no longer wanted the piece he had agreed upon, a normal piece about the book and *McSweeney's*. He now wanted coverage of the coverage, and he wanted it to be contrarian. Which is unsettling, because now editors are dictating the content, and the writer's interpretation of her subject, not according to the truth, but in reaction to whatever else is out there. Again, all things I've done as an editor and a writer, but hard to take being the subject.

CB: What was the soundtrack for writing this book?

DE: I'll talk about one song I listened to.

Every so often, I leave Brooklyn and rent a room in whatever motel I can find in central Connecticut—the usual *no phones, no email, get some work done goddamnit* motivation. When I was really needing to finish this book, I stayed out there, at a motel on the highway frequented by prostitutes and their men, for about a week. Shortly after getting there, I realized that I had forgotten any kind of music-playing device, and my CDs. Which is a problem, because I listen to music every second I work, all played on a little Sony portable thing a friend left at my house a few years ago.

So after a day of losing my mind with the silence and sounds of porno playing in adjoining rooms—it came standard at this motel—I finally remembered that my computer has a built-in CD player. (I am always slow to come to such realizations.) So I went out to the Wiz off the highway to buy a CD or two, and ended up getting Beth Orton's *Central Reservation*. Then I did what I always do: I latched on to a particular song, in this case "Sweetest Decline," and listened to that one song, on a continuous loop, for the next six days. No joke. I tend to try to wear a song out, to rid myself of it. But that song, I still haven't solved. I still listen to it for days on end.

CB: I see that you reviewed Lorrie Moore's *Birds of America* for *Salon*. I see that you are a Lorrie Moore fan. I see some similarities between yourself and Moore, the way you both are able to plumb the souls of your "characters," and you both are (in your words) "funny and mean." Your thoughts?

DE: Lorrie Moore was my first huge infatuation, writer-wise. I was in college when someone gave me *Anagrams*, and after that I devoured everything she wrote. For a while I was writing a lot like her, but soon enough realized that I couldn't write as carefully as she does—I'm too hyper and messy, I guess.

But the main thing I like about her is that she has, in interviews, made the case that any book without humor—and I'm paraphrasing horribly here—isn't really accurately reflecting human experience, because everyone laughs, all the time. Try going to the store to buy a newspaper without the clerk bantering with you. Or even in the saddest relationships, when someone slams a door and gets in her car, it's as likely as not that she's going to come back, because she forgot her keys, and you're both going to laugh, even when you want to kill each other. It's always there.

So when people point out Moore's sense of humor, and how very funny things happen in her very sad stories, it's not so much that she does what she does, but why don't others do it more often?

CB: Would you ever want your book to be turned into a movie under any circumstances? If so, what would those circumstances be?

DE: It's a really hard thing, that notion.

As you may know, there are people in Los Angeles willing to pay a great deal of money for this story. Enough money to make real a lot of *McSweeney's*'s [how weird does that look?] dreams, chiefly the hope that we could make *McSweeney's* into a publishing company, producing a dozen or so books a year, on top of the quarterly. Beautiful, odd, uncommercial books that otherwise will never see the light of day. But then I'd have to live with this movie, and even if it's a good movie—and I am pretty sure, given who has expressed interest, that those making it would be good-movie-making people—Toph and I still have to walk around, forever, having been characters in a movie. It would be endlessly surreal, and I'm not sure it would be worth it.

But I haven't ruled it out. But I would hope, desperately, that they wouldn't try to make a faithful adaptation. There wouldn't be a way to do that well. So if someone made sort of a corollary work of art, taking the book as a starting-off point for something more strange and structurally odd, that might be good.

CB: What are you reading right now?

DE: Right now I'm doing a lot of research into the history of the fetus in medical drawings, so I have a lot of old books and anatomy manuals around.

Actual-book-wise, I'm in the middle of something called *Chang and Eng*, by Darin Strauss, due out in the summer. It's a novel about the lives of the famous Siamese twins of the nineteenth century, and so far it's really great. Extremely vivid and evocative, but very funny, too. I mean, these men, who were repeatedly almost killed because of their freakdom, ended up living in North Carolina, married to sisters. The story gets weirder and weirder.

I love historical fiction, though I read too little of it. You know what else is great? Gore Vidal's *1876*. I also recommend to everyone George Saunders's new book, *Pastoralia*. And Sarah Vowell's *Take the Cannoli*.

CB: Does your social life revolve around *McSweeney's*?

DE: No. My social life revolves around the same friends I've had since fifth grade, most of whom live out here or in San Francisco. I almost never do media-oriented events, because I get incredibly tired of talking about magazines and publishing. I like hearing about babies and football, which is what my longer-term friends like talking about. Very few of my best friends have any interest in any of this stuff. They roll their eyes.

CB: Do you think boys will like your book more than girls, or do you think it might be an even draw?

DE: So far it seems like a draw. The odd thing is that anyone likes it at all, I think. Older people, who I figured would hate it, have been very kind. It's all really confusing. I tried to make something ugly and I guess I failed.

CB: Are you happy?

DE: Yes. No. Yes.

CB: What has been the response at readings you've done so far? I've read that you're kind of uncomfortable reading in public. Is that going away?

DE: I had never read aloud before last week, in San Francisco, where I started the book tour. I don't come from that tradition, the creative-writing-class/seminar/school tradition, where you write and read aloud and are critiqued. So all this is new. But I have been to a ton of readings, and always found them a little unnecessarily boring, even when I've really liked the author reading. So I try to entertain a little, with guest speakers and audience participation.

For the first New York reading I had two go-go dancers, male and female, who danced on a table behind me while I read. I think that went over pretty well. Afterward, we chartered a bus and took about fifty attendees to a bar near the Newark airport. Everyone got blitzed, and some of the people, strangers before the bus, ended up hooking up at the bar. It was pretty great.

In San Francisco I had a fireman open the show, Lt. Fernando Juarez of the SFFD, who spoke for about ten minutes about fire safety in the home. When he said "stop, drop, and roll" I almost fainted. Maybe I'm just trying [to] distract people from my own poor oratory skills. But he had brochures, too, and everyone likes a good brochure.

CB: Are you interested in writing fiction next?

DE: Yes. Fiction will save me from myself.

CB: Some people kind of get off on creating a flurry of both positive and negative press. You seem to be able to use humor as a diversion for the rest of your life; why not now?

DE: When I was in San Francisco, I had a cartoon for about five years that ran every week. I got lots of hate mail, lots of nice mail. And the hate mail rarely affected me. But for some reason—and I've talked to other writers who say the same thing—with certain projects you can become more sensitive, unwillingly. Maybe I'm just tired.

CB: Anything special planned for your Portland visit? Should we expect a straight reading or something a little more riotous?

DE: No plans yet. I tend to put the shows together the day before, so we'll see. But I recommend everyone bring their boots.

Brother Knows Best

Amy Benfer / 2000

Let it be known that Dave Eggers does not want to be interviewed.

In the past month, the editor of *McSweeney's*, a literary quarterly that even *Harper's* magazine editor Lewis Lapham thinks is hip, and the author of a "memoir-y kind of thing" called *A Heartbreaking Work of Staggering Genius*, has been interviewed by the *New York Times*, the *Village Voice*, *Time* magazine, and assorted publications too numerous to mention.

Michiko Kakutani, the famously cantankerous *New York Times* book reviewer, has agreed that Eggers's talent is "staggering," as have writers David Foster Wallace, Rick Moody, David Sedaris, and David Remnick (who published an excerpt of his book in the *New Yorker* under the title of "Here Come the Orphans!" earlier this year). His readings are standing room only, the new issue of *McSweeney's* sells out as soon as it arrives (shipping is rather slow, as Eggers decided to have them printed in Iceland), and even his publisher ran out of review copies of the book a week before its publication date.

The book in question, Eggers's first, is about a boy (Dave Eggers) raising another boy (his brother, Christopher, called "Toph"). The Eggerses' parents died of cancer within thirty-two days of each other, leaving Dave, then twenty-one, as the surrogate parent of Toph, then eight. They leave their home in the wealthy suburb of Lake Forest (outside Chicago) and follow sister Beth, then twenty-three, to Berkeley, where she attends law school.

The story is, as one might expect, "heartbreaking," tragic, and inspirational, but as Eggers tells it, it is also funny, lyrical, and liberating, full of madcap escapades and slapstick humor. In Eggers's telling, this story of orphans making their way in the world resembles a Pippi Longstocking fantasy gone wild. He acknowledges that along with the sense of being hard-done-to comes the existential freedom to redefine the entire notion of family: Life assumes a "sense of mobility, of infinite possibility, having suddenly found oneself in a world with neither floor nor ceiling."

It's a true story, more or less, and Eggers is relentless in detailing which parts are more true than others: In his preface he walks the reader through the various changes he's made in dialogue, characters, location, and time. He even finagled a highly idiosyncratic copyright page out of Simon & Schuster: After claiming that the book is a work of fiction, mostly due to the limits of memory, he acknowledges that most things, people, and incidents described are real "because, at the time of this writing, the author had no imagination whatsoever for these things, and could not conceive of *making up* a story or characters—it felt like driving a car in a clown suit."

The relationship between Dave and Toph, now twenty-nine and sixteen, pivots around a self-conscious declaration of their unique status—"We are pathetic. We are stars."—and the sort of workaday banalities and love found in any parent-child relationship. Their house is messy, and they spend a lot of time sock-sliding (Dave provides diagrams of the best routes) and playing Frisbee. Dave threatens to pick up women at parent-teacher conferences and worries that Toph will fail because he is always late for school. Dave goes out drinking with friends and spends the entire evening terrified that Toph will be murdered by the babysitter.

In between, Dave and his friends—many of them old friends from Lake Forest who moved to California for various reasons—start a magazine called *Might*. And Dave tries—and fails—to become a character on MTV's *The Real World*.

Eggers hemmed and hawed, but he finally agreed to be interviewed for *Mothers Who Think*, on the grounds that *Salon* is "family"—he was once the editor of the *Media Circus* site—and on the condition that we both talk about being young parents. (I am the twenty-six-year-old mother of a ten-year-old.)

Amy Benfer: So, you don't want to do this interview.

Dave Eggers: I thought I reached a point where I could never do it again, maybe a month ago. I've had a couple of ridiculous interviews. People who just want to ask me about *The Real World*, stuff like that.

AB: So what about *The Real World*? Were they up for having you and Toph? Would you have allowed Toph to move into the *Real World* house?

DE: I don't know. I'm just lucky that we all came to our senses before something bad happened. I was never that serious about it. I wouldn't have lasted more than a week, probably.

But I fantasize about a lot of things. On the way here, I was thinking about going to Mars, but it didn't mean much. There is a lot of time during the day to think about a lot of things. In the book, I think that some people are misinterpreting my idle thinking as serious thinking. But I'm thinking about twelve things at once, a hundred thousand times a day. Most people do, I would imagine. But you just choose to write certain things down. I picture my death twenty times a day. But doesn't everybody briefly picture things like that? You have to be true to how active your brain is.

AB: Do you think people treat your idle thoughts differently because in the midst of your idle thinking—about *The Real World*, about death—you also have custody of a small child? Do you think that people are judging you, wondering what will happen if your child gets caught playing out your idle thinking?

DE: Well, there's a choice. A child could be raised by Quakers or Mennonites in Pennsylvania. I think there is a strange American Puritanism, of course, that's always there, right below the surface, that favors incredible simplicity and austerity for the raising of a child.

And I did too in a way. I really believe strongly that kids should be spared the runoff of their parents' lives and problems. Chris [Toph] didn't know—nor will my own kids—about my problems at work, or that I broke up with a person. I didn't want to burden him with stuff like that.

AB: How did you avoid that, especially as a single parent? How do you avoid him being around you when things happen?

DE: Well, he would *meet* people. If I were seeing someone, he'd go out with us. I only really took him out with people that he's known since he was born. These people are all his relatives, basically.

When I grew up, I didn't know anything about anything. I didn't know a swear word until I was like, thirteen, maybe. I couldn't possibly utter one until well after that. We couldn't say the word *God* in the house. We'd have to say, "Mom, Bill said the word *dog* backwards."

I remember my first friend in the world—who was at the reading in Berkeley the other night—when we were like, eight or nine, asked me what "balls" were, just to test me. And I thought really hard about it, and I was like, "Well, it's gotta be . . . your butt." I couldn't say "butt" at the time; I had to say "rear end."

I didn't know the first thing about drugs until maybe college. My parents didn't idly talk about adult things and problems of the world and that kind of thing to us, and burden us with stuff. We were left to be kids.

It was the same way, as much as possible, with Toph. He didn't see anything. And I believe in this. There were a few people, my age or my sister's age, that didn't know how to act. Some people are really fucked up around kids. They think kids need to be deflowered intellectually. I remember a good friend of Toph's in Berkeley, when he was about ten, knew absolutely everything about every conceivable drug-related subject—all the terms, all the slang. I had no idea what he was talking about. I don't know where he got it. Maybe from his brother, maybe there was some talk in his home. The stuff that came out of his mouth was so old and icky and dirty. It was sort of sad, I think.

AB: You mention in the book a mother who talks about allowing her son to smoke pot at home. She looks to you, thinking that as a young, hip parent, you will understand. Do you feel that other parents had the expectation that you would be more lenient than you actually were?

DE: Yes, I think a lot of parents assumed that our house was a young bachelor pad, chaotic sort of thing. At one point, a neighbor of ours in Berkeley thought that when Toph didn't want to play with her son. Toph and my older brother, Bill, and I were just sitting around, and she burst into the house—unannounced, without knocking—and she said: "What's going on? Just tell me what's going on!" like really thinking that she was making a drug bust or something, just because Toph was avoiding her son, who was kind of dorky.

There was some of that, but usually once I would talk to them, the other parents were really incredibly nice and generous. I liked talking to them about parent stuff.

These were private schools. The parents in particular at San Francisco Day School were like, wonder parents. These guys were all just incredibly active and smart and they think hard about everything. I would recommend that school to anybody.

All the schools were rather generous. People were always nice to us. I went to public school all my life and all through college and I liked it. Toph went to private schools because we were never sure where we'd be living. They have endowments, they have people who are well off, who are paying more so that people with less can join in on the fun.

AB: I've found that people who are writers or in magazines or doing hip, creative, interesting stuff have a horror of parenting at a young age. These are the people who won't have kids—if at all—until their late thirties, at least. Do you feel that you did the same things you would have done as a young adult, regardless of your parental status?

DE: Roughly. I think about this a lot. It's an issue of the chicken or the egg. I never went out a whole lot. Never more than once a week, usually. I always attributed that fact to the conviction I had that something horrible would happen to my brother if I left, obviously, and that I would pay for it for the rest of my life. But a lot of it had to do with work. I like working. I like staying home and working on things and pretending to work on things. And half the time I prefer hanging out with Toph at home to just going to a bar. We had real fun. We had Ping-Pong.

AB: It sounds like you had pretty strict rules about dating. For instance, you never had people sleep over.

DE: Oh, never. Never. It would be just too weird. It got comical here and there. He *met* many people that I dated, as any child of divorce will meet his mother's dates.

If someone's not comfortable around your child, that's sort of a weeding out. I think that there's some issues there. To think that kids are some other species that you have to act a certain way around, to be nervous around. I've had people who were very nervous around my twelve-year-old brother. Whatever. And that's a problem.

AB: But you also said that you don't want them to act the same way they would around adults, right?

DE: Well, yeah. But there's a pretty easy balance. You treat a kid with respect, and as an adult you talk to them as if they're smart people. But you don't throw at them the trappings of adulthood and, you know, the darker stuff. I've seen people throw that at kids—they prick them. Parents do too. They lean on them too hard with their own problems. They don't need that. They want to know their parents are pretty invincible. And then they want to play. That's it, you know. Let them play.

They certainly don't want to think, "I hope Dad doesn't break down again." Growing up, my parents were pretty invincible. And that's important. That allows you stability in your brain to develop other interests outside your family. No kid should have to worry, "Where am I going to be tomorrow?"

And that's primarily in the formative years, I would say, like from zero to eight, maybe. Those years should be trouble-free.

Obviously, my mom was a master, so she took care of that with Toph. So by the time he and I got together, it was pretty easy. She had done all the real work.

AB: So do you feel that you were pretty consistent? Do you feel that you raised Toph the way you felt your mother would have done?

DE: Yeah. Absolutely. She was a parenting genius. I'm not the only one who would say that. She taught for many years and had hundreds of kids, and I think almost all of them would say that. You define a genius as someone who almost never has to second-guess what their instincts say, who knows things without ever having to be told them. Obviously, a lot of people are like that, parenting-wise—parenting is an instinctual thing—but a lot of people aren't. And lot of people have to read books.

AB: What do you think about parenting manuals?

DE: I've never read a word of one. Nor will I ever. I'm sure that there are a lot of helpful ones out there. I don't know much about it, though. That's a different world. Like my mom, I kind of feel like I know it all, and I'm not going to let someone tell me what's what. But I don't read any self-help anything. It's a genre I know nothing about.

AB: Why did you decide to leave Chicago?

DE: Gotta go. You can't stay and fester in the community of your childhood. I don't want to say that it's always bad—*fester* is a tough word to use—but you know, because you have a young 'un with you, it doesn't mean you can't move. And *do*. And I think in the long run, your child is going to respect that.

AB: But how did you justify that to yourself? You decided that you were going sell the house, sell the furniture, take your child out of school, and move across the country to a place neither of you had ever lived before.

DE: We couldn't afford to stay there. This was Lake Forest. This was not a cheap place to live.

AB: But the Bay Area isn't exactly cheap, either.

DE: In Berkeley, we were paying about a $1,000 a month for a house. Beautiful little street, nice neighbors, which I imagine would have beat our mortgage out there in Lake Forest by a mile. And my sister, Beth, was in law school out in Berkeley, so everyone had sort of put their life on hold for a while anyway. So at that point, if you're a kid, and you're eight, do you want to be in a town where everyone knows exactly what happened to your parents? Or do you want to move?

So we got a fresh start. In a few weeks in our new school, no one knew anything. Kids don't care.

AB: But clearly they picked up on the fact that you were a lot younger than the other parents.

DE: Yeah, sure, they picked up on that. But that just made it more fun.

AB: I once lived with an old friend from high school. That was hard. I think we are especially vulnerable as single parents. We think that it will be easier to live with other people, but once you are sharing space with another person, your child becomes their roommate, too. And then they assume parental rights.

DE: And you want to strangle them. The people around people like you and me are under a lot of weird stresses. They don't know what it's like. They sometimes want to second-guess you, which makes you want to throw them off a cliff. And I have severed relations here and there with people. I mean, after six years of doing this stuff and then they try to second-guess me: It's like, "Well, I'll see you in hell."

But we have young friends. And a lot of times, their ignorance comes through. Obviously, ten years down the road, they're never going to second-guess the decision of a fellow parent. Nor would they now second-guess the decision of a forty-year-old parent. But they feel like they can do that with us. And that's a problem. Because nobody knows better.

AB: But on the one hand, there you are walking around the PTA meetings saying, "We're special, we're different, we're better, we're stars, we're the thing, we're the *new* thing. We're the thing that nobody here can ever be because we're young and free." You want it both ways, right? Because you also want to have the fabulous power of reinventing parenthood in a way that seems more interesting. And yet you don't want to lose the authority that comes from seniority and experience.

DE: They're not at all mutually exclusive.

AB: Why not?

DE: Just because you're reinventing it? By innovating it, do you mean that you lose your grip on authority?

AB: By insisting that *you are not them*. You define yourself as not being an older parent: You are not old, dumpy, boring, unable to play soccer. But at the same time (in the book), when you have to prove your own authority to a friend, you scream, "I am a forty-year-old mother. Don't ever forget that."

DE: Right. You want it both ways. Obviously. You want the moral authority. But you think that you know a bit more because you're closer to the age. You probably think that your fellow parents are woefully out of it, and don't know what's what. I mean the closer you are to your daughter or brother or sister's age, the more you feel like you can relate. And that means the world when you're raising a kid, right?

AB: But there's also the danger that being too cool of a parent will cause your child to rebel.

DE: I never rebelled. Not in any conventional way. I wanted to please my parents. When I liked an album, I wanted them to like it too. I was desperate to make connections with them, and I really liked doing that. So I don't ever identify with the idea that you try to upset your parents in some deliberate way. I didn't understand that. I never thought of it as an antagonistic relationship. It's not that way with Toph and I because we're part of the same thing. It's a partnership.

AB: Do you feel that it's more of a partnership because you are his brother, not his parent?

DE: No. It's always been exactly the same. We've never been like brothers, like brothers who grew up together. It's always been a hybrid of brother and parent ever since he was born. And it's still that way.

I think that for people in our children's situation, it's less likely for them to rebel.

AB: The problem is that being a single parent, especially a young single parent, you are told that you don't have the moral authority, that because you are more like a pal than a parent, your child is more likely to lack the stability that a nuclear family provides, and more likely to have problems.

DE: Well, there's nothing on paper that can tell you how someone's going to turn out. I think most of the damage is done by the time the kid is four years old. I believe very strongly in that.

AB: Which means that you never could have done any damage. It was all set up by the time you became Toph's guardian.

DE: Sure. Don't blame me.

No, I do think that the seed is planted in the first couple years. If the kid grows up in a loud or stressful household, they're going to absorb that. At the developing stages, all external input has infinitely more influence than it does later on. I have so many vivid memories from when I was three that mean nothing. Why do I remember exactly how Uncle Ted threw me in the pool? And I can't remember what I did yesterday.

Most of that stuff happens really early on, and the only solution to anything like that is love. And if a child is provided enough love at all times, and he knows it, then fuck everything else. There's just no way that you can go wrong. That's the only thing that's ever lacking, I think. Are you very clear to this person always that they mean absolutely everything to you and you're behind them 100 percent? After that, it's simple. Who cares about laundry and the house and what kind of food you eat?

AB: Well, some people would say that that's exactly what matters. That this is how kids get their sense of stability: Knowing that the house is clean and the laundry is done and the food is there is all part of the care and maintenance to provide a happy home.

DE: No, that's a smokescreen. That's for people who don't know what they're doing. That stuff helps, sure. It's nice to grow up in a house where everything is taken care of. Does it make a damn bit of difference if your parents are reluctant to express their affection to you? No. You're going to end up shooting people from a tower in Texas. No matter how clean your laundry is. Take John Wayne Gacy: I'm sure his house was immaculate. It just all has to do with constant, unconditional love, as corny as that sounds.

AB: So do you think that you're ever going to have other kids?

DE: Oh yeah, sure. I love kids. I'm going to have a bunch of kids.

AB: But do you feel like you could be in a serious relationship with somebody and consider having children with them while Toph is still in the house?

DE: No, you're right there. Pretty soon he'll be in college. I'm not saying I'll do it anytime soon. But I'll do it. I'm never anywhere near as happy as I am when I'm in a house full of kids. I was just visiting a friend of mine who just had a baby. I had a reading in Berkeley. And there was just no *way* I wanted to go to that reading, not with this cute little thing. He smiled all the time and I had him on my lap and I was just like, I'm crazy to leave. I've spent most of my life around little kids. It's certainly better than spending it around adults—so boring. No offense to you guys.

AB: Why is it that everyone hates to admit to being adults? Why is it that no one wants to admit anymore that there are cool things about being an adult?

DE: I don't think that it is cool. It basically just means that you've accepted the fact that you're slow and boring. Really. I have a lot of friends who do accept it: "I wear these clothes, because I'm an adult now." Good God!

AB: Most people would say that the truest sign of being an adult is becoming a parent, regardless of your age.

DE: No, not at all. I would say that it's completely unrelated. I mean, there are things about parenting that will mature you, for sure. But you know. Tell me something: When you meet people, do you draw a line between those who have been through stuff, who know what it's like to struggle on a daily level to get things done? I mean, at twenty-six, some of your friends must be incredibly immature by comparison. I used to always divide people like that. I would find that those whose parents had been divorced, if a parent had died, I could identify with them better. Any sort of breakage in the family unit will mature someone, will sober them a little bit. And they will understand that things aren't always just so.

You probably find people who want to judge you, right?

AB: Oh sure. But what I think is strange is that although you say that you do end up seeking out people who have some sort of breakage, these are the same things that you say you don't want to expose your own children to. So this is the question: If you believe that hardship matures you, makes you interesting, and if you don't believe in exposing your own children to hardship, are you then in danger of raising boring children?

DE: No. They'll absorb enough. Your daughter and my brother will know enough to know that they are—unusual—but there's no reason to pound it home. You have to allow them to think that they're just as good and just as normal—or in our case, *better*—than anyone else. You're special. You're chosen. But what you never want to do is use your situation as an excuse to wallow or fail. It just means that you're that much more. It's all an advantage.

Because, do you want to be like everybody else? I think that's the question that you have to ask yourself, ask your daughter. And I think that people who would judge you and your daughter—and I'm sure that the things that were said to your daughter are similar to the things that were said to Toph, because you're different. Or, "You're the one with no dad." Or, "You're the one with no parents." Or, "You're the one whose house is filthy." Or, "You live in an apartment."

It's a badge of honor, though. Soon enough, they'll realize that. Kids like to be considered normal so they can go ahead and get on with their lives and not have to worry about that. But soon enough, it turns 180 degrees, and the more normal you are, the more likely you are to be predestined for some boring, predetermined life.

It's just like growing up with a silly name. Like one of my friends was Giacomo Calliendo. And we had another kid in high school named Gonzolo Chocano. And my best friend in the world is named Flagg. And you get all the shit in the world for that. But at this point, who would you rather be: Giacomo, Calliendo, or Dave?

It's the same thing with your upbringing. Who wouldn't envy someone who was brought up on ships sailing the Pacific? Or was brought up in Nova Scotia? Normalcy is okay to a point—but what do you get for it? Nothing. You've lived your life in a normal way. And then, you've got a problem. Because what have we been seeking this whole time? Anonymity and normalcy? I mean, you're dead and you're glad that you were so normal? And you're glad that your familial structure was as normal as possible and your parents were just the right age? Strange thing, you know. Very strange.

And in the end, at least in the existential sense, you only have what you have, you know. Unless you're saving it for some other world, and I don't know anything about that. I don't know if there's some other world. So you try to make it as interesting as possible here.

AB: So if you later decide to have kids at a sensible age, in your late thirties, with a stable income, a good career, and a nuclear family, then what do you do?

DE: You have to manufacture chaos.

AB: Exactly.

DE: That's a recurring theme in the book: the manufacture of chaos. Trying to make seemingly safe lives seemingly dangerous to satisfy that primal urge for danger.

AB: And yet, I know many forty-year-old mothers who tell me that they are just as insane, just as unconventional as I am. Is there really a divide between young parents and forty-year-old mothers? Or are we forty-year-old mothers?

DE: We can't possibly be. I think kids feel the difference. And they see the difference, when we show up at parent-teacher conferences.

AB: I love the parent-teacher conferences in your book.

DE: I didn't even go into them all the way in the book. At times, there would be three of us: me, my older brother Bill, who is an archconservative, and then my sister, Beth, who is way Left. And we would be barraging them with questions about their curriculum. We all thought we were so smart. And we were the same age as most of these teachers, so we felt like we knew the game, we knew what was up with them. But we also had the moral authority to question them on the very foundation. So it was fun.

Boy Raises Man: Dave Eggers and His Heartbreaking Work of Staggering Genius

Stuart Wade / 2000

From the *Austin Chronicle*, March 3, 2000. © 2000 by Stuart Wade. Reprinted by permission.

1. Know This about Dave Eggers. He:

Grew up in suburban Chicago and attended the University of Illinois.

Quit school at twenty-one and moved to San Francisco after both of his parents died within five weeks of each other.

Assumed the role of father to his kid brother, Toph, then eight years old (now sixteen), the pair now residing in Park Slope, Brooklyn (they have another brother, Bill, based in Austin).

Cofounded now-defunct *Might* magazine (best remembered for its bogus postmortem of *Eight Is Enough* star Adam Rich, who is still very much alive) and created quirky, acclaimed anti-magazine *McSweeney's*.

Has written a highly praised memoir, *A Heartbreaking Work of Staggering Genius* (Simon & Schuster, 480 pp., $23)—from which he forced his publisher to remove the subtitle, "A Memoir," and that deconstructs the memoir form even as it exploits the Eggers family's personal tragedy.

Can boast jacket blurbs for said book contributed by several famous Davids, including *New Yorker* editor David Remnick, fiendishly intelligent writer David Foster Wallace, and humorist David Sedaris.

Has a goofy acronym for his book: AHWOSG.

Is currently writing a novel and will appear at BookPeople Monday, March 6, at 7:00 p.m.

2. Hear His Terrible, but Wise, and Yes, Often Hilarious, Story:

Eggers's mother died of stomach cancer after a long battle, his father of lung cancer after a brief one. In the book, which retains much of *McSweeney's* retrofit intelligence despite the obvious tragedies at hand, Eggers dismantles not only memoir literary convention, but also the appalling American tradition of the mediagenic "survivor" strolling pensively to a gravesite as TV cameras roll. Eggers is honest about all of it: his pain, his acute self-awareness, even the exhilaration of having been cast out, an orphan, amid descriptions of himself and Toph playing beach Frisbee; staging "belt-whippings" intended to shock neighbors; of Dave trying to go on dates; of being a quasi-parent among the mothers and fathers of Toph's schoolmates. And while he's busy providing the book's many sly asides—such as an in-depth listing of menu items the brothers cook in their often filthy apartment—time and again, the author illustrates the powerful bond the boys share and explains precisely why he and Toph feel bulletproof, chosen, and owed by society.

3. Admire as Mr. Eggers Redefines "Margins":

What is that page called before the dedication page of a book? The one that contains the copyright information and disclaimers about "persons living or dead"? Front matter? Frontispiece? Living or dead guy page? Do not fail to read this page, because it—with its hidden, jokey text inserts in small print ("all events described herein actually happened, though on occasion the author has taken certain, very small, liberties with chronology, because that is his right as an American") and despite not technically even being part of the book that is to follow—illustrates what's to come, what the author does better than anybody. He does a little dance in the margins.

4. Laugh Heartily as Our Hero Adds Levity with Witty Asides:

Not only does the book include "Rules and Suggestions for Enjoyment of This Book" ("Skip the table of contents if you're short of time"); not only does it include a special fictional offer the author says is quite serious—send him your copy of the book and he'll send you a floppy disk containing the entire digital manuscript, but with all names and locations changed; not only does AHWOSG include a twenty-plus-page set of acknowledgements (e.g., "the author acknowledges the brave men and women serving in the United States Air Force") and the actual, working telephone numbers of three of the author's former girlfriends; but also, superheroes and superhero imagery figure prominently throughout. And hey, who doesn't love superheroes?

5. Please Enjoy This Original Eggers Drawing:

6. Witness Mr. E's Pyrotechnic Prose:

Ignore, if you must, the book's occasionally intrusive technical in-novation. Go beyond the first moment where a slice of dialogue actually breaks out of authentic-sounding conversation between the author and his brother—actually lifting right off the page, twisting and metastasizing right before your eyes—and AHWOSG will still make you laugh and think, all while you're being gut-punched with grim descriptions of losing parents far too soon, of struggling to assume the role of parent, yet still somehow main-taining your own identity as a single person in your twenties:

"We are always late, always half-done. All school forms need to be sent to me twice, and I have to hand them in late. Bills are paid in ninety days minimum. . . . Our relationship, at least in terms of its terms and its rules, is wonderfully flexible. He has to do certain things for me because I am his parent, and I have to do certain things for him. Of course, when I am called upon to do something I don't want to do, I do not have to do it, because I am not, actually, his parent. When something doesn't get done, we both shrug, because technically, neither of us is responsible, being just these two guys, brothers maybe, but we hardly even look alike, making duty even more questionable. . . . It is an unsaid mission of mine . . . to keep things moving, to entertain the boy, to keep him on his toes. . . . There is a voice inside me, a very excited, chirpy voice, that urges me to keep things merry, madcap even, the mood buoyant. . . . It's a campaign of distraction and revisionist history-leaflets dropped behind enemy lines, fireworks, funny dances, magic tricks."

7. Pause to Ponder Whether the Author Is Trying to Have It Both Ways:

Yes, AHWOSG often sidesteps grief and even undermines its critics by slyly layering the self-deprecation. In Eggers's hands, however, it works. (Gape in horror at the true details of the author's ill-fated tryout for MTV's *The Real World*, San Francisco cast. Experience immeasurable relief as our hero fails to earn the opportunity to burn himself into America's cerebral cortex as the SF cast's Tragic Guy—as the White Dude Other than Puck.) In these often humiliating asides regarding his own selfishness, depravity, or paranoia, Eggers remains genuine. Even his line-item breakdown of Simon & Schuster's six-figure advance, given for him to exploit his own parents' deaths, is but one of numerous moments pointing to a groundbreaking use of self-awareness and irony in memoir.

8. Treat Yourself by Reading:

McSweeney's, the quarterly (with a companion website at http://www.mcsweeneys.net) that calls itself a "repository of odd things one could never shoehorn into a mainstream periodical, and might be too quirky for other journals."

9. Know This at Last:

Eggers is a gracious and funny person who loves working into the wee hours and has been known to send email messages after 3:00 a.m. To one such recent after-hours query, the author responds:

Austin Chronicle: Can you think of a question you'd like to be asked?

Dave Eggers: I honestly don't know why no one asks about my career as a Hollywood makeup artist. After all, I did spend twelve years doing that, after my stint in Korea, and I won quite a few honors for my work, including the R. Thalstein Award for Special Achievement in Miniseries Makeup. But no one wants to talk about any of that. You know, I think it's indicative of the prejudices people have against Hollywood makeup artists. It kind of sickens me. I mean, when will we stop and realize that we're all people, even if some of us are ugly and malformed, and some of us are at the cutting edge of Hollywood makeup artistry?

AC: Is writing a heartbreaking work of staggering genius more difficult than doing publicity interviews?

DE: Doing interviews, obviously, gets old. When doing interviews gets old, you stop making sense and you start doing things like I just did above, just to entertain yourself. But this, in Austin, will be my last interview and my last reading, so for that I'm happy. Then I can go back to the ER and get back to what I should be doing—saving lives.

AC: Can you tell us what the novel you are now writing is about?

DE: The novel will include these parts:

—A gray whale who works in the Bronx, at the Social Security office

—A group of one hundred children attached by long filaments of skin

—Planks with nails hammered through them
—Mexican water taxis
—Monogamy
—Talking trees
and
—The sounds your ears hear when underwater.

Dave Eggers Needs a Vacation

Erik Himmelsbach / 2000

From *LA Weekly*, March 3–9, 2000. © 2000 by Erik Himmelsbach-Weinstein. Reprinted by permission.

Anywhere would be fine, but an escape from the planet Earth would be the first choice of the author, fried from book shilling and media glare. "I'm just tired by life. I just want to get off this planet and go somewhere else," Eggers says by phone from the Brooklyn apartment he shares with his younger brother, Toph, now sixteen. Amid constant yawns and throat clearing, a punchy Eggers explains his journey from founder of a long-gone, little-seen Gen-X magazine (*Might*) and editor of an obscure, quirky literary journal (*McSweeney's*) to a reluctant member of the publishing establishment.

LA Weekly: You're not a big fan of memoirs. Why, then, did you write your own?

Dave Eggers: I would never pick up a book that said "memoir." I hated the word; I thought it was silly. On the one hand, it seems sort of obscene to allow yourself to write a book about your own life. Then there's a more powerful and true sentiment, which is: Good fucking God, why not? Why do we hesitate to ever tell a true story, what are we saving it for? This is a very strange private theory of mine, but I believe everybody thinks that when we die and go up to heaven we get to tell everybody about our lives down here. But I don't believe in God or the afterlife or anything like that. If you're not going to hurt anybody and if everybody in the story is cooperative and everybody agrees to have that story told, then why not tell the story?

LA Weekly: Considering the high sob potential of your life, there's very little sorrow and pain in your book.

Eggers: There's this suspicion that, oh well, Toph and I were both much more fucked up than I'm saying. But that's not the truth. We chased each other around the house with squirt guns. That's the truth of it. Some people don't like that we weren't walking around bawling all day. I can't apologize for that. We went to California and we had a really great time.

LA Weekly: Because of the loss of your parents, you wrote about feeling like you were owed. Did you really feel bulletproof?

Eggers: On the one hand, you feel invincible, because you feel emboldened by all this in a way, chosen. On the other hand, there was that precariousness, where you feel like anything can happen and you're sort of teetering. I don't think you ever really shake that feeling. I have a friend that was in a crazy car accident, who rolled like six times on the highway. Put him in any car now, and he's always a wreck. White knuckles on the wheel: it's the same kind of thing. You get close to stuff, and you know how close it is.

LA Weekly: *Might* and *McSweeney's* show a healthy disdain for the kind of popular media canonization that currently swirls around you. Are you ambivalent about the attention you're getting?

Eggers: Yeah, it sucks shit. This is the worst. Having somebody call you the literary "it" boy—that's very painful. We had done interviews promoting *Might* and *McSweeney's*, and it was fine, but I never thought I'd get so sick of this stuff. Also, you get burned by a couple people who are friendly and nice, and then they lie about you in print and turn things around in a way that's just appalling.

LA Weekly: Perhaps it's your penance, since *Might* was renowned for taking the piss out of people.

Eggers: I did an interview with Joan Didion once, and she was incredibly nice and charming, and I wrote about it in a plain sort of way for *Salon*. Then I turned around and wrote a piece for *Might*, where I kind of made the whole thing sort of ugly. I got in a few jabs at her—oh well, her recent books just don't have the resonance of *The White Album* or *Slouching Towards Bethlehem*. This was a hero of mine. Who the fuck am I to take a jab at her? But you justify it to yourself—well, I'm just as good as Joan Didion, or I'm the journalist, and my opinion of her is very important. What an asshole I was. I'm having that done to me all the time. It's been interesting to see all that happen from this perspective and see the same tricks that I used to pull as a young asshole being pulled on me. The ultimate result is that the book sells more copies, and all of a sudden *McSweeney's* has all this money. So, as of the next issue, we get to pay people and we get to continue. We were deeply in debt. Now I can take care of that debt. We can pay people and publish books—we're publishing four books by the summer. That's the whole point. If I need to be sacrificed in order to do that, that's fine.

Dave Eggers: An Interview

Saadi Soudavar / 2000

From the *Harvard Advocate* 135, no. 4. © 2000 by the *Harvard Advocate*. Reprinted by permission.

In 1993 Dave Eggers founded the now defunct Gen-X sneer of *Might* magazine. After a brief stint at *Esquire,* Eggers returned in 1998 to the avant-garde of the magazine world with the eccentric banality of *Timothy Mc-Sweeney's Quarterly Concern* (www.mcsweeneys.net). Eggers's first book, the best-selling memoir *A Heartbreaking Work of Staggering Genius,* was published in February of this year by Simon & Schuster to rave reviews. The following is an email transcript of a Q & A exchange with Eggers in which he is prompted to "rant" by the mention of the phrase "selling out."

Date: Fri, 28 Apr 2000 17:06:27 -0400 (EDT)
From: Saadi Soudavar <soudavar@fas.harvard.edu>
To: McSweeney's <mcsweeneys@earthlink.net>
Subject: Attn David Eggers: Harvard Advocate Interview

Dear David,

I'd first like to say that I hope that, by the time you get these questions, you've extricated yourself from under the perfidious yoke of those Massachusetts McSweeneys. Talk about a McFaustian bargain! We've got a light question for you before we get to the ones culled from the more serious elements of our staff.

0) In his appreciation of your work in the online magazine *Feed* (www.feed mag.com), Keith Gessen suggests that you might have been able to handle Puck had you been chosen for *The Real World* instead of that sniveling weakling Judd. But in your book you seem to be a little startled by Puck,

even cowed. What do you think? Could you have put Puck in his place and kept his scabbed-up fingers out the peanut butter?

A HEARTBREAKING WORK OF STAGGERING GENIUS

1) One of the most interesting aspects of AHWOSG is the consistently self-deprecatory tone. In the preface, for example, a list precisely maps out all the symbolism in the work. On one level, this undercuts the obvious amount of work that's been put into the book by suggesting that the book can be reduced to a very basic level of meaning. But it also functions to point out how much more complicated the book is than the chart makes it seem. The book has been criticized for precisely this reason: in the guise of self-deprecation, it's self-aggrandizing. What are your thoughts on this and, in general, the relation of the author to the text?

2) I'm curious as to what you were reading while writing this: your style is not that of the average memoir writer. Resemblances to David Foster Wallace's essays have been noted, and by their inclusion in *McSweeney's*, similarities are suggested to the style of Lawrence Weschler and Paul Maliszewski (and others published in *The Baffler*). Much greater parallels might be drawn, however, between your nonfiction and the work of the classic American metafictionists: the dialogue in Donald Barthelme, the narrative conniving in John Barth, or the character sketches in Pynchon. How much do you see your style as a reflection of your influences?

3) *Selling out? Good? Bad? Not the issue?*: What has surprised you about your book's reception? How do you explain the backlash to all the hype about you? It doesn't seem to be about your work, but more about you. Simple jealousy? Media saturation? How does it differ from other pop media backlashes?

4) Having attracted this much commercial attention with your book, the lit-crit establishment can't be far behind—a slew of theses here at Harvard were written on David Foster Wallace after *Infinite Jest* came out, a book received in somewhat the same way that yours has been. What's your attitude toward the inevitable critical discussion of your work (this interview . . .)? The aesthetic of *McSweeney's*, if one can be defined, seems to be one endorsing the pure joy of reading a story. Does criticism miss the point?

5) What's up with the cover art of AHWOSG? Are Komar & Melamid for real?

6) Have you optioned or considered optioning the movie or television rights to AHWOSG? Who would you like to see cast (specifically as yourself) and direct? If it became a television series would it be an hour-long drama, half-hour sitcom (with laugh track or without?), or some hybrid?

Okay. Let's talk about *McSweeney's.*

McSWEENEY'S

7) My favorite piece ever to appear in *McSweeney's* is Gary Greenberg's article on his attempts to meet and use the Unabomber. It's not, of course, about the Unabomber so much as about the cultural and media uses he was put to. It was really a very human and very careful look at what the magazines do to people, and it's really hard to imagine that article appearing anywhere else. Do you have any favorites yourself, pieces you think typify what *McSweeney's* is going for?

8) Well, and what is *McSweeney's* going for? Reading your book, one can't help be struck by your very messianic conception of *Might*'s mission; that, Josh Glenn notwithstanding, you weren't just making fun of people, that you were, in your way, saying something, though it wasn't clear what, exactly. I somehow sense that there's less of that in *McSweeney's.* Do you agree? Without putting you in the position of explaining what *McSweeney's* is "saying," I would like to ask where you want *McSweeney's* to go, what you think its place is in the history of the universe.

9) There is talk afoot in the land, Dave, that *McSweeney's*, content-wise, no longer differs much from smart journals like *Conjunctions* or *Epoch*. Even from the *New Yorker*, for that matter. Which is not to imply that, were the *Harvard Advocate* to receive a story from George Saunders, we would put our street cred above our commitment to excellence, a commitment from which we have not wavered in over 130 years of excellence. But still: Are you concerned that you're not publishing as many unknowns as you had been? And killed pieces? Are you taking any steps—are there any steps to be taken—to keep shit real?

10) One of the remarkable things about *McSweeney's*, especially before the whole AHWOSG extravaganza, was the enthusiasm it seems to have unleashed—it was obviously a revelation to all of us who'd become, painful as

it was, fairly accustomed to the polite, handsome literary journal that consisted primarily of academic poetry. But it's also drawing in people who've not been interested in literary magazines, which is remarkable, because it is so literary, much more so than *The Baffler* or *Hermenaut*, for example. I suppose what's especially shocking about all this is that young hipsters are so excited about an aggressively textual project. I mean, the only pictures you've used are for Lawrence Weschler's "Convergences." Your readings have been phenomenally successful. Do you think people are really interested in hearing stories? And reading texts?

11) My final question is a multipartite monster, so please feel free to jump in here whenever. The real issue at hand, Mr. Eggers, is whether you're on the side of the good guys or the bad guys. Certainly the fact that there's no advertising in any *McSweeney's* production augurs for the former; but you've motivated this several times by saying that ads are "ugly." In a similar vein, you've lavished great care on the design of the magazine, and in issue 4 you take this further still, both by creating a beautiful magazine and also devoting quite a bit of space to discussing the aesthetic wholeness of literary texts. Are you hewing a sort of politics from the scattered shards of aestheticism? George Saunders's horrifying story—the most horrifying to date—in issue 4 makes a clear distinction between the dehumanizing aspects of modern work and the humanizing impulses that remain nonetheless. Saunders is also pretty clear about equating the unhuman part of the equation with murder, specifically with, like, organized mass murder. In my hopeful moments, I feel like *McSweeney's* is trying to carve out the human space in our culture. In moments of dark suicidal despair, I think *McSweeney's* is just trying to sell a lot of magazines by being so pretty and "authentic." Which do you think it is? And if it is to carve out a human space, why do you think it makes sense to do this on aesthetic grounds? And if this is more or less to the point, can you also explain the extent to which you feel *McSweeney's* does more than simply reverse the design formula of the glossies (black/white instead of color, text instead of image, content instead of advertising, etc.)?

Date: Wed, 3 May 2000 17:08:15 -0400 (EDT)
From: David Eggers <mcsweeneys6@earthlink.net>
To: Saadi Soudavar <soudavar@fas.harvard.edu>
Subject: Re: your mail

Saadi:

Here are my answers. At the end is an addendum that's explained down there. All of this is long, but you can't edit without my permission. So let me know if you want to, though I hope you don't.

DE

1) Well, anyone who has criticized the book for the self-aggrandizing aspect—and I must admit I haven't seen any such review (though I stopped reading reviews a while ago)—are simply echoing my own criticisms, so it's hardly worth comment. As a longtime critic myself, I anticipated all the possible angles a reviewer might take and incorporated them into the acknowledgments. So there were no surprises in terms of any reservations or comments anyone made, given that I was much harder on the book than anyone else could possibly be. As for the last part of the question, I can't answer it—much too general.

2) I had never read a memoir before writing this thing, so that's probably why it doesn't read like one. There's really nothing more crippling than reading too much of a genre before working within it. But while writing the book, I did read Mary McCarthy's *Memories of a Catholic Girlhood*, which was a fairly devastating take on the form, in terms of how impossible it is to write compelling nonfiction without lying a great deal. Otherwise, my influences are mostly people I read in college—Nabokov, Tom Wolfe, Vonnegut, Didion, Lorrie Moore, Vidal, Wilde. The influence of Wallace is always overstated, and he'd agree readily—the similarities are very superficial. Barth, Barthelme, sure. Pynchon? I don't see it.

3) I address the "sellout" word later on (see addendum). As for the so-called backlash, I can't say I'm aware of one. I did expect something like that to happen, but I haven't seen anything yet. Where is it manifest? I haven't been looking, of course, but if there has been a backlash, it must be a very small or quiet one, because it hasn't shown up on my radar.

4) I think criticism, more often than not, completely misses the point, yes. The critical impulse, demonstrated by the tone of many of your own questions, is to suspect, doubt, tear at, and to take something apart to see how it works. Which of course is completely the wrong thing to do to art. I used

to tear books apart, and tear art exhibits apart—I was an art and book critic for a few years in San Francisco—but my urge to do that was born of bitterness and confusion and anger, not out of any real need to help or edify. When we pick at and tear into artistic output of whatever kind, we really have to examine our motives for doing so. What is it about art that can make us so angry? Is it healthy to rip to shreds something created by an artist? I would posit, if I may, that that's not really a healthy impulse. Now, as far as I know, out of maybe one hundred or so reviews that I've been made aware of, my own book has received only one negative example. That's pretty lucky, especially when you consider that Wallace, for example, has gotten pretty abused by some people, people who for the most part don't have the patience his work requires. But criticism, for the most part, comes from the opposite place that book-enjoying should come from. To enjoy art one needs time, patience, and a generous heart, and criticism is done, by and large, by impatient people who have axes to grind. The worst sort of critics are (analogy coming) butterfly collectors—they chase something, ostensibly out of their search for beauty, then, once they get close, they catch that beautiful something, they kill it, they stick a pin through its abdomen, dissect it and label it. The whole process, I find, is not a happy or healthy one. Someone with his or her own shit figured out, without any emotional problems or bitterness or envy, instead of killing that which he loves, will simply let the goddamn butterfly fly, and instead of capturing and killing it and sticking it in a box, will simply point to it—"Hey everyone, look at that beautiful thing"—hoping everyone else will see the beautiful thing he has seen. Just as no one wants to grow up to be an IRS agent, no one should want to grow up to maliciously dissect books. Are there fair and helpful book critics? Yes, of course. But by and large, the only book reviews that should be trusted are by those who have themselves written books. And the more successful and honored the writer, the less likely that writer is to demolish another writer. Which is further proof that criticism comes from a dark and dank place. What kind of person seeks to bring down another? Doesn't a normal person, with his own life and goals and work to do, simply let others live? Yes. We all know that to be true.

5) Can't say I understand this question. The work of Komar and Melamid is in the collections of every major contemporary-art-collecting art museum in the world. There is no artist alive today doing work that's more important. They're carrying on the work of Duchamp, and they're more skilled as artists to boot. So yes, they are for real.

6) Had this been asked in another, less glib, way, I would have answered.

7) My favorite pieces were all written by Paul Collins. His series, which chronicles the lives of various hopeless dreamers of the nineteenth century, will soon be a book, called *Losers*. It's the closest stuff to what I wanted *McSweeney's* to be about.

8) Not sure about the Josh Glenn reference. Did you mean John Glenn? Otherwise I'm confused—should I know a Josh Glenn? I knew a Jodi Glenn in college, but I don't think you'd know her. Anyway, yes, *Might* had a messianic mission, for about three months. After that, it was a vehicle within which to publish things we found important or made us laugh. *McSweeney's* has no political goal. We only want to publish work that we like, and to do so with an attention to the craft of book and magazine production. Art made with mission statements is not art.

9) See addendum.

10) I'll address the readings portion of the question. Simply put, our readings are so well attended because they're fun. I don't like being bored, but most readings are aggressively boring. There is an assumption, in LiteraryLand, that readings must be sober and slow and long and serious. The spoken-word contingent sometimes improves upon this, but usually in a horribly pretentious way. So what we do is simple: we make sure alcohol is available, to ourselves and the audience, and then we have fun. And part of that involves breaking out of the author-at-the-podium-turning-pages schtick; we figure if five hundred people are going to come out, you might as well have some shit happen. Thus, at our last reading, in Brooklyn, Arthur Bradford, who accompanies his stories with guitar playing, broke his guitar against a wall, John Hodgman was interviewed by a man in a caveman costume, and, during intermission, I carefully cut the hair of five attendees. Then everyone stayed until two, most people were drunk, and lots of people hooked up with each other. All good, and all at a reading.

11) I address some of this question in the addendum, but I want to address the "sell a lot of magazines by being pretty and 'authentic'" part here. Honestly, Saadi, what the fuck are you talking about? You're applying principles of mass marketing to a money-hemorrhaging literary magazine produced out of my apartment. Please. No one here is trying to sell a lot of magazines.

Why would we be making a literary magazine in the first place, if sales numbers were our goal? And why would we be printing this thing in Iceland, and printing only twelve thousand copies? Jesus, son, you have got to stop tearing apart and doubting the people who are obviously, clearly doing good work. I mean, who the fuck do you believe in? *The Baffler* is nice-looking, too, and they print *twenty thousand* copies. Does that put Tom Frank in league with Tony Robbins? I'm exasperated. Saadi, you have to trust me, and you have to trust Tom Frank, because Tom Frank, for example, matters. If Tom Frank, tomorrow, agreed to be in a commercial for the Discover Card—as Kurt Vonnegut did a few years ago, for whatever reason—you would still have to trust Tom Frank and respect him, because he has for a decade been doing work that matters, and you have no idea about his motivations or needs or state of mind when he say okay to the Discover gig. I am giving you really good advice, here, Saadi, and offer it to other readers of the *Advocate*, because I wish I had the same advice pounded into my head at your age, when I was a bigger, more smug and suspicious asshole than you— I was the biggest asshole of all. To me, everyone was a sellout. Any band that sold over thirty thousand albums was a sellout. Any writer who appeared in any mainstream magazine was a sellout. I was a complete, weasely little prick, and I had no idea what I was talking about, and goddamn if I don't wish I could take all that back, because I knew nothing then, just as you know nothing now. You simply cannot judge someone, especially someone whose work you have respected, when they disappoint you, superficially, once or twice. Think of the fuckheads who turned their back on Dylan when he started using electric guitars, for Christ's sake. What kind of niggardly imbecile would call Dylan Judas when he plugged into an amp? What kind of small-hearted person wants an artist to adhere to a set of rules, to stay forever within a narrow envelope which we've created for them?

Now, the addendum.

First, a primer: When I got your questions, I was provoked. You expressed many of the feelings I used to have, when I was in high school and college, about some of the people I admired at the time, people who at some point disappointed me in some way, or made moves I could not understand. So I took a few passages from your questions—those pertaining to or hinting at "selling out"—and I used them as a launching pad for a rant I've wanted to write for a while now, and more so than ever since my own book has become successful. And the rant was timely, because shortly after getting your questions, I was scheduled to speak at Yale, and so, assuming that their minds might be in a similar spot as yours, I read this, the below, to them, in slightly less polished form. The rant is directed to myself, age twenty, as much as it is to you, so remember that if you ever want to take much offense.

You actually asked me the question: "Are you taking any steps to keep shit real?" I want you always to look back on this time as being a time when those words came out of your mouth. Now, there was a time when such a question—albeit probably without the colloquial spin—would have originated from my own brain. Since I was thirteen, sitting in my orange-carpeted bedroom in ostensibly cutting-edge Lake Forest, Illinois, subscribing to the *Village Voice* and reading the earliest issues of *Spin*, I thought I had my ear to the railroad tracks of avant-garde America. (Laurie Anderson, for example, had grown up only miles away!) I was always monitoring, with the most sensitive and well-calibrated apparatus, the degree of selloutitude exemplified by any given artist—musical, visual, theatrical, whatever. I was vigilant and merciless and knew it was my job to be so.

I bought R.E.M.'s first EP, *Chronic Town*, when it came out and thought I had found God. I loved *Murmur*, *Reckoning*, but then watched, with greater and greater dismay, as this obscure little band's audience grew, grew beyond obsessed people like myself, grew to encompass casual fans, people who had heard a song on the radio and picked up *Green* and listened for the hits. Old people liked them, and stupid people, and my moron neighbor who had sex with truck drivers. I wanted these phony R.E.M.-lovers dead.

But it was the band's fault, too. They played on Letterman. They switched record labels. Even their album covers seemed progressively more commercial. And when everyone I knew began liking them, I stopped. Had they changed, had their commitment to making art with integrity changed? I didn't care, because for me, any sort of popularity had an inverse relationship with what you term the keeping "real" of "shit." When the Smiths became slightly popular they were sellouts. Bob Dylan appeared on MTV and of course was a sellout. Recently, just at dinner tonight, after a huge, sold-out reading by David Sedaris and Sarah Vowell (both sellouts), I was sitting next to an acquaintance, a very smart acquaintance married to the singer-songwriter of a very well-known band. I mentioned that I had seen the Flaming Lips the night before. She rolled her eyes. "Oh I really liked them on *90210*," she sneered, assuming that this would put me and the band in our respective places.

However.

Was she aware that the Flaming Lips had composed an album requiring the simultaneous playing of four separate discs, on four separate CD players? Was she aware that the band had once, for a show at Lincoln Center, handed out to audience members something like one hundred portable tape players, with one hundred different tapes, and had them all played at the same time, creating a symphonic sort of effect, one which completely devastated everyone in attendance? I went on and on to her about the band's accomplishments, their experiments. Was she convinced that they were more than their one appearance with Jason Priestly? She was.

Now, at that concert the night before, Wayne Coyne, the lead singer, had himself addressed this issue, and to great effect. After playing much of their new album, the band paused and he spoke to the audience. I will paraphrase what he said:

"Hi. Well, some people get all bitter when some song of theirs gets popular, and they refuse to play it. But we're not like that. We're happy that people like this song. So here it goes."

Then they played the song. (You know the song.) "She Don't Use Jelly" is the song, and it is a silly song, and it was their most popular song. But to highlight their enthusiasm for playing the song, the band released, from the stage and from the balconies, about two hundred balloons. (Some of the balloons, it should be noted, were released by two grown men in bunny suits.) Then while playing the song, Wayne sang with a puppet on his hand, who also sang into the microphone. It was fun. It was good.

But was it a sellout? Probably. By some standards, yes. Can a good band play their hit song? Should we hate them for this? Probably, probably. First *90210*, now they go playing the song every stupid night. Everyone knows that *90210* is not cutting edge, and that a cutting-edge alternarock band should not appear on such a show. That rule is clearly stated in the obligatory engrained computer-chip sellout manual that we were all given when we hit adolescence.

But this sellout manual serves only the lazy and small. Those who bestow sellouthood upon their former heroes are driven to do so by, first and foremost, the unshakable need to reduce. The average one of us—a taker-in of various and constant media, is absolutely overwhelmed—as he or she should be—with the sheer volume of artistic output in every conceivable medium given to the world every day—it is simply too much to begin to process or comprehend—and so we are forced to try to sort, to reduce. We designate, we label, we diminish, we create hierarchies and categories.

Through largely received wisdom, we rule out Tom Waits's new album because it's the same old same old, and we save fifteen dollars. U2 has lost it; Radiohead is too popular. Country music is bad, Puff Daddy is bad, the last Wallace book was bad because that one reviewer said so. We decide that TV is bad unless it's *The Sopranos*. We liked Rick Moody and Jonathan Lethem and Jeffrey Eugenides until they allowed their books to become movies. And on and on. The point is that we do this and to a certain extent we must do this. We must create categories, and to an extent, hierarchies.

But you know what is easiest of all? When we dismiss.

Oh how gloriously comforting, to be able to write someone off. Thus, in the overcrowded pantheon of alternarock bands, at a certain juncture, it became necessary for a certain brand of person to write off the Flaming Lips, despite the fact that everyone knew beyond a shadow of a doubt that their music was superb and groundbreaking and real. We could write them off because they shared a few minutes with Jason Priestley and that terrifying Tori Spelling person. Or we could write them off because too many magazines have talked about them. Or because it looked like the bassist was wearing too much gel in his hair.

One less thing to think about. Now, how to kill off the rest of our heroes, to better make room for new ones?

We liked Guided by Voices until they let Ric Ocasek produce their latest album, and everyone knows Ocasek is a sellout, having written those mushy Cars songs in the late eighties, and then—gasp!—produced Weezer's album, and of course Weezer's no good, because that "Sweater" song was on the radio, right, and dorky teenage girls were singing it and we cannot have that and so Weezer is bad and Ocasek is bad and Guided by Voices are bad, even if Spike Jonze did direct that one Weezer video, and we like Spike Jonze, don't we?

Oh. No. We don't. We don't like him anymore because he's married to Sofia Coppola, and she is not cool. Not cool. So bad in *Godfather 3*, such nepotism. So let's check off Spike Jonze—leaving room in our brains for . . . who??

It's exhausting.

The only thing worse than this sort of activity is when people, students and teachers alike, run around college campuses calling each other racists and anti-Semites. It's born of boredom, lassitude. Too cowardly to address problems of substance where such problems actually are, we claw at those close to us. We point to our neighbor, in the khakis and sweater, and cry foul. It's ridiculous. We find enemies among our peers because we know them better, and their proximity and familiarity means we don't have to get off the couch to dismantle them.

And now, I am also a sellout. Here are my sins, many of which you may know about already:

First, I was a sellout because *Might* magazine took ads.
Then I was a sellout because our pages were color, and not stapled together at the Kinko's.
Then I was a sellout because I went to work for *Esquire.*
Now I'm a sellout because my book has sold many copies.
And because I have done many interviews.
And because I have let people take my picture.
And because my goddamn picture has been in just about every fucking magazine and newspaper printed in America.

And now, as far as *McSweeney's* is concerned, *The Advocate* interviewer wants to know if we're losing also our edge, if the magazine is selling out, hitting the mainstream, if we're still committed to publishing unknowns, and pieces killed by other magazines.

And the fact is, I don't give a fuck. When we did the last issue, this was my thought process: I saw a box. So I decided we'd do a box. We were given stories by some of our favorite writers—George Saunders, Rick Moody (who is uncool, uncool!), Haruki Murakami, Lydia Davis, others—and so we published them. Did I wonder if people would think we were selling out, that we were not fulfilling the mission they had assumed we had committed ourselves to?

No. I did not. Nor will I ever. We just don't care. We care about doing what we want to do creatively. We want to be interested in it. We want it to challenge us. We want it to be difficult. We want to reinvent the stupid thing every time. Would I ever think, before I did something, of how those with sellout monitors would respond to this or that move? I would not. The second I sense a thought like that trickling into my brain, I will put my head under the tires of a bus.

You want to know how big a sellout I am?

A few months ago I wrote an article for *Time* magazine and was paid $12,000 for it. I am about to write something, one thousand words, three pages or so, for something called *Forbes ASAP*, and for that I will be paid $6,000. For two years, until five months ago, I was on the payroll of *ESPN* magazine, as a consultant and sometime contributor. I was paid handsomely for doing very little. Same with my stint at *Esquire*. One year I spent there, with little to no duties. I wore khakis every day. Another *Might* editor and I, for almost a year, contributed to *Details* magazine, under pseudonyms, and were paid $2,000 each for what never amounted to more than ten minutes' work— honestly never more than that. People from Hollywood want to make my book into a movie, and I am probably going to let them do so, and they will likely pay me a great deal of money for the privilege.

Do I care about this money? I do. Will I keep this money? Very little of it. Within the year I will have given away almost a million dollars to about a hundred charities and individuals, benefiting everything from hospice care to an artist who makes sculptures from Burger King bags. And the rest will be going into publishing books through *McSweeney's*. Would I have been able to publish *McSweeney's* if I had not worked at *Esquire*? Probably not. Where is the $6,000 from *Forbes* going? To a guy named Joe Polevy, who wants to write a book about the effects of radiator noise on children in New England.

Now, what if I were keeping all the money? What if I were buying property in St. Kitts or blew it all on live-in prostitutes? What if, for example, I was, a few nights ago, sitting at a table in SoHo with a bunch of Hollywood slash celebrity acquaintances, one of whom I went to high school with, and one of whom was Puff Daddy? Would that make me a sellout? Would that mean I was a force of evil?

What if a few nights before that I was at the home of Julian Schnabel, at a party featuring Al Pacino and Robert De Niro, and at which Schnabel said we should get together to talk about him possibly directing my movie? And what if I said sure, let's?

Would all that make me a sellout? Would I be uncool? Would it have been more cool to not go to this party, or to not have written that book, or done that interview, or to have refused millions from Hollywood?

The thing is, I really like saying yes. I like new things, projects, plans, getting people together and doing something, trying something, even when it's corny or stupid. I am not good at saying no. And I do not get along with people who say no. When you die, and it really could be this afternoon, under the same bus wheels where I'll stick my head if need be, you will not be happy about having said no. You will be kicking your ass about all the no's you've said. No to that opportunity, or no to that trip to Nova Scotia, or no to that night out, or no to that project, or no to that person who wants to be naked with you but you worry about what your friends will say.

No is for wimps. No is for pussies. No is to live small and embittered, cherishing the opportunities you missed because they might have sent the wrong message.

There is a point in one's life when one cares about selling out and not selling out. One worries whether or not wearing a certain shirt means that they are behind the curve or ahead of it, or that having certain music in one's collection means that they are impressive, or unimpressive.

Thankfully, for some, this all passes. I am here to tell you that I have, a few years ago, found my way out of that thicket of comparison and relentless suspicion and judgment. And it is a nice feeling. Because, in the end, no one will ever give a shit who has kept shit "real" except the two or three people, sitting in their apartments, bitter and self-devouring, who take it upon themselves to wonder about such things. The keeping real of shit matters to some people, but it does not matter to me. It's fashion, and I don't like fashion, because fashion does not matter.

What matters is that you do good work. What matters is that you produce things that are true and will stand. What matters is that the Flaming Lips's new album is ravishing and I've listened to it a thousand times already, sometimes for days on end, and it enriches me and makes me want to save people. What matters is that it will stand forever, long after any narrow-hearted curmudgeons have forgotten their appearance on goddamn *90210*. What matters is not the perception, nor the fashion, not who's up and who's down, but what someone has done and if they meant it. What matters is that you want to see and make and do, on as grand a scale as you want, regardless of what the tiny voices of tiny people say. Do not be critics, you people, I beg you. I was a critic and I wish I could take it all back because it came from a smelly and ignorant place in me, and spoke with a voice that was all rage and envy. Do not dismiss a book until you have written one, and do not dismiss a movie until you have made one, and do not dismiss a person until you have met them. It is a fuckload of work to be open-minded and generous and understanding and forgiving and accepting, but Christ, that is what matters. What matters is saying yes.

I say yes, and Wayne Coyne says yes, and if that makes us the enemy, then good, good, good. We are evil people because we want to live and do things. We are on the wrong side because we should be home, calculating which move would be the least damaging to our downtown reputations. But I say yes because I am curious. I want to see things. I say yes when my high school friend tells me to come out because he's hanging with Puffy. A real story, that. I say yes when Hollywood says they'll give me enough money to publish a hundred different books, or send twenty kids through college. Saying no is so fucking boring.

And if anyone wants to hurt me for that, or dismiss me for that, for saying yes, I say Oh do it, do it you motherfuckers, finally, finally, finally.

Eggers Surprised by Success—
Author to Read from
Staggering Genius

James Sullivan / 2001

From the *San Francisco Chronicle*, April 2, 2001. © 2001 by the *San Francisco Chronicle*. Reprinted by permission.

Writer Dave Eggers treats his celebrity like a gold lamé suit: It's amusing, absurd and, in his mind, not quite appropriate.

Readers and critics, however, have been dazzled by Eggers's wryly titled *A Heartbreaking Work of Staggering Genius*. The surprise bestseller has sold three hundred thousand copies to date, the paperback is just out with three separate cover designs, and New Line Cinema paid $2 million for movie rights. The author reads tonight at City Lights and tomorrow at All Saints' Church.

By turns riotously funny and every bit as moving as the title implies, the memoir details the author's struggles to raise his younger brother after both their parents died of cancer. The story takes place in the Bay Area, where Eggers moved from Chicago with a few friends and founded the short-lived, sorely missed humor magazine *Might*. The writer, returning to the Bay Area after a stint in New York, now publishes an offbeat quarterly called *McSweeney's* (online at www.mcsweeneys.net).

In February, the Eggers book was back in the news when the author had a high-profile run-in with a *New York Times* reporter over a story about the paperback publication. He agreed to participate in this interview via email.

Q: You sent your story out into the world, and the world devoured it. Were you prepared for the public side of your life?

A: I never expected more than a *Might*-sized audience—mostly prisoners and grad students—to read the thing. I completely didn't expect older readers to have any interest at all. But once it started selling well, I braced myself. And as much as I thought I could predict what would happen and why, the good stuff and the bad, I was surprised again and again. It's been an almost entirely positive thing—people I meet are so astoundingly kind. I don't know where all these people came from.

Q: Were you reluctant to use the word *memoir*?

A: I'm not such a fan of the word. I've never read a memoir, actually, outside of M. McCarthy's. I didn't think the term—which evokes tell-alls by Golden Era film stars—really applied to my book, especially after I removed the scenes with me and Esther Williams.

Q: What's next?

A: I'm trying to finish a book that will, I'm thinking, be shelved in the fiction aisle. But the distinctions seem sort of meaningless. The two genres—literary nonfiction and fiction—are like fraternal twins. You can barely tell them apart.

Q: There has been an almost inordinate amount of attention paid to the business end of your book—your unconventional publishing ideas, your publishers' willingness to accommodate them, your movie deal. Is it misguided?

A: I think people have been attentive to it all because with *Might* and with *McSweeney's*, we've been fairly determined not to make any money. So when my book did well, people wondered what the hell was happening. But I am interested in the hows of making things, the economics of putting books together. At *McSweeney's* we're trying to take that whole process apart, to see if there's a better way to do it, to make things more comfortable for writers and the relationship between reader and writer more direct.

Q: Are there aspects of celebrity that you find yourself enjoying?

A: The success of the book has enabled us, with *McSweeney's*, to do a lot of the stuff we like to do. We'll publish ten books this year, and that makes us happy. We opened a little store that sells taxidermy supplies. And my family's been able to give away money. That's nice—to be able to redirect money that you don't deserve or need.

Q: How does your particular Bay Area differ from the clichés?

A: The weird thing is that it doesn't. I like it for all the clichéd reasons. I like the hills. I like the raw surf. I like the bridges. I have nothing new to say about it, I'm afraid.

Q: Given your experience, are you more or less inclined toward actual parenting?

A: Just about everyone I know is pregnant, so I guess I'm slow. But I'm no less inclined generally. I plan to have about eight of the suckers and use them as an excuse to put off work.

Q: Your book has been cited as a distinct product of turn-of-the-century America. Is it ominous to think of yourself in terms of the superstar-generation writers, both good and bad?

A: I guess it can be a horrible curse. But I knew that going in. I knew I was writing stuff that would probably make me cringe in a year. It already makes me cringe.

Q: What's the status of a potential movie version of the book?

A: We're proceeding with the original plans—to set it in the year 2067, after a crazy virus has killed all the good-looking people. Samuel L. Jackson has tentatively agreed to play me, though there'll have to be some tweaking of the story line to accommodate him. For example, instead of working at a magazine with his friends, he'll be with an elite CIA outfit full of young women and dog-men. It'll be great. Everyone's excited.

Q: Is Iceland (where *McSweeney's* is printed) really as happening as the Brits claim?

A: I don't spend much time in Reykjavik, so I'm the wrong guy to ask about the social life. When we go, we drive around in the fjords, through the interior, which is like the moon and Arizona and Mongolia combined. The only problem is the prices. The place is way too expensive—an orange will cost you about $120.

Q: You once wrote marketing slogans for *The Chronicle*. Anything you're especially proud of?

A: Nothing I did there was very memorable. I was thankful every day I wasn't canned.

"So I've Rambled": Dave Eggers Discusses the State of Publishing, *The Onion*, and Irony in an Unedited Email Interview

Joshua Tyree / 2001

From the *Daily Page*, April 30, 2001. © 2001 by Joshua M. Tyree. Reprinted by permission.

Dave Eggers's moving memoir *A Heartbreaking Work of Staggering Genius* has become a best-selling "National Curiosity." Eggers will read from the new paperback edition at the First Congregational Church on March 27 at 7:00 p.m. The reading benefits HospiceCare Inc. of Dane County. Seven dollars will be donated to HospiceCare for each copy of the book sold. The event is sponsored by University Book Store and is free.

Interviewer's note: Mr. Eggers only conducts interviews by email and insists that these exchanges only be published uncut, and with minimal window dressing. We were flattered to receive Eggers's belated responses to my questions. But they doubled my word-limit for the piece, and we got no reply to our request for a shorter version. We were wary of the recent vitriolic controversy between Eggers and *New York Times* writer David Kirkpatrick (visit the McSweeneys.net "Clarifications" page for the gory details). Respecting what appears to be a healthy distrust of journalists after this bitter episode, we held strictly to the pre-arranged rules, resisting the idea of publishing a shorter version of the Q & A in the print version of *Isthmus*. It appears here uncut.

Joshua Tyree: Call out to those who are thinking of coming to your reading/benefit.

Dave Eggers: Please come to the event if you're not picky about your entertainment options. This event should not be your first choice. Come if all your good options have fallen through.

JT: As an admirer, I might have wished a less-quick fame on you. Has publicity made things easier or more difficult? Are you sick of it, or does it make you thrive?

DE: Quick fame? I'm thirty-one, good God. I've been doing this stuff forever. The publicity is largely a very good thing. It helped the book sell, which made *McSweeney's* able to publish the journal, and the books, and everything else. Every cent put into *McSweeney's* has come from AHWOSG, so I really can't complain.

JT: I reread the paperback AHWOSG much more critically in light of the groundswell and subsequent erosion of your outsider aura. The book itself is as great as ever, but are you worried about backlash, knife-sharpening for the next book?

DE: Nah.

JT: Tell Madison about your plans for the new "April Book" of fiction, and the next "musical" *McSweeney's* (based on *McSweeney's* website info)?

DE: I'm still trying to finish that book. The new issue of *McSweeney's* comes with a CD soundtrack composed by They Might Be Giants, with contributions by M. Doughty and Philip Glass. It's really amazing—stories and essays by Ian Frazier, Zadie Smith, Lydia Davis, Mark O'Donnell, lots more. Plus forty-five songs.

JT: In the new appendix to the paperback AHWOSG, you say, "True community cannot be political." You have also said that large publishing conglomerates have little influence on peoples' actual lives. Really? I feel like the media giants are giving people less interesting dreams, which is why I find things like *McSweeney's* and David Foster Wallace so refreshing. Do you think it's just a matter of getting more heartfelt stuff to the people? Or, whatever glimmers, is this too optimistic?

DE: Well, if I may be so bold, look at your question there. You say that you find *McSweeney's* and Wallace refreshing. But Wallace is published by a large tendril of a huge conglomerate. As are some of the best writers of the day—George Saunders, Lethem, almost everyone. The thing is, I don't like conglomerates, but not because they threaten me in some way, or because good art is not being made because of them. Good art will absolutely never be made by companies, so we should just stop worrying about them with regard to art and books and music. Individuals make art, and sometimes we let companies profit from that. But I only question the dogma that posits that large companies control our lives, threaten us all, and try to stamp out all that is good. It's overly simplistic.

I had sort of an online discussion with a guy who lamented the state of publishing, claiming that good books weren't getting published by the big guys, etc. But since when were the big publishers ever interested in smaller, difficult books? Not all that often. Small publishers publish small books, and big publishers publish big ones. And sometimes big publishers take big risks on weird books. A lot of writers who started at *McSweeney's* have sold their (very offbeat) books to large publishers. Arthur Bradford wrote a collection of stories about people who interact in strange ways with dogs and slugs and other animals, and Random House is publishing it. Paul Collins wrote a collection of articles about obscure and failed inventors throughout history, and St. Martin's is putting it out. Both are books of dubious commercial appeal, but they're good books, and the companies were able to buy them because they have deep pockets with which to take risks. So it's nuanced. If they hadn't stepped forward, these guys wouldn't have their work bound and distributed. And that's the most important thing: Is the work getting to readers? I think it is. Worthy books are getting published.

But I'm going to double back for a second and ask a related question we need to ask: Do we want or expect conglomerates to make our best art? Do we want or expect the best books to be coming from gleaming buildings in Manhattan, and our best movies to come from Hollywood?

Sometimes they do. They very often do. But why worry about these companies at all? It's like lamenting that Dr. Pepper doesn't make more innovative beverages, or Menudo doesn't make more groundbreaking music. A good deal of the best things, in any form, will almost always come from outside these places, in one way or another.

In your own city, you have *The Onion*, which was started by a few people with a little money, and now they're doing pretty well. But they could have gone to New York right away and asked some publisher for the initial funding, and they would have been quickly refused. Or, if funded, the publisher/investor would have changed everything quickly and dramatically, until it sucked. So the *Onion* people could have complained about how terrible corporate America was, and how they weren't given a chance, etc. But instead *The Onion* did it on their own, the way they had envisioned it, and a huge audience responded to the purity of their vision, and how fucking perfect everything they did was. Now huge publishers pay *The Onion* extravagantly to do exactly what *The Onion* wants to do. The lesson is, if you make something good and it finds an audience, you'll always have the option of getting money people to pay you to continue doing exactly what you're doing.

So I've rambled.

But the core of it is that we shouldn't feel threatened by these companies. Of course, this is completely aside from any environmental and labor-related issues; I'm only talking about creative stuff here. That's the difference I try to point out. But again, it's a matter of perception. There are chain coffee shops all over—do we find this just annoying or see it as a sign of the apocalypse? Every day, in my old neighborhood in Brooklyn, brought a new, independent café, so I didn't worry so much about it all. No one's preventing anyone from starting new ventures.

And no one's been preventing *McSweeney's* from getting weird books into stores. We work primarily with independent stores, because that's where we know most of our readers get their books, and where the owners are most knowledgeable. And they've been incredibly supportive. So my feeling is the climate is pretty good for writers, and for any kind of do-it-yourself venturers. I just hate hearing people use conglomerates as a crutch, a catch-all evil-doing entity that's making the world unsafe for art. It's easier now than any time in history to make and disseminate any form of art, and in our hearts we all know it.

JT: In the appendix you also attack how people (over)use and misuse the term *irony*. Two points, address either, both, or neither:

[Point #1]: Are you "against" irony as some kind of agent of cultural decay that keeps fearful people hiding behind cleverness and not being heartfelt?

DE: No, not against irony. I'm against the usage of the word to cover pretty much anything with any offbeat combination of humor and pathos. Clever is good, but clever is distrusted. They Might Be Giants, for example, are often called *too clever* or *ironic* because their music is smart. I don't think we should punish people for being smart, or for eschewing a straight ticket of Earnest or Not-Earnest. The only people who label stuff one way or the other are those who aren't giving themselves enough time to understand.

JT: [Point #2]: Didn't you forget "dramatic irony" (i.e., when the audience watching a play knows something about the plot—like in, say, Othello—that the characters don't)? I ask because I think maybe, psychologically speaking, people misuse the term *ironic* to describe their lives as if an invisible audience were jeering at them and God/Fate/Chance were deliberately setting up obstacles in their path. Do you want to go into this?

DE: Good point. I won't elaborate.

Speed Merchant

Jon Casimir / 2003

From the *Sydney Morning Herald*, March 8, 2003. © 2003 by Jon Casimir. Reprinted by permission.

The interviewee: Dave Eggers, thirty-two.

Made his name: As the author of the hugely successful *A Heartbreaking Work Of Staggering Genius* (2000), in which he described the experience of being a twenty-one-year-old left to bring up his eight-year-old brother after their parents died of cancer.

Also known for: Editing and designing the deservedly hip *McSweeney's* literary journal, a quarterly (of sorts) that attracts big-name authors and arrives in a new and imaginative format each time. He also oversees the increasingly ambitious McSweeney's book-publishing arm.

Other interests: He volunteers regularly at 826 Valencia, a writing lab for San Francisco school students.

New book: *You Shall Know Our Velocity!*, his first novel. It's the story of Will and Hand, two young men who, upset by the recent death of their best friend Jack, set out to circumnavigate the world in a week. On their trip they dispense, almost randomly, $80,000 that Will received for allowing his silhouette to be used in an advertising campaign—money he owns but does not feel entitled to.

The deal: Eggers rarely does interviews and consented to this one on the understanding that it be presented in question-and-answer format.

Q: When you released *Velocity* through McSweeney's in the US, instead of a major publisher, some people said it was a ploy to sell more books [for them], even though you could have had a much more lucrative deal elsewhere. Why do you think people, journalists mainly, have been so suspicious of your motives?

A: Well, a few—and I do think it's a scant few—journalists don't think they're doing their job unless they question the motives of everyone, any time anything out of the ordinary is done. Not long ago, one of [J. D.] Salinger's biographers claimed that Salinger's reclusiveness, and his unwillingness to publish again, was itself a ploy to keep *The Catcher in the Rye* selling well. It was ludicrous. I mean, poor Salinger can't win. If he does interviews and publishes books, then he wants fame, money, etc. If he goes into seclusion, he still wants fame, money, etc.

It gets ridiculous after a while, and I just feel that those kinds of people—those who make claims like that—are really, always, constantly, overthinking everything. They're trying to figure out fame; they're trying to figure out why the public likes a certain writer, or musician, or actor; and often they assume that there's something beyond chance or talent or a simple connection between audience and artist at play.

Q: You shun media attention but do readings and public appearances. Is this your way of accepting that people want more connection with authors of books they love?

A: I love meeting readers; that's about the size of it. My favorite thing is to talk with the people who read a lot—just regular readers who love books. The media part of it often doesn't have much to do with books; it's wrapped up in so many other things—hype, distortion, weird motives, etc. So it's more dubious and fraught than the more simple and personal experience between a writer and a reader. That's why you find a lot of musicians who love to play live, but who don't do interviews.

Q: You studied painting, didn't you? You studied journalism, too. Your first published book was a memoir. Were you always heading toward fiction?

A: Never. I was really only interested in nonfiction. When I was studying art, my paintings were representational, and usually political. A lot of the paintings I did in high school, for instance, were about class, and I trained myself for ten years to be able to draw photo-realistically. I wanted to be able to get there, and then distort, if need be. I wanted to do [Diego] Rivera–like murals, huge tableaus of the state of the country—documents of contemporary life. Somewhere along the way, I found that I was better able to make things look the way I envisioned with words—more so than with paint. And, even then, it was all journalism for many, many years. The fact that I'm writing fiction now is very strange, and I fully admit I'm learning as I go along. God save us all.

Q: After the wrench of *Staggering Genius*, how liberating was making most of it up?

A: Incredibly liberating.

Q: You had to travel the world for *Velocity*. Did you do it in the same time frame as the characters, mumbling Hunter Thompson–style into a micro-cassette recorder taped to your bicep?

A: Did he do that? I didn't know that. But, yes. I traveled with a friend, in about the same time frame. And I'm a dedicated user of tape recorders. I just wrote a new story that takes place on Kilimanjaro, and brought the tape recorder with me, and was glad I did, though it's hard to make out what I'm saying half the time, with all the heavy breathing. It was a long walk.

Q: What is your own attitude toward money? You put a lot of the paper-back and film monies from *Staggering Genius* into McSweeney's, 826 Valencia, and other charities. Do you share Will's feeling that this stuff was windfall you couldn't justify?

A: I guess all I can say is that I like to keep the funds in circulation. I'm impatient about money. I want to see it do things, right away. Generally, I'd rather it didn't pass through my hands, if it's not absolutely necessary. I just started writing a book about the Lost Boys, a group of Sudanese refugees now living in the US (and many in Australia, actually), and, for that, the money—from Penguin—is just being paid directly to the Lost Boys Foundation, for college scholarships and other support services. I just didn't want it coming to me. Those guys need it and will do good things with it.

Q: There's a randomness to the movements of Will and Hand. They have plans, but the plans are napkin-sized. Does this state of being appeal to you? Are you a big believer in serendipity?

A: I think I am. Whenever I travel, I do it without a plan in mind, and usually without a map. I don't pack a whole lot or think too far ahead. A rental car is the basic thing, then I head in the general direction of wherever seems interesting, and then, once there, I get lost on purpose. It's the only way to travel. It's so rare when the designated tourist stops are any more interesting than random locations half a mile away.

Q: What strikes me about your writing is the perpetual motion. The hall-way sliding in *Staggering Genius*. The jumping between speeding cars in *Velocity*. What is it about movement that makes you want to capture it in words?

A: Well, I wish I knew. You nailed something there, because I've been noticing how often movement, and speed, is involved in the stuff I do. I'm trying to cut down a bit on that. But, then again, I just finished a story about surfing, so there you go—I can't escape it. I guess, on a basic level, I'm interested in speed because speed makes me feel more alive. It's the opposite of

JON CASIMIR / 2003 **61**

writing, which involves so much stasis. You sit down and you want to write about heroism, but what's heroic about writing? It's a weird paradox. Speed, and writing about it, is the closest I can come for the time being.

Q: Why did you write *Velocity*, as compared to, say, taking all those days off and going to the park?

A: I thought of it as a political book. There are dead-serious opinions at the core of that book, below the wandering and the guys steering a car with their tongues. So I got the book out relatively quickly, about six weeks after I finished writing it, because I felt like it had something to say, in the context of where we are, in terms of the First World vis-a-vis the Third, and our roles as individuals—as representatives and beneficiaries of the relatively incredible wealth of our nations—in that relationship.

Genius Loves Company:
A Conversation with Dave Eggers

Christopher J. Lee / 2005

From *Rain Taxi Review of Books* 10, no. 1. © 2005 by *Rain Taxi*. Reprinted by permission.

If there is a word to describe Dave Eggers, it is commitment. This is a central theme to his best-selling memoir *A Heartbreaking Work of Staggering Genius* (2000), a chronicle of family and responsibility that broke away from conventions of the genre to redefine its emotional and stylistic range and to become a Pulitzer Prize finalist in general nonfiction in the process. His first novel, *You Shall Know Our Velocity!* (2002), evinced again a commitment to exploring the contingencies of personal relationships, and to literary form and the possibilities of reinvention, by updating the friends-on-the-road novel established by Twain and Kerouac. Such commitment to literature has been additionally expressed in his ongoing McSweeney's enterprise, an effort that harks back to the heyday of the *Paris Review*, with its stable of acclaimed and lesser-known writers contributing to print and online versions of the journal, as well as an independent press that has published such luminaries as Lydia Davis, Jonathan Lethem, and William T. Vollmann. Profits from this venture have gone to yet another commitment, a community outreach program in both San Francisco and Brooklyn, known as 826 Valencia and 826 NYC, respectively, that has given young people the opportunity to pursue creative writing after school, a quixotic notion these days for sure, but nevertheless a growing success. Amid these various responsibilities, Eggers remains a committed writer. With the recent publication of his first short story collection, *How We Are Hungry* (McSweeney's Books, $22), and a collaborative effort on contemporary philology with Jonathan Safran Foer, *The Future Dictionary of America* (McSweeney's Books, $28), we spoke about his work to date, how he spends his time, and, yes, his various commitments.

Christopher J. Lee: So, to begin, I have to ask: Is the ever-expanding McSweeney's empire part of some master plan dreamed up a long time ago, or has its development been more organic, a set of contingencies that happened to line up in a feasible manner?

Dave Eggers: McSweeney's is as randomly planned an organization as is humanly possible. We never think more than six months ahead, really, though we're beginning to have to think more future-like soon. 826 Valencia, and the organizations like it, or that spring from it, in other cities, necessitates our planning more, and looking as far as five years ahead. But overall, we just see what work there is to do and then we try to do it well.

CJL: Yeats, somewhat famously, made a distinction between life and the work of making art, saying that the true artist must choose the latter completely. I'm curious if you have a different perspective. What is "work" to you? How do you find balance amid the various activities you're involved in?

DE: I've read lots of different sayings about how artists have to be hermetic, and that if they have any involvement with people or the world, it takes away from the art. It's all sort of ridiculous, though, isn't it? How can an artist of any worth lock themselves in an attic? I guess there are the Emily Dickinsons and Henry Dargers, who prefer to be more or less alone, and their work benefits from isolation. But then there the Orwells, Hemingways, Mailers, Sontags, Lowells, and so many others, who choose a more *engagé* existence, because they feel a basic responsibility to participate in the world. Thoreau actually has a nice quote that punches the Yeats quote in the stomach: "How vain it is to sit down to write when you have not stood up to live." I was, for a while, the sort of guy who spent twelve hours a day in front of the computer, thinking everything I was doing was all-important. But it almost killed me; I ran out of things to write about and felt totally disconnected

I fear this is how we end up with so many people writing about the movements of molecules inside their homes. I personally need a lot of interaction with people, and involvement with the world, to keep me honest and inspired.

CJL: This is clear in your current work. In reading your recently published collection of short fiction, *How We Are Hungry*, I was struck by the global sensibility that is also on display in your novel *You Shall Know Our Velocity!* Put differently, unlike other writers of your generation such as Rick Moody, A. M. Homes, and Jonathan Franzen, you seem less concerned with making new inroads into American suburbia, instead showing a greater affinity with international writers like Haruki Murakami—a situation of Defoe or Conrad in a pop, iPod world. Is this a fair description? What thematic concerns compel you?

DE: I guess I wasn't so sure I could add much to the literature of the suburbs, however you might define that (and not that Franzen, Moody, and Homes do only that; they do lots more). I felt like I took on the idea of the suburb in *A Heartbreaking Work of Staggering Genius*, and I wasn't sure I had much else to say about the concept. So I started taking fictional people, many of whom grew up in the suburbs in the Midwest, and began throwing them around the world. It's a fairly easy device, on one level—the fish-out-of-water proposition. I've been interested in travel for a while, because I had a weird evolution, in terms of my attitude about it. I grew up going on a lot of road trips with my mom and siblings, but I didn't leave the country till I was twenty-six. And I didn't really start traveling much until I was about thirty, at which point I did a lot of it. I guess I still haven't gotten over the shocking inequity travelers experience in most parts of the world. Great beauty surrounding great poverty. And generally, because I grew up in the suburbs, and am in a house most of many days, I feel like it's not very interesting material to write about all the time. When I sit down to write, I want to go somewhere and bring readers somewhere they don't necessarily know. That said, I do have another semi-suburban novel cooking; it'll be much more comic than anything I've done in book form.

CJL: I once read that Raymond Carver wrote short fiction because he never actually had the time to write a novel. At times he would sketch out stories while sitting in his car in a parking lot waiting for his children. Is your turn to short fiction influenced by similar circumstances of time? Or is there a different pleasure in writing short fiction that you don't find in a novel or creative nonfiction?

DE: My short stories came about because, after many years of writing a few stories a year, there were enough stories for a collection. The longer stories were written far before life got busier with 826 Valencia and other things. If anything, I have more time generally to write now than I did when I was younger and working two jobs while living with my brother. Now things are relatively more settled.

CJL: You've written in several genres, edited others, and invented some new ones. Does genre mean anything to you? Is it a door or a wall?

DE: I don't want it to mean anything. Definitions of styles, genres, movements, and all that—they're extremely problematic for me. As a matter of fact, I'm answering your questions while I'm stalling on something I'm supposed to be writing, because I can't get the style right for it. I would really love to find a way to fuse all the things I like to do—journalism, fiction, painting, comics, design—but I can't figure out exactly how. Until then, I guess I sometimes struggle in the borderlands between some of these forms.

CJL: In connection with this, I liked the concept of *The Future Dictionary of America* and the definitions by poet David Berman in particular (floorganization, SRV Afterlife, Wappletism). I'm curious how this project came together.

DE: Jonathan Foer had put on an event, Downtown for Democracy, with a bunch of writers giving readings in New York. It was a big deal, and it raised a lot of money to beat Bush in 2004. Afterward, he and Nicole Krauss and I started talking about doing the same sort of thing—harnessing all the disconnect in the book world and putting it into some form of book protest. Foer came up with the dictionary structure, and I happened to have already designed a template for a dictionary (for an abandoned novel). So we used that template and got a lot of help from Françoise Mouly on the rest of the design and production of the book. It all came together very quickly—about two months, really—but it ended up doing really well; I think we raised about $250,000 for voter registration drives in Florida and Ohio.

CJL: When considering your work as a whole, the expression *zeitgeist* comes to mind. *A Heartbreaking Work of Staggering Genius* essentially embraced the rage for memoir happening in the 1990s and in due course managed to define that moment; *You Shall Know Our Velocity!* and *How We Are Hungry* seem to be reaching for something similar, the very use of *You, Our,* and *We* suggesting a collective movement of some kind. *The Future Dictionary of America* and the general popularity of *McSweeney's* can also be seen as manifestations of a zeitgeist. Is this something you think about? Do writers create zeitgeist moments, or do they capture them?

DE: I guess it's possible for writers to assist the creation of movements, but it's pretty rare now. Books don't have the fueling power they once did, I don't think. Music might be better suited to getting people going in one direction or another. But I admit that I've always been interested in movements, and I've always been pretty optimistic about the things that can get done when a lot of people paddle in one direction. I don't consciously try to define any group of people, but I can't deny that sometimes I would hope to inspire or motivate a group of people. Sometimes you can do that pretty well with a book, since you're in someone's head for so long.

CJL: So why do so many women dig Roxy Music?

DE: Women love falcons, and there's that falcon on the cover of that one album. I think that's what it is—the falcon.

CJL: Before we finish, I understand you are working on a new book about the "lost boys" of Sudan. Can you talk about this project?

DE: I'm writing a biography of a young man named Achak Deng (he went by "Dominic Arou" for a while—long story). He's one of about three thousand young Sudanese refugees now living in the US, and his story is biblical in scale and depth of suffering. But the book does have a somewhat happy ending: he and I went back to Sudan last year and were able to find his parents, who were still alive. He hadn't seen them in seventeen years.

CJL: Finally, in the spirit of the times, complete this sentence: Paper is . . .

DE: sexy; off-white paper is sexier.

Citizen Dave: The *Stop Smiling* Interview with Dave Eggers

JC Gabel / 2006

From *Stop Smiling*, issue 27. © 2006 by *Stop Smiling*. Reprinted by permission.

Stop Smiling: What is your earliest memory of growing up in Illinois?

Dave Eggers: Well, I was born in Boston and I lived in Brooklyn Heights until I was three. Then we moved to Chicago, to a suburb called Lake Forest, and we lived there until I went to college. Where we grew up—this is going to sound like a joke to anybody who knows Lake Forest—I didn't realize the reputation of the town until I left for college. I wasn't ignorant of the fact that it was a comfortable place to live, but to us it was just a very Huck Finn place to grow up. It sounds insane to say because it's a well-manicured, just-so WASP suburb. But when you're a kid, you don't know about that kind of stuff, and of course you can't choose where you grow up. We were out in a part of town where it's mostly ranch houses. It's fairly close to the highway. Most of it was undeveloped back then, so there were these vast fields. There was a creek in the back of our house, and all of my friends lived on one side of the creek or the other. So we waded in the creek, we swam in the creek, we would take boats down the creek. In the winter we walked to each other's houses on the frozen creek. We thought of it as the Mississippi River, but it was actually something called the Skokie Valley drainage ditch. I remember that town being all about the natural world. We rode our bikes everywhere. We went to the beach all the time—winter, summer, fall, whenever. The town was comfortable, but I didn't know it was fancy. My friends' parents were teachers—one of them owned a frame shop. Our next-door neighbors were carpenters. Eventually, I came to know there was real money in the town, but it wasn't in my neighborhood.

SS: When did you start going into the city?

DE: When I was thirteen I took classes at the Art Institute, and all through high school—summers, weekends, and nights—I would take the train. I lived on it—the Northwest Line. It stopped not too far from my house and went straight into that Helmut Jahn building. I would walk toward the lake, to Michigan Avenue. I loved that.

SS: F. Scott Fitzgerald mentions Lake Forest in the first chapter of *Great Gatsby*.

DE: That's when it was a place where people had summer homes. That was as far as we knew. All we cared about was Mr. T. He was the only celebrity we knew there—and the Bears. Actually, that was a big claim to fame—that the Bears practiced there. Willie Gault lived down the street from me, and that was incredible. We never saw him, but we heard he lived there.

SS: You were in the same high school class with Vince Vaughn.

DE: We went to school together from fifth grade on. We were friendly, with a lot of mutual friends, but we didn't socialize much. In high school, he hung out with the football players, but he was also a bridge with the artsy people. He hung out with the football guys—they called themselves the Hammerheads, with T-shirts and everything—but he was also in the school plays, emceed the talent show, all that. So I really think he united different factions, to a degree that he ended up being the class president. His joke is that it's the only reason they didn't flunk him out of school. It wouldn't look good for the high school to flunk the class president.

SS: Were you a smart aleck in high school, or were you shy?

DE: I was in between. I was a pain in the ass to my gym teachers, but I wasn't the most outgoing guy, at least for a few years. I joined a lot of clubs eventually. I was really introverted for a while. I was covered in acne. I hit puberty late. My hair got curly and dark. I grew up with blonde, straight hair. It's so sad—such a cruel joke. You get used to it. I had a couple of years of adolescent angst. Then I did the usual stuff: I joined the literary magazine, the yearbook, the newspaper. I played soccer. I hung out with the painters, spent all my free time in the art room. I had a lot of really supportive teachers, and they helped get me more engaged with the world and feel valued. I keep in touch with most of them.

SS: Did you consciously pick the University of Illinois knowing that you were going to go into journalism?

DE: No. I thought I was going to a small college out East. I didn't get into some of the places I wanted to, and the few places I did get in were expensive. My family had three kids in school, and my dad had been out of work, so we all went to public schools. I didn't even visit U of I. I'd never been to

Champaign, but everybody in Illinois applies there. It wasn't even on my radar as a place where I would actually go to school. It was close to home, but it was in the middle of nowhere. The first time I saw it was when I went down there to stay.

SS: Were you alarmed by how big the school was?

DE: I was freaked out mostly by the landscape, because water is important to me. Topography and trees are important to me. Champaign is pretty empty—at least the campus. I remember the drive alone really depressed me. My freshman year roommate was alarming, I guess. He was twenty-one years old, a fifth-year senior. He was bald and sweaty and drank crazily. He thought he was the reincarnation of F. Scott Fitzgerald. Every night he would drink when he was writing. This was before anybody had computers in college, so he would type on a manual all night. He would drink a case of Little Kings beer every time he sat down to write. That's what got him primed. Then one night he woke me up and he said, "I think I can tell you. I trust you. I'm the reincarnation of F. Scott Fitzgerald." He wasn't saying, "I write like him" or "I'm as good as him." He actually thought he had been chosen as the vessel for the soul of Fitzgerald. He was from the West Side of Chicago, with a heavy accent and everything. I don't remember reading anything he wrote, because we only lived together a semester. I do want to say I liked U of I. I liked everyone there and I learned a lot. I recommend it to anybody if they can deal with being in the middle of nowhere. I studied painting for my first three years, and I had a studio, but my last year I got serious and took journalism courses, and that's technically what I graduated with a degree in. Although I didn't quite graduate officially until two years ago.

SS: When you left Chicago after your parents passed away, did you think you were ever coming back?

DE: Sure. The weird thing is, I loved it there. I really liked high school. I liked the town I grew up in. I have tons of friends still there. I have a lot of ties there. I just didn't have a family life there. It wasn't some place I was escaping. When you leave a place, sometimes it's because of the accumulated weight of everything you've seen and done there. You're ready for a fresh start. I think sometimes you can too closely associate that with a place, as opposed to people or the fact that you broke up with somebody there—like, it's Chicago's fault that Cindy left you, or whatever. But I never had that. I was just ready to move. My parents had just died, and it was time to leave for a while. Besides, I didn't have a whole lot of choice in the matter.

SS: Why San Francisco?

DE: My sister was about to start law school at Berkeley and had deferred a year while my parents were sick. So when it was time to leave Chicago, my little brother and I followed her to California. We knew that we'd live near each other and she would share parenting responsibilities.

SS: Is it correct that Timothy McSweeney was someone who had the same last name as your mother's maiden name and was writing letters to your family saying, "I'm a relative."

DE: Yeah. My grandfather was an ob-gyn, and he'd overseen the birth of this baby who was adopted by a different McSweeney family. My grandfather was named Daniel McSweeney. It was just a coincidence. There were a lot of McSweeneys in Boston. Later on in life, this baby grew up and was looking for his birth parents and somehow thought my grandfather was his real father. My grandfather was dead at that point, so Timothy looked for the next of kin, and that was my mom.

SS: It wasn't some kind of Carl Solomon–type character. He was honestly looking for his parents?

DE: He was a troubled guy. He wrote his letters from institutions. He's still institutionalized now. He was really hoping for his true family. When we named the magazine *McSweeney's*, I didn't think he was a real person. I didn't know the backstory.

SS: You discovered it along the way?

DE: We discovered it when we had an intern named Ross McSweeney, who is Timothy's nephew. Timothy McSweeney is a real person. Ross had started interning a week before, and we were all out at a bar or something, and he said, "I might be related in some way." I said, "Yeah, we're both from Boston. There are a lot of McSweeneys—maybe somewhere down the line, we're related." He said, "Well, yeah. Actually, I think that Timothy is my uncle." He told the whole story. Timothy is his father's brother. He's seen him in the last few years. He's still in a home somewhere; it's very sad. He was very talented. He was an artist, went to Johns Hopkins, eventually taught there.

SS: Is there one writer you read in high school or college that you've clung on to?

DE: Lorrie Moore. I read her when I was interning at *Chicago* magazine. One of the older editors gave me one of her books. I was an editorial intern for the front section. The editor that was there, Richard Babcock, came on the same year I interned, and he's still there. I interned one summer. I liked magazines, I guess. I wasn't sure what I was going to do. I did research. I spent a lot of time researching an article called "Custom Made Chicago"— where in the city you could get custom chairs, shoes, clothes. It was a typical intern project, I guess. Later on, when I got really serious about writing, Saul Bellow was the person who I idolized more than anybody else. The writing I like best is by writers who capture the enormity of the experience of life, everything you can see and feel in life, everything all in one galloping sentence or paragraph. He does that on every page—everything from the emotional turmoil someone feels after being cuckolded by his wife, on the same page as him thinking about the entire history of Western thought, on the same page as how his protagonist feels about the natural world while he's holed up in a cabin. Bellow casts a net around all of life and makes you feel like that's what it is to be alive. He's describing it. It's maximalist. It's a lot more in tune with what I would want to read, rather than something that's real minimal and sparse and nihilistic.

SS: Which of his books is your favorite?

DE: *Herzog.* With *Henderson the Rain King* second, I guess. *Augie March* after that.

SS: Getting back to your books—you travel a lot promoting them. Do you still like doing book tours?

DE: I don't always love getting up in front of a microphone. I'm not a performer by nature, but I love meeting readers. I could sit there and talk to people all day. Books are very personal. To meet somebody who's spent all that time with what you've written—I'm affected by that, I'm moved by it. I'll talk to anybody because I feel like they've given me a lot. I always feel a strong connection with any reader that bothers to read what I do and comes out to see me. It hits me hard. It's just that as I get older I don't like traveling as much.

SS: With the *McSweeney's* project, you had no idea it would grow into what it is, likewise with 826 Valencia. Did you ever outline on paper what you were thinking about doing?

DE: No. Nothing close. The scale of everything is so small. And they're all sort of disconnected to each other in a natural way. It would be one thing if any given project made money, but these are all money-losing propositions, or they just barely break even. Every time we think about doing something like, "Let's put out a monthly magazine," the first thought is that it's stupid. It's insane. Then we think, "Well, what if we did it on a really small scale and we have one paid employee and everybody else is part-time? Will it work?" So we do the math and think about how we can pull it off without losing money. And it's always about scale. With *McSweeney's* I thought the most we would ever do was four issues. After four we thought, "Okay, eight." It was just an effort to experiment with the form. I had a lot of friends who couldn't find a home for some of their work, so it was like, "Let's try to make a vehicle where these unusual things could be published." It was fun. People sort of liked it. Then we thought, "As long as it's interesting, as long as we're developing, as long as it's challenging or if we're reinventing it, we'll keep going." That went on longer than we thought. And the addition of Barb Bersche and Eli Horowitz and Jordan Bass and all the people who have helped along the way—they keep coming up with new ideas, and that's why it stays alive. We have a poetry issue coming out that's all the work of a former intern. I couldn't care less where the ideas come from. Whoever has the best idea, or whoever has it and can follow through, should do it. I've always wanted it this way, but also we can't afford to do it any other way.

SS: The pirate supply store in San Francisco was originally conceived because you had to have a commercial storefront in order to function legally in that particular space—is that right?

DE: Yeah. It's zoned for retail. At 826, the landlord wanted retail or a restaurant.

SS: When you were first gutting the place, it looked like a pirate shop?

DE: Yeah. After we gutted the building, the floors were nice wood, and then there were nice whitewashed beams underneath acoustic tile that we tore down. It had the look of the hull of a ship and it just made us laugh. Barb and I and her old boyfriend gutted the place. We thought it could be funny, and it just kept making us laugh. Along the way, we thought, "Kids might like this, too, and it could attract them."

SS: The location is central to a lot of schools in the vicinity.

DE: We're in the middle of the highest concentration of schools in the city. Ninety-five percent of the kids that come to 826 after school walk straight from school. For the workshops later on, most walk or ride their bike or get a ride or take the bus, but it was the perfect place. It was my favorite neighborhood in the city, and the schools there were up against great challenges. We have a lot of families that moved to the US not long ago, and the parents don't speak a lot of English, and the kids have to assimilate as much as they can. We knew that there would be a big English-as-a-second-language component.

SS: What else are you working on?

DE: We're working on a book about Hurricane Katrina, for one. This is part of our Voice of Witness series. A few years ago, I gave an introduction when Studs Terkel came and spoke at Berkeley. I grew up reading him. My dad loved his work, so it was an amazing experience. Around the same time I was asked to teach a course at UC–Berkeley at the Graduate School of Journalism. We thought, "What if we take oral history as the foundation?"

At the same Terkel event, I met Lola Vollen, a physician and human rights expert who had worked a lot in Bosnia. She also started the Life after Exoneration program and worked with the wrongfully convicted after their release. I met her at that Studs Terkel event, and we started talking about the same thing. "Where do you hear the voices of the wrongfully convicted, and other human rights victims? There should be a book out there where you can read their oral histories." So right then and there, at the Terkel event, we thought, "Okay, we'll make a book." That became the course at Berkeley that we taught, and the resulting book was *Surviving Justice: America's Wrongfully Convicted and Exonerated.* Now Voice of Witness is a series where we use oral history as a way of illuminating these human rights crises. I hope it works. We're trying to make it teachable, too. We work with high school teachers at making it teachable at that level and the college level.

SS: Did it ever occur to you that you might one day be in the role of a teacher—at your own space and at the college level?

DE: I probably won't teach college again any time soon. It took far more time than I accounted for. But I always wanted to teach. My mom taught little kids, and my sister was a teacher for a while, and a lot of my best friends taught after college. I've kept in touch with so many of my high school teachers and even my grade school teachers, so it felt like a world I was pretty connected with still. It was something that was always on my mind, I guess—even before 826. The idea of teachers' salaries had been on my mind because I had a couple of good friends who had to quit teaching in the city because the salaries weren't in keeping with how they could live.

SS: So now you're helping coordinate 826 tutoring centers all over the country. There's the one we've been talking about in San Francisco, but there are new branches in Seattle, New York, Los Angeles, Ann Arbor, and Chicago. What is the theme for the Chicago storefront?

DE: It'll be a supply store for those who have to work undercover—spies, CIA, KGB agents—people like that. The front will be nondescript, and there'll be nothing exciting in the window, because if you're a spy you don't want to be seen going into a spy supply store. Instead, there'll be a big sign outside that says "The Boring Store," in big neon lights. And then it'll say, "Nothing is inside, move along, nothing to see here"—something like that. Then there'll be a roll of masking tape in the window or something incredibly boring, but when you go inside it'll be very high tech. But the tutoring center has been open all year. The tutoring always comes first, and the storefront is a way to raise money and entice kids. Each center differs depending on the city. Los Angeles doesn't have a storefront. Seattle has one, and they've got more space than any of the others. New York has a storefront. Ann Arbor doesn't. It just depends. The organizers in each city can interpret the idea however they want to. The storefront ended up being a way to raise money. It helps pay the rent, and it brings people in. Instead of being a nonprofit hidden and tucked away into a corner high-rise, which a lot of nonprofits are, it's on the street level, so people can walk by, they can see what's going on, kids can walk in and discover it that way.

SS: You're about to venture into film. You've adapted *Where the Wild Things Are*. Spike Jonze is directing the film. Can you tell me about that?

DE: I love that book. I love Maurice Sendak. I read everything he did when I was young doing my own drawings—I wrote and illustrated my own books when I was a kid. He was my idol. When Spike was starting to work on the film, he had known Maurice for years. Together they talked about what would be a good fit, and Maurice thought Spike would be the one to do the best job with it. At some point, Spike called me to help him write the screenplay, but it's really Spike's vision. Spike had a whole arc in mind and a way he wanted to tell the story. So I'm helping shape and put on paper what Spike and Maurice together want to make of it. I'm the third wheel—just sort of happy to be along.

SS: You mentioned illustrating and making books when you were younger. Did you know you might someday go into publishing?

DE: Not as a kid, really. I guess in high school I started liking the idea. It's the same reason we publish so many student books and newspapers at 826, because of the feeling of empowerment you get when your work is out there. I remember that feeling when I would write and design and put out something. It's real and tangible and you're able to disseminate it in whatever small quantity—there is a real feeling of empowerment and connection. That was the difference with painting, at least in my experience. It wasn't as much about connection. It was more of an isolated kind of life, less social. That's why I spent more time in publishing. So we try to give that same experience to the students.

SS: I think it's important that people understand the process. They might not think of it as so daunting if they did understand. Is that what you hope people come away with?

DE: Yes. Even when we were doing *Might* magazine we used to host kids from the YMCA and teach them Quark, Photoshop, Freehand, other programs. We taught them these things to sort of say, "It's not out of reach." Everything from doing your own newspaper or book to doing a magazine, to designing your own album cover.

SS: It's unbelievable what's happened in the last ten or fifteen years with desktop publishing. You can make ten copies of something and make it look as professional as if you'd made a hundred thousand.

DE: We've seen it happen with so many kids. We've just finished another book with a bunch of students at Galileo High School, a huge public school that serves low-income students from all over the city. Probably 25 percent of them go to college. But they worked on this book together, with hundreds of tutors. These kids spend hundreds of hours, lunches, after school, weekends, and holidays working on seven or eight drafts of a five-page essay. All for no credit. A lot of times they're seniors, and it's too late to use it on their college applications, but they all want to see their work in print, just to have it in a real paperback book that will stand forever, that can be read by their families, teachers, friends, and available in stores, even Amazon. Their parents can see that it's real, and the students see that their thoughts are worth this sort of dignity. We try to dignify the work and honor it in that way. And the experience can be totally life-changing. It was for me, and I think it is for a lot of these students.

The Rumpus Long Interview with Dave Eggers

Stephen Elliott / 2009

From *The Rumpus*, June 9, 2009. © 2009 by Stephen Elliott. Reprinted by permission.

The Rumpus: We both went to the University of Illinois in Champaign-Urbana. We didn't know each other, but we both ended up as writers living in San Francisco. What's the connection? Is U of I the best university in the country?

Dave Eggers: The weird thing is that I knew your sister Victoria while we were in school. She and I worked at the *Daily Illini* together. I guess you and I didn't meet until maybe 2002 in San Francisco. You used to come talk to my high school classes at 826 Valencia. Wait, I didn't answer the question.

Is Illinois the best state and the best state school? I don't think anyone's ever debated either of those questions. Not seriously, at least. Illinois is the best state, and U of I is everyone's favorite university located in east central Illinois.

Rumpus: This book, *Zeitoun*, is coming out very close to *Away We Go*.

Eggers: It's weird, because they happened over such a long period of time. I don't know; I was working on *Zeitoun* back in 2006. That book was pretty slow-going. It took an incredible amount of research. And the first draft of *Away We Go* was written in 2005. So both have been sort of slow processes. It's odd that they both landed this summer, but it didn't seem right to push *Zeitoun* back to 2010 just because the movie was scheduled this summer.

Rumpus: *Zeitoun* is nonfiction, set during Katrina in New Orleans and its chaotic aftermath, as seen through the eyes of a Muslim American family, the Zeitouns, who were living Uptown during the storm. I didn't hear about *Zeitoun* until a few weeks ago, when you printed a copy for me, which I briefly considered selling on eBay. You were pretty quiet about it.

Eggers: Sometimes we [at McSweeney's] don't do galleys for my own books. I always blow the deadline to get galleys done. Usually there's only a month or so between when the book's done and when the hardcovers come back from the printer, so we sometimes skip the galley step—galleys cost a lot of money, and we don't have that kind of budget. So we print a few, and they're about twenty dollars each to print at Kinko's or wherever, so it's hard to justify all that expense when the actual hardcovers are coming back from the printer in a few weeks. And this book was meant to be out back in March or April anyway. I just kept fiddling with it, and it took longer than expected to get finished.

Rumpus: But you always fiddle until the last minute. I remember that from working on *Happy Baby* with you and also publishing *Where to Invade Next* with McSweeney's.

Eggers: Yeah, the McSweeney's publishing system allows that. We vet books as thoroughly as anyone, but then when they're ready to go to press we send them to press. There's not much of a delay between when they're ready and when they're available to readers. For *Zeitoun*, the gap was about six weeks. We sent it to press in mid-May, and it'll come out in early July, depending on how far from the printer we need to truck the books. The printer's in Canada, so maybe if you're in Canada you'll get it at the end of June.

Rumpus: The book is about Abdulrahman and Kathy Zeitoun, who have lived in New Orleans for a long time. Abdulrahman stays in the city during the hurricane, and afterward he begins to canoe around the city trying to help people. How did you meet the Zeitouns?

Eggers: We have this series of books called Voice of Witness, where we use oral history as a window into human rights crises. Back in 2005, right after Hurricane Katrina, a group came together in New Orleans and elsewhere, and they interviewed New Orleanians about their experiences before, during, and after the storm. The book became *Voices from the Storm*, edited by Chris Ying and Lola Vollen, and one of the narrators in that book was Abdulrahman Zeitoun.

Right after the book came out, I was in New Orleans to visit the New Orleans Center for the Creative Arts—this incredible high school for the arts—and while I was in town I met up with Abdulrahman and his wife, Kathy. We started talking, and pretty soon it was clear that there was a lot more to his story than we'd been able to cover in *Voices from the Storm*.

Rumpus: This book is nonfiction.

Eggers: It is. That's my background. My degree—from our sacred alma mater, U of I—is in journalism, and that's what I did for a living for a long while, so I still have that instinct that says to follow a story if it seems like it hasn't been fully told. So I started doing more interviews with the Zeitouns.

Rumpus: And?

Eggers: And their story intrigued me from the start, given that it's at the intersection of so many issues in recent American life: the debacle of the government response to Katrina, the struggles facing even the most successful immigrants, a judicial system in need of repair, the problem of wrongful conviction, the paranoia wrought by the War on Terror, widespread Islamophobia . . .

Rumpus: How was it working with the Zeitouns? How involved were they?

Eggers: They're really a beautiful family, and we worked on the book together for a long time. With a book like this, I think you get the most accuracy when you involve your subjects as much as possible. I think I sent the manuscript to the Zeitouns for six or seven reads. They caught little inaccuracies each time. They have to live with the book, of course, as much as I do, so I needed their approval. With *What Is the What* and with this book, I consider the book as much theirs as mine. So they were intimately involved in every step, as were their extended families. We had many months to get everyone's approval over everything, to make sure it was accurate.

Rumpus: The anniversary of Katrina is coming up.

Eggers: We definitely knew that, and didn't want to release the book too close to that. It's such a horrific anniversary that we didn't want to seem to be timing the release to coincide with it in any way. I meant to get it out in April. It was scheduled for April, but it wasn't ready in time.

Rumpus: You're setting up a nonprofit for *Zeitoun* the same way as with *What Is the What.*

Eggers: With the help of some lawyers working pro bono in New Orleans, we're setting up a foundation to distribute the funds from the book.

Rumpus: So you're not being paid.

Eggers: Not for this, no.

Rumpus: Is this the same or different from the Valentino Achak Deng Foundation? And who runs that organization?

Eggers: The VAD Foundation is actually using the funds to build a school complex in his hometown. And that's really Valentino's doing. I think I had to do about 1 percent of the work involved in the foundation. We set up the parameters of the foundation, and the rest was Valentino's doing. He hired Greg Larson—his foundation director here in the US—and from there it's been those two guys, and a few volunteers, and all the teachers and builders Valentino's hired in Sudan. Valentino has an incredible organization in his hometown, and he's built it entirely himself.

Rumpus: Greg Larson was a student of mine, and I recommended him for the internship at McSweeney's, which led to him applying for the job with Valentino. I'm not trying to take credit. I'm just saying.

Eggers: Greg's incredible, and the two of them together are a real force of nature. Those two guys, and their builders in Marial Bai, have done what I think no one else could have done, which is break ground on a twelve-building educational complex in a remote part of southern Sudan and open his school within nine months of that groundbreaking. They started classes at the beginning of May. It's the first secondary school in the region. I mean, that's just astounding to anyone. NGO workers and people we know in the government of South Sudan are all flabbergasted. The minister for education for the government of South Sudan just flew to Marial Bai a few days ago, just to see this school that Valentino built. There are pictures on his website.

Rumpus: And the Zeitouns will do the same kind of thing? A foundation and projects in New Orleans?

Eggers: It'll be different this time. The Zeitouns already have a business they run, and they have five kids, so they're not in a place where they want to start and run a new nonprofit. So the Zeitoun Foundation will be mostly a grantor. Funds from the book will go to the foundation and then flow to a bunch of nonprofits already working in New Orleans. There are so many great organizations there already that it didn't seem necessary to start another from scratch. Better in this case to help nurture the work already being done.

Rumpus: I guess people will want to know why you chose nonfiction for this and fiction for Valentino Deng's story in *What Is the What.*

Eggers: I definitely concede that it's odd, given they're both forms of bi-ography. But with Valentino's story, there were too many events and time periods that we had to cover, but were so long ago, that Valentino's memories weren't sufficient for nonfiction. So in some cases I had to take an event about which he might have remembered a skeletal amount, and then flesh it out a bit given the historical record and personal observation and some re-creation of dialogue. *What Is the What* is Valentino's true story, but it's not strict nonfiction in that we can say, Yes, back in 1988, on October 31, Valentino was standing in this one spot. But of course all the events in *What Is the What* are based closely on Valentino's experiences.

Rumpus: Including the attack that begins the book?

Eggers: People sometimes ask me if I think that's where the fiction comes in. Valentino was attacked in his home in October of 2005. And when he was, that's when I thought that Valentino's life in America, and all the continuing struggles of that life, should be part of the book. Until that attack,

I'd planned on having the book end when he reached the United States. It would have been a very different book and a simpler one. But after knowing Valentino for three years at that point, it was clear that the story didn't end with a simple and triumphant story of a refugee getting to the United States.

Rumpus: Zeitoun's story is also one of an immigrant's struggle. But it's nonfiction this time.

Eggers: Because Zeitoun's story is so recent, and there was so much documentation available, and I could interview so many of the people involved; I could recount the events sufficiently to write it as nonfiction. But in a few ways, their stories are similar, in that they're incredibly hardworking people who are victimized by societal indifference.

Rumpus: One of the things that really struck me in *Zeitoun* was that I really felt I was there in a way. Or rather I could see what the world looked like to a man sleeping on his roof in a tent, half of his home underwater.

Eggers: Zeitoun's experiences right after the storm are surreal, and very quiet—the opposite of the chaos we saw on the news reports. The Zeitouns live in a neighborhood called Uptown, which is a few miles from the downtown/Superdome area of the city, and even farther from neighborhoods that were harder hit, like the Lower Ninth Ward. So Abdulrahman Zeitoun stayed behind in his house in this quieter neighborhood, and his experiences were very different from what we often see or hear about. He had an experience that was kind of postapocalyptic in a way: everything very quiet, where he was canoeing around, seeing few people, helping neighbors and pets who were stuck in the upper floors of houses.

Rumpus: How much time did you spend with Zeitoun and Kathy and in New Orleans? How hard was it to do the research for this book? What were the obstacles?

Eggers: The book took about three years, and the Zeitouns were deeply involved in every step of the process. So we spent a lot of time together in New Orleans, and over the phone, and via email. And I was able to go to Syria and meet Abdulrahman's family there, and spent some time with his brother Ahmad, a ship captain in Spain. Ahmad was a wealth of information and is a meticulous record-keeper. I had to get to know the whole extended family because Abdulrahman's life before New Orleans figures into the story too. I had to go to Syria and see where he grew up and visit the ancestral home of the family, on this island off the coast, Arwad Island.

Rumpus: You do a great job at giving the different perspectives of different people in New Orleans during Katrina. There was a lot of fear, and some people in government, some police officers, might have overreacted. But you go out of your way to contact those people and find out what their experience was like. Some of the people who made mistakes also saved lives, often in the same day.

Eggers: It was strange, because even the police officers I talked to who made mistakes, they talk about how chaotic it was, and how they came into the city with bad information. All the media coverage was so dire, and there was so much talk of lawlessness that they came in with the idea that they were coming to a war zone. Tens of thousands of cops and soldiers came to the city heavily armed, with riot gear on, machine guns, armed helicopters, tanks, everything. And then they arrived and found just a lot of desperate people needing food and water and rescue. Every law enforcement officer I talked to said the same thing, that they came in with a mission to restore order, and they ended up spending all their time doing search and rescue.

Rumpus: Could you talk about some of the misperceptions that occurred during Katrina? Particularly the government's willingness to believe that terrorist cells working with al-Qaeda could be on the loose intentionally exacerbating the chaos in the aftermath of the storm?

Eggers: There's a very interesting document available online—or it was last time I checked—called "How Terrorists Might Exploit a Hurricane." It was issued by the Department of Homeland Security in 2003. It actually goes through all the possibilities for terrorists who might swoop in after a hurricane and somehow make things worse. This was just indicative of the madness of Homeland Security, which had absorbed FEMA after 9/11. In the nineties, FEMA was a freestanding agency and was run exceedingly well by James Lee Witt. It was dedicated to actually helping people after disasters. But when it was folded into Homeland Security, its focus was altered, and anti-terrorism sucked out all the air from the room. There are some incredible stories about local governments being unable to get the attention of FEMA unless there was some terrorist component to whatever natural threat they faced.

Rumpus: How do you mean?

Eggers: There are a couple great books that detail this. There's a fantastic one called *Disaster: Hurricane Katrina and the Failure of National Security*, by Christopher Cooper and Robert Block. It's very lucid and reads like a thriller. It details how after 9/11 the focus of FEMA moved from the relief from hurricanes and floods and fires to this overarching anti-terrorism agenda. It became hard for cities and states to get any FEMA money or attention unless there was an anti-terrorism component to whatever they asked for. It was absurd. And that's partly why the response to Katrina was so botched. The agency had been recalibrated for anti-terrorism; response to actual natural disasters didn't figure so well into their new mindset. And that's why, in part, the government response to the disaster was overwhelmingly a military one. Instead of search and rescue, they sent tens of thousands of heavily armed soldiers, all of them expecting widespread rioting or some version of urban combat.

Rumpus: Were there obstacles in writing *Zeitoun*? Were there any documents you were unable to get to?

Eggers: There were some obstacles, but I had some help in New Orleans from people who work with the courts down there. Billy Sothern, a great writer and lawyer who defends prisoners on death row, was helpful all the way through and connected me to some of his colleagues, who helped get some documents I couldn't otherwise access. But really the book is about this family and what they went through. Most of the research consisted of interviews with them and then the research in Syria and Spain.

Rumpus: Did you read the Qur'an? You excerpt it a few times.

Eggers: I read a few editions of the Qur'an, trying to find an edition that reflected what all Arabic speakers talk about—the incredible beauty of the language. I found what I consider a phenomenal translation by Laleh Bakhtiar. Her edition is recent, and it's called *The Sublime Quran*. The way she brings it into the English language, it's incredibly powerful and beautiful. I know it's still a far cry from hearing it in Arabic, but still, this is the edition I've been pushing on people.

Rumpus: What are you working on now?

Eggers: I guess we've talked about this newspaper idea. We're putting out a newspaper prototype. It'll be an issue of *McSweeney's*, but it'll look and read like a daily newspaper and will cover the news on the day it appears.

Rumpus: You have a lot of optimism about print in general.

Eggers: Well, there are still a billion books sold every year. And there are about a billion newspapers printed every day. I understand when people are worried about aspects of the business, and as a small and always struggling publisher, we worry at McSweeney's too, but there's an element of doomsaying that's just premature. The Kindle, for example, has a comparatively tiny portion of the overall book sales, but I have friends who already assume that new books won't even be printed on paper in a year or two. It's kind of extreme, and it ignores a fair bit of reality.

Rumpus: I know a lot of your optimism comes from your working with kids at the 826 centers.

Eggers: The students we serve at 826, by and large, just aren't addicted to electronic media—not in the way we're led to believe all kids are. Most of our students don't have cell phones of their own, and they don't have computers at home. So they come into 826, and they work with paper and pencil on their homework. Honestly, that's about 80 percent of what we do. Even at the high school level, the students we work with aren't soaking in the internet all the time. To some extent all the doom about the printed word is a class thing. Wealthier kids who can afford their own phones and computers are probably spending more time online, and in some cases, less time with books, but the kids we work with are honestly pretty enamored of books and newspapers. It means a lot to them to have their work between two covers, an actual book that they can see on a shelf next to other books. There's a mystique about the printed word. And the students who come into 826 every day really read. These middle schoolers have read everything. Judy Blume came into the center in San Francisco one day, and she was mobbed. Fifty kids swarmed her. They practically tackled her. Same thing with Daniel Handler, who writes the Lemony Snicket books. These are by and large kids whose parents immigrated here from Latin America, and English isn't spoken at home. But they've read all thirteen Lemony Snicket books. So I have optimism about print because I see these kids and how much they love to read. And they work on our student newspapers and anthologies and a dozen other print projects. They really have a thing for print. And I do too. I fear sometimes we're actually giving up too soon. We adults have to have faith. And we have to rededicate ourselves to examining what in any given issue of our daily papers is really speaking to anyone under eighteen. That's a challenge. I was just in Chicago, and the *Tribune* there does all kinds of very interesting stuff to reach out to younger readers. It's something that we all have to think about.

Rumpus: So you're not looking at a post-paper world.

Eggers: My admittedly strange opinion is that we need to try harder with print. We can't just give up on it. Inevitably there will be some loss of newspaper readership, but even that will stabilize. Not everyone wants all their news online. Do we all want to look at screens from 8:00 a.m. to 10:00 p.m.? There's room in the world for both online and paper. It doesn't have to be zero-sum. I guess that's one of the things that's always frustrating to hear, that the rise of the internet means the death of print. There's always this zero-sum way of painting any given industry or trend, while the reality will be more nuanced. I think newspapers that adjust a bit will survive and still do great work. But we do need to give people reasons to pay money for the physical object. The landscape right now does require that we in the print world try harder. We have to think of the things that print does best, and do those things better than ever before. We need to use the paper, maximize the physical product.

Rumpus: Could you talk a little more about this newspaper you're putting together? What's involved?

Eggers: I come from a newspaper background, and I still get most of my news from newspapers and magazines. So we've been spending a lot of time at McSweeney's just running numbers and starting to make a prototype, trying to prove that there can be a way to run a newspaper in 2009 without losing your shirt. And so far we're pretty sure we can create a workable model. It'll look different in some ways, but it'll be a true newspaper, where journalists are paid well to hold their government accountable, where they have time to do enterprise journalism, to seek out stories all over the world and write them well and at length. But we're just doing a prototype. It'll just be a one-off thing, but we'll be providing all the information you'd need to replicate it, in terms of the economics of it. The hope is that, for example, the folks formerly at the *Rocky Mountain News* might band together and put out a print newspaper again. It doesn't have to be a billion-dollar enterprise. We'll have a business plan included in the issue, hoping to prove that there's an opportunity for smallish newspapers of high quality to exist and stay in business. The business model will be a bit different than some of the bigger papers, but the emphasis on investigative journalism, and great writing, on the best photography and design and all the things that newspapers can and should do—all that will still be there.

Rumpus: Do you feel you'll be competing with internet sites?

Eggers: No. I mean, there's that zero-sum thinking again. I actually don't think newspapers and the internet need to compete with each other. I think that we're heading to a point where the two media will each do what they do best and coexist peacefully. I really think we're all in it together, all of us who care about journalism, so we should all be thinking of what's best for journalism—and that, I think, is to find a sustainable model for news-gathering on the web and on paper. There are probably workable models out there for both, and we're going to be concentrating on the newspaper side of things. We're not making any claims beyond that.

Rumpus: So that comes out in the fall, the *McSweeney's* newspaper prototype?

Eggers: We've been working on it for about five months and will spend the rest of the summer on it. Then it'll come out one day, ideally in September.

Dave Eggers's Heartbreaking Work of Staggering Reality

Andrew O'Hehir / 2009

From *Salon*, July 16, 2009. © 2009 by *Salon*. An online version remains in the *Salon* archives. Reprinted by permission.

For better or worse, Dave Eggers will always be known as the author of the quasi-fictional memoir, *A Heartbreaking Work of Staggering Genius*, a 2000 bestseller that recounted his experiences raising his little brother after the sudden deaths of their parents. (He began writing it, I should note, while employed as an editor at *Salon*.) That sudden rise to literary celebrity threatened to turn Eggers into a Generation-X cult figure or avatar of sincerity, but viewed in retrospect he handled the lightning strike of success about as well as anyone could. He has refused to be trapped by the highly self-conscious literary voice of that book and, more impressive still, has tried to turn his success toward real-world ends.

Eggers has founded a magazine and a publishing house, funded a wide range of youth-literacy programs through his 826 Valencia center, and co-directed an oral history program called Voice of Witness, focused on permitting survivors and witnesses of human rights abuse to tell their stories. Among various other things, Voice of Witness sparked *Zeitoun*, Eggers's latest nonfiction volume. You couldn't write a book more different from *Heartbreaking Work* if you tried. Like his 2006 novel, *What Is the What*, which was based on the life of a Sudanese refugee, this is a work of testimony, and almost of ventriloquism.

Its protagonist is Abdulrahman Zeitoun, a Syrian immigrant turned New Orleans contractor and landlord who stays in the city when the rising waters of Lake Pontchartrain rupture the levees in late August of 2005. Zeitoun finds himself nearly alone in an eerily quiet drowned city, which he patrols for several days in a secondhand canoe. Along with a loose network of other New Orleanians who remained through Katrina, Zeitoun rescues stranded elderly people, feeds abandoned dogs, and grills lamb with friends on the roof of his flooded Victorian in the historic Uptown district.

Although Zeitoun has stayed behind primarily to protect his own property—while his American-born wife, Kathy, and their four children drive north to stay with relatives in Baton Rouge—he comes to see his mission in New Orleans as something much larger. While the outside world receives grossly exaggerated reports of anarchy and violence, Zeitoun finds a sense of purpose in a city that is underwater but largely at peace. A devout Muslim, he begins to wonder whether God has chosen him as a servant and witness in this dire emergency.

After a group of heavily armed men and women, wearing uniforms with no identifying badges, burst into a rental property that Zeitoun and his friends are using as a staging area, he has ample time to repent of his sinful pride. He disappears into a quasi-legal bureaucratic nightmare that resembles a Kafka story but is all too real. Kathy does not hear from him for weeks, and given the hysterical news coverage, assumes the worst. Is Zeitoun's life insurance paid up? Can she begin again without him?

Zeitoun is a story about the Bush administration's two most egregious policy disasters—the War on Terror and the response to Hurricane Katrina—as they collide with each other and come crashing down on one family. Eggers tells the story entirely from the perspective of Abdulrahman and Kathy Zeitoun, although he says he has vigorously double-checked the facts and removed any inaccuracies from their accounts. At first, as a reader, I felt some resistance to this tactic—could the Zeitouns possibly be as wholesome and all-American as Eggers depicts them?—but the sheer momentum, emotional force, and imagistic power of the narrative finally sweep such objections away.

In many ways, *Zeitoun* is an old-fashioned journalistic yarn, an oral history rendered in literary form that seeks both to inspire and outrage its readers. Entirely free of authorial asides, its innovative quality lies in its thoroughgoing rejection of the "me journalism" that has dominated reporting for three decades or more. Eggers presents it as a collaboration between him and the Zeitouns, similar in method to his collaboration with Valentino Achak Deng on *What Is the What*. (That book was presented as a novel, Eggers says, because it contained numerous reconstructed scenes from many years earlier, whereas *Zeitoun* is strictly nonfiction.)

I knew Dave Eggers many years ago (although not especially well) when we both worked at *SF Weekly* in San Francisco. I remember him as a quiet and serious young man who was evidently smart and ambitious, and who had some strange domestic situation involving his little brother. (I didn't know the details.) It's safe to say that a lot has changed in his life since then. Among his upcoming projects is a prototype daily newspaper (discussed briefly below) and an all-ages "novelization," to use his word, of Maurice Sendak's *Where the Wild Things Are*, to be published this fall alongside the release of Spike Jonze's movie version, which Eggers scripted. He called me the other day from the San Francisco office of McSweeney's, his publishing imprint.

Q: I notice that you've been inviting people to appeal to you for a pep talk on the future of the printed word, which we're all very worried about. So if I were to write to you and say, "Dave, cheer me up about the future of writing," what would you say?

A: *Salon* still exists, thank God. I think there's a future where the web and print coexist and they each do things uniquely and complement each other, and we have what could be the ultimate and best-yet array of journalistic venues. I think right now everyone's assuming it's a zero-sum situation, and I just don't see it that way.

Our students at 826 Valencia still have a newspaper class, where we print an actual newspaper, and we do magazine classes and anthologies where they're all printed on paper. That's the main way we get them motivated, that they know it's going to be in print. It's much harder for us to motivate the students when they think it's only going to be on the web.

The vast majority of students we work with read newspapers and books, more so than I did at their age. And I don't see that dropping off. If anything the lack of faith comes from people our age, where we just assume that it's dead or dying. I think we've given up a little too soon. We [i.e., McSweeney's] have been working every day on a prototype for a new newspaper, and a lot of what we're doing is resurrecting old things, like things from the last century that newspapers used to do, in terms of really using the full luxury of the broadsheet newspaper, with full color and all that space.

I think newspapers shouldn't try to compete directly with the web, and should do what they can do better, which may be long-form journalism and using photos and art, and making connections with large-form graphics and really enhancing the tactile experience of paper. You know, including a full-color comic section, for example, which of course was standard in newspapers years ago, when you'd have a full broadsheet Winsor McCay comic. So we'll have a big, full-color comic section, and we're also trying to emphasize what younger readers are looking for, what directly appeals to them. It's hard to find papers these days that really do anything to appeal to anyone under eighteen, and the paper used to do that all the time. I think there will always be—if not the same audience and not as wide an audience—a dedicated audience that can keep print journalism alive.

Q: Turning to your new book, talk about what drew you to the story of Abdulrahman Zeitoun and his family. Didn't they come to you through the Voice of Witness program?

A: That's right. The idea of Voice of Witness is to let survivors and witnesses of human rights abuses tell their story at length. It started with a course that I co-taught at UC–Berkeley journalism school back in 2003. The first book that came out of it was *Surviving Justice*, which was about exonerated prisoners in the United States. Right when we were publishing *Surviving Justice*, Katrina hit.

So we contacted a network of people living near New Orleans, in Houston and Baton Rouge and other cities where New Orleanians had gone, and put *Voices From the Storm* together. That book was thirteen or so narrators telling their stories and woven into a day-by-day narrative. One of the narrators was Zeitoun. I was immediately struck by his story, and the next time I was in New Orleans I met up with him and Kathy. I started talking to him to find out what he might not have been able to tell in that five- or six-page section, and it was clear there was a lot more there. Slowly, over the next six months, we began exploring whether there was a way to tell his story in book form, going back to Syria and exploring his life as an immigrant and a New Orleanian.

Q: It's interesting, and in some ways challenging, that you tell the story entirely from the Zeitoun family's point of view. There's none of the pretense of authorial objectivity or neutrality that conventionally goes with journalism. You're not issuing opinions or analysis from on high.

A: That's true. But that's not to say that it's not factual. If they misremembered something, we corrected it. If they said something that was provably and demonstrably incorrect, we didn't print it. But it's third-person quotes, very much through their eyes, as opposed to my take on things, where I come down and give my perspective on their story and the storm and its aftermath. I didn't feel like I had a place in this narrative, other than to help structure the story and make it compelling and readable. It's an effort to disappear into the narrative, which I was also trying to do with my earlier book, *What Is the What*. In both cases, I felt like I was most useful being out of the picture.

Q: Which is certainly interesting considering that your first book, the one for which you are still best known, is an autobiographical, self-aware, and even self-referential work. Was it important to you as a writer not to repeat that?

A: Yeah, I think so. After that first book, I wrote some stories that had protagonists that were close to my sensibility or my background. And then I just, to some extent, got that out of my system and wanted to do something new. Not that I would rule out writing in the first person in the future, but I started out as a journalist, and that's what my training and degree was in. I missed it for those years. Fiction was actually new to me. This is just a return to the basic training that I had, where one tries to use whatever skills one has to facilitate the telling of a story that you find important and that you might be able to bring to a wider audience.

Q: This is even closer to journalism than *What Is the What*, right? That was about a real person but was classified as fiction, whereas *Zeitoun* is nonfiction.

A: They were very similar processes, actually. *What Is the What* is incredibly close to Valentino's life story, and all of the major milestones in his life take place the way that they're described, but it was necessary to reconstruct dialogue and paint scenes that took place fifteen years ago. If we were restricted to nonfiction we couldn't, you know, prove what the weather was like on a given day. In this case, because it was so recent we really could prove everything, and the memory was so fresh that we were able to call it nonfiction. Otherwise, the processes—in terms of working in close collaboration, working with their memories and their subjective point of view—all those things were very similar.

Q: It's worth mentioning that in both cases you're deflecting your author's royalties to some combination of third-party nonprofits and charities, right?

A: Yeah. I just felt funny, in both cases, benefiting materially from it. I have friends who work in nonprofits down in New Orleans, and there's a lot of need there still. More than ever, really, because we're at the stage where some of the work that they're doing and the city in general is getting kind of forgotten. So we thought that if something good can come out of what the Zeitouns went through, then maybe it had some purpose. That was really the main motivating factor, I think, for the family to go into it and to cooperate, as painful as some of these things were to delve back into. Certainly we did go deeper than one's daily memory could go and the kind of version you tell yourself.

Q: I can see why your writer's radar got lit up by this story—the combination of Hurricane Katrina, the post-9/11 era, and a Muslim family. It's kind of an amazing microcosm of the twenty-first century in America, isn't it?

A: Yeah, no kidding. You know, there's a new graphic novel called *A.D.: New Orleans After the Deluge* by Josh Neufeld, and one of his protagonists is also Muslim American. Their story, like that of the Vietnamese American community in New Orleans, was a lot less told. And it's a legacy of the War on Terror, this mentality that an overwhelming military response was the solution to a humanitarian crisis. It just felt like a real manifestation of the Bush years. FEMA was folded into Homeland Security, and that became a disaster. And then, because of the military response and the perception that law and order was the first order of business, you had the suspension of pretty much all rights. Martial law was more or less enacted in New Orleans, and then you have one man who is just caught between all these lines, all these lumbering forces.

Zeitoun was among thousands of people who were doing "Katrina time" after the storm. There was a complete suspension of all legal processes, and there were no hearings, no courts for months and months, and not enough folks in the judicial system really seemed all that concerned about it. Some human rights activists and some attorneys, but otherwise it seemed to be the cost of doing business. It really could have only happened at that time; 2005 was just the exact meeting place of the Bush-era philosophy toward law enforcement and incarceration, their philosophy toward habeas corpus and their neglect and indifference to the plight of New Orleanians.

Q: It's a completely horrifying story, and I felt like my jaw was on the floor the whole time once I realized where it was going. But Zeitoun actually got out relatively quickly compared to some people, right?

A: There were hundreds of people that did months in jail, and I'm sure there are dozens of cases of prisoners who did over a year in various jails and prisons around Louisiana, where no one even knew where they were. It's unprecedented in American history, I think, this wide a suspension of habeas corpus. I don't think we've seen that since the Civil War.

Q: I wonder whether the most damaging long-term consequence of the Bush administration is that by and large Americans are ready to accept things like this, which would have seemed like science fiction ten or fifteen years ago.

A: I think there was a dark age, right in the middle there, from 2003 to 2006 especially, when anything seemed possible and nothing was surprising. Kathy felt so relieved when she found out that Zeitoun was in prison, like, "Well, I know where he's at and he's safe and he's alive." But for his family in Jableh, Syria, and his brother in Spain, that was even more worrying. That their brother, a Muslim from Syria, was in an American prison. It was really brought home when I met his family there and learned that they were gathered around the TV and phone for weeks, worried about what might happen to him in an American prison. I don't think anyone in the Middle East would have normally thought, before 9/11 and before Bush, that that was the worst situation somebody could be in.

Q: One of the ingenious things about the way you tell the story, from Zeitoun and Kathy's perspective, is that it outflanks the reader's preconceptions, or maybe even your preconceptions, about what a Syrian immigrant and his Muslim wife would be like. You don't have to come in as an author and say, "Hey, listen! They're normal people; they watch TV." You're just presenting their lives and we ride with them.

A: Yeah, that was one of the goals. The first time I met them I was just in their living room, and Kathy had just bought a big-screen TV on sale from Sam's Club, and the kids were all over the place and their pets were running around. They had chickens at the time. They might even have been watching *Pride and Prejudice.* They were just so incredibly all-American in so many ways. And just such a warm and a funny family, where there's all the family chaos that you want. From the beginning, the idea was to de-exoticize the Muslim American experience and cover the commonalities.

Kathy and Abdulrahman have a really fantastic marriage and a fantastic family, and I wanted to get that across in a seamless way, so that their plight becomes the plight that anyone might have gone through. Certainly it wasn't all Muslims who were caught up in the aftermath of Katrina, so in a way it is everyone's story.

Q: If there is any silver lining to their story it seems like Zeitoun's ancestry and ethnicity played only a minor role in the way he was treated. There's a really crazy period where the guards are telling him, "You're al-Qaeda, you're Taliban." But it doesn't last that long.

A: I interviewed two of the police officers that arrested him, and I put it to them: Did his accent or his name have anything to do with it? And they very convincingly denied it. They might not have even heard him speak. Gross indifference and incompetence played as much a part as ad hominem suspicion and incarceration with intent. So much of this is just systemic dysfunction.

Q: The contrast between the first part of the book, when all kinds of random people in New Orleans are trying to help each other through this painful and destructive experience, and the second part, when the world of authority comes down on them like a ton of bricks, is just amazing. It seems like, if the cops and military had simply stayed out of New Orleans altogether, everything would have been much better than it was.

A: You know, I've heard that thesis before, and it's fascinating. Zeitoun's friend Todd Gambino counts his rescues at about two hundred—the number of people he plucked off of rooftops and porches and second-story windows and then brought to safety. There were all these incredibly heroic citizens and good Samaritans going around helping. But there were so many police and Coast Guard and National Guard who did phenomenal work too. It's just that overall, as a result of all the misinformation spread by the media, those going in really expected a war zone. All these National Guardsmen, some of whom came from Afghanistan and Iraq and had been trained in house-to-house searches, came in, and they were all hyped up, expecting the worst. There was this sense that martial law is in place. We're going to clear out this city at all costs, and we're going to cast the net pretty widely. So they came down with unnecessary force. Coupled with a nonfunctioning judicial system, that produced some mind-boggling human rights violations.

Q: You know, on the failure of the media and public officials to paint an accurate portrait, that still has not been addressed. Having written a couple of times about the film *Trouble the Water*, I can attest to the fact that there are a lot of people out there, among *Salon*'s readers, who still believe that there really was rape and pillage in New Orleans, that armed men were shooting at helicopters and all that stuff.

A: Yeah, there are those that think that it's some sort of liberal or left-wing apologist baloney to say otherwise. But all the statistics bear out that crime was grossly exaggerated. They predicted hundreds of bodies in the Convention Center and the Superdome, and they found only one murder among both. More than any other event in recent history, this exposed the quiet racism that's right there under the surface, these assumptions.

Everyone's willingness to accept the idea that a city would turn into this chaotic war zone in the aftermath of a storm, it really necessitates a long soul-searching for everybody that bought into that. Zeitoun's relatives believed it too, and thought that the major danger he faced was being preyed upon by these lawless gangs of young men. And that's the twist in the book, that I'm hoping people don't see coming. But maybe I'm already giving it all away [*laughs*].

Dave Eggers Interview:
The Heartbreak Kid

John Preston / 2009

From *The Telegraph*, December 29, 2009. © 2009 by *The Telegraph*. Reprinted by permission.

There was a time not so long ago when Dave Eggers didn't do interviews. Or rather, he would only do them by email. This was after a row with a *New York Times* journalist that ended with Eggers calling him a "bitter little b-----d." All of which makes me feel rather nervous as I wait outside the office at his British publishers, where Eggers is waiting.

He turns out to be a chunky, outdoorsy-looking man of thirty-nine, wearing hiking boots and with dark, curly hair that's only partially tamed by a center parting. But he seems in a thoroughly affable mood—even if this will later be punctured by long bursts of frowning introspection.

For all his affability, Eggers, you suspect, has a pretty dark side—which will hardly come as a surprise to anyone who has read his first book, *A Heartbreaking Work of Staggering Genius*. In the book, Eggers described how, aged twenty-one, he brought up his eight-year-old brother Christopher—"Toph." This was after their parents both died of cancer within weeks of one another.

Ten years after it was published, Eggers is a literary star. He's written a novel, film scripts, two nonfiction novels, and numerous short stories.

He's also founded the most influential literary magazine in the United States, *McSweeney's*. But childhood—his own childhood—still churns away inside him, which is why he teamed up with film director Spike Jonze to make the recent film version of Maurice Sendak's *Where the Wild Things Are*. As well as writing the script, Eggers has also written a novel, *The Wild Things*, a kind of companion piece to the movie, but very different from it.

Eggers remembers first reading *Where the Wild Things Are* when he was five and being absolutely terrified. What scared him so much? "Argh . . ." he says, throwing up his hands. "I just reacted with pure terror. But then I used to hide under the couch during *The Wizard of Oz*. I think what frightened me the most was that I couldn't work out if the Wild Things were nice or nasty. There was a moral ambiguity to them which really disturbed me."

His own upbringing was much less riven with uncertainty—at least on the surface. Eggers grew up in a prosperous Chicago suburb where his father was an attorney and his mother a schoolteacher. But behind the happy facade, all was not well: his father drank and spent long periods out of work.

"I can remember very clearly being seven or eight, which is the age the boy, Max, is in the book. And when I was raising my brother, that started off when he was eight—so it's a very vivid moment that I've thought about a lot. I can remember feeling responsible for my mother's happiness. If she was sad, I would think: 'Can I do my robot maneuver and make her happy?' And slowly you come to realize that there's only so much you can do."

Eggers's childhood was also weirdly cloistered. In all the time he was growing up, his parents never went out in the evening. "Not once. Isn't that extraordinary? But while mom and dad were incredibly caring, it was also a very chaotic household where everyone fought about everything. So I know what it's like to internalize all that chaos.

"For years, I resisted keeping any kind of schedule. Because my parents were very rigid and everything happened at a set time every day, I really fought against that. I mean, I didn't even have a wallet until I was twenty-seven."

When Eggers wrote *The Wild Things*, he basically turned himself into Max—except that the young Dave Eggers was much, much wilder than his fictional counterpart. "I think I was pretty crazy, looking back. For instance, when I was a kid we used to do stuff like soaking tennis balls in kerosene and playing football with them. At the same time, though, I remember being quite good in school and also fairly docile. So there are all these weird contradictions that are hard to reconcile."

But he probably wouldn't have written the book had he not got a phone call from Sendak, now eighty-one, the original creator of *Where the Wild Things Are*. "Maurice was very involved in the film, and he told me that people had been talking about a novel based on the screenplay. He asked me if I'd do it. I had to think about it, but I thought it might be a good place to explore all those thoughts that I've had about childhood."

Eggers has a breathy, laconic way of talking that gives everything he says a carefully measured air, a sense of being repeatedly pored over. He's plainly pored over *Where the Wild Things Are* in microscopic detail—first as a terrified child and now as a father. He and his wife, the writer Vendela Vida, have two small children, a girl and a boy.

"I wrote it between our two children being born. I wanted to write something that might have the same sort of effect on a kid as the books I read when I was young had on me. I can remember exactly where I sat when my teacher first read Roald Dahl's *James and the Giant Peach*. It's like the cement is still wet when you're that age; every little mark can become permanent."

Fatherhood has brought other changes, too. When Eggers first started writing, he used to do so between midnight and 5:00 a.m.—always in what he calls a desperate, overcaffeinated, blood-strewn, tear-your-own-ear-off sort of way. "I had this romantic idea that I had to be at the end of my rope. But now with kids, I have to work bankers' hours. Believe me, it's hard to think of anything less romantic—or more sedentary."

Given the success Eggers has had—President Barack Obama recently recommended his 2006 book, *What Is the What*, to his cabinet—it comes as quite a surprise to hear him say that he's never had any confidence in his work.

"Even now, when I start something, I never think I'll ever be able to get to the end, or that it will make any sense," he says. "Actually, *The Wild Things* is the first book I've ever written where I enjoyed it. Normally, there'll be about one day a month where I think: 'Wow, I had a good time today.' But with this, I just sat there chortling away."

Eggers was in his midtwenties when he started on *A Heartbreaking Work of Staggering Genius*, and if his confidence remains shaky now, it was in a far worse state then. "I remember turning in some chapters to an editor, and when he said he liked them, I said, 'What are you talking about?' I even accused him of not doing his job properly.

"Then when it came out, I felt so conflicted—partly because the title was so ironic. I just thought it would be funny to give the book this grandiose title when, of course, it's a disaster. I thought about three people would read it and that would be the end of it."

Except it didn't quite work out like that. Even now, Eggers says, barely a day goes by without someone coming up and saying how much the book means to them. Not that this makes him feel much better.

"I've had a really complicated relationship with it for some years. In a lot of ways the guy in it is me, but also he isn't. We were very private people, my family, and that kind of self-revelation is something that was not in any way native to them. In a lot of ways, writing it was an act of rebellion."

One of the reasons Eggers feels so ambivalent about *A Heartbreaking Work of Staggering Genius* is because of what subsequently happened to his sister, Beth. When the book was published, she accused him of downplaying her role in their brother's upbringing and beefing up his own. She later recanted, saying she'd made a dreadful mistake—"I'm so embarrassed. I was having a terrible LaToya Jackson moment." Then, in November 2001, Beth Eggers committed suicide.

Eggers has never talked about his sister's death. But it seems telling that he's opted to write two books since in which trust has played the key role. In both *What Is the What* and *Zeitoun*—out here next March—he is telling someone else's story.

What Is the What is the autobiography—albeit written by Eggers—of a real-life Sudanese refugee who was separated from his parents, trekked across large swathes of Sudan, and eventually came to the US.

Zeitoun is the story of a Muslim family from Syria. Abdulrahman Zeitoun stayed in New Orleans during Hurricane Katrina, after which he saved the lives of several survivors, only to be interned as a suspected terrorist.

"As far as I was concerned, I was there to tell their stories," Eggers says. "But if there was something they didn't want in, then obviously I'd respect that. I suppose the most important thing with both books was to do no harm—unless it was harm to the Bush administration, which I was absolutely fine with."

When he's not sitting on his couch being sedentary, Eggers leads an extremely busy life. He's the founder of 826 Valencia, a tutoring center in San Francisco where children between the ages of six and eighteen can go to develop their writing skills. He also has a shop in San Francisco that sells nothing but pirate gear.

Then there's McSweeney's, which publishes a quarterly literary magazine, a website, a monthly magazine called *The Believer*, and a quarterly DVD magazine, *Wholphin*. All Eggers's proceeds from *What Is the What* went to Sudanese refugees in the US, while those from *Zeitoun* are going to the Zeitoun Foundation, which is helping in the rebuilding of New Orleans.

Eggers has also become a tireless campaigner for the power of the printed word in an internet age. His magazines aren't afraid of publishing novella-length stories, and his books luxuriate in the kind of playful design that could never be reproduced on a screen.

To hammer the point home, Eggers recently published the *San Francisco Panorama*, a 320-page, full-color broadsheet newspaper; it sold out immediately.

He's clearly seeking to do as much good as possible, and I wondered how much his faith in human nature fluctuates between optimism and despair. "I think I'm far too hopeful and trusting. That's something I got from my mom. Because I grew up with this naive expectation of people doing right, I get shocked by every little violation. But however naive I might be, I do feel that books have a unique way of stopping time in a particular moment and saying, 'Let's not forget this.'"

He breaks off. Our time is up. "I'm sorry," he says. "I'm babbling again. That's the thing with me, you see. I never end tidily. I just kind of trail off . . ."

An Interview with Dave Eggers about *Zeitoun*

Anis Shivani / 2010

From the *Colorado Review*, Summer 2010. © 2010 by Anis Shivani. Reprinted by permission.

Anis Shivani: It seems to be a long road for a writer, from the Eggers of 2000, who gave us *A Heartbreaking Work of Staggering Genius*, which defined irony, self-consciousness, detachment, and cool for members of a certain generation, to the Eggers of 2009, who gives us commitment, political engagement, objectivity, and heat, meaning dissatisfaction with how procedures of justice and fairness have fallen by the wayside. Define for us, please, how you crossed from where you were as a writer to where you are now. What were some of the important way stations, and did you encounter resistance in yourself to broadening your scope to the extent you have?

Dave Eggers: I've definitely moved around a lot, I guess. I was trained as a journalist, and in and out of college I did everything from straight news to features to editorial cartooning and art criticism. When I wrote my first book, I was twenty-nine, and that was sort of a miracle for me; I had no previous expectations that I would ever write or publish a book. So I was surprised that it came together at all. After that, I was still working as a journalist, but somewhere along the way I started exploring fiction, albeit fiction that still, for the most part, had a strong basis in research and journalism. For example, when I hiked up Mt. Kilimanjaro, I brought a tape recorder and camera and documented the trip pretty thoroughly, unsure what would become of the material. I ended up writing a short story, fiction, about it, though all the details are real. It's an actual account of hiking up the Machame route of the mountain, with a fictional character and background laid over. Anyway, on the one hand my work hasn't shifted a lot, in that it's always been about people feeling somewhat out of place in new worlds, driven to a large extent by forces beyond their control. But these last few books, because they're both forms of biography, bring me closer to my journalistic roots. And they're both less about bringing attention to the form of the writing than they are about bringing attention to the story itself.

Shivani: Please talk about how *What Is the What,* in particular, fits into the progression to *Zeitoun.* Why do you think more writers in the last decade haven't seized the opportunity to write about human rights? Do you think it puts the writer outside establishment bounds in some ways to take up this most important of all subjects?

Eggers: Well, I think there are some fantastic writers working on issues of human rights. One of my heroes is Samantha Power, whose *A Problem from Hell* was crucial to me, along with Philip Gourevitch's book about the Rwandan genocide. Those two books realigned my thinking in a lot of ways, and I read them just before I was asked to write the biography of Valentino Deng. The writers I studied a lot as a journalism student—Orwell, Mailer, Didion, Vollmann—were writers who moved fluidly between fiction and nonfiction, and could even work in different styles of journalism, from very personal reportage to more traditional newspaper-style journalism. Whether or not it's outside the bounds of the establishment, I'm not sure. The establishment itself shifts mightily every five years or so, it seems.

Shivani: *Zeitoun* is very much the kind of book George Orwell might have written, in his own mélange of reportage and imagination, had he survived to the modern media age. Orwell wanted to expose the fissures between language and truth, the failed modalities upon which the vast architecture of oppression is built. Specifically with respect to *Zeitoun,* how would you explain the function of the writer in a time of information overload? What is the condition of facts today?

Eggers: You know, Orwell is a towering figure in my life; it's pretty astounding how many tools there were in his toolbox. His journalism influenced his fiction, of course, and vice versa, and I'm sure what he saw of war and oppressions large and small gave him little patience for totalitarian regimes, small progressions toward that way of life, or the way even a supposedly benevolent state can slowly or quickly crush the spirit. That's always been an interest of mine, the fight between the individual and the machinery—governmental or corporate or otherwise—that grinds us up. I don't know, it's an interesting time right now, in that I think there's some pretty intense complicity in some of the aspects of technology that are openly dehumanizing and ultimately oppressive. The main operating force working against Zeitoun is one that Orwell explored a fair amount, which was the routineness of certain injustices and evils. It's not even banal, really, so much as it is routine, and driven by a lack of courage and imagination more than anything. The guards in charge of keeping Zeitoun in an outdoor cage couldn't imagine that he might be innocent. To allow for that possibility requires great courage, and of course any doubt in a guard's mind in the fallibility of the system might dismantle that system. The glue of the prison-industrial complex is the presumption that the system works. That is, that once a guard receives a prisoner, he must assume he's guilty. But what if that isn't true? What if no particular link in the chain can be relied upon?

Shivani: *Zeitoun* is a story of modern apocalypse—which in many ways is not limited to Hurricane Katrina or New Orleans but continues in countless instances of indignities and violence, whether they get noticed or not—that refuses to fit the contours of apocalypse familiar from recent fiction and film. Should we rethink apocalypse? Do we miss something crucial about our reality if we don't?

Eggers: Katrina left New Orleans in an apocalyptic state, plain and simple. If you saw the Lower Ninth Ward, Gentilly, and Lakeview after Katrina, you saw apocalypse in the US on a scale I don't think we've ever seen before. Maybe the burning of certain cities during the Civil War would compare, or the San Francisco or Chicago fires at the turn of the twentieth century. I don't know. So many New Orleanians suffer from post-traumatic symptoms, and it's no wonder. But I think the rest of the country is perhaps unwilling to recognize that New Orleanians quite literally experienced the end of their world. It's not something you get over in a few years.

Shivani: Where do you think the disregard for basic human rights procedures the American character has displayed in the last several years comes from? Do you see an end to this, or is the situation likely to build on momentum, so that we become more and more unrecognizable as a country? Have we already crossed the point of no return? *Zeitoun* is obviously a warning of worse yet to come; certain inherently illiberal (to put it mildly) tendencies inevitably come to the fore with the least instigation. Any future hurricane or natural disaster or terror attack seems sure to provoke similar intolerance, and lack of shame about it, as the residents of New Orleans experienced after Hurricane Katrina. Why isn't there an Army-McCarthy hearings moment?

Eggers: There's a fantastic book called *The Lucifer Effect*, by Philip Zimbardo, the man who designed the Stanford Prison Experiment back in the seventies. I know most people know about this experiment, but for those who might not: In that experiment, a bunch of average Stanford students were placed in a faux-prison setting, where some of them were told to be guards and some were told to be prisoners. They were to live that way in a closed dorm for a week or so. And though they weren't given a whole lot of rules or guidance to fill their new roles, they quickly devolved into a very base state, where the guards were sadistic and callous, and the prisoners had assumed their own guilt and status as entities less than human. This was all within a few days; the change in all of these students was so dramatic and quick that Zimbardo had to shut the experiment down far ahead of schedule. So Zimbardo's book, written a few years ago, connects what happened in that experiment to what happened at Abu Ghraib, where you had a group of similarly young soldiers, also operating without any meaningful guidance. All the while, the soldiers were working within an overall atmosphere where Iraqis—prisoners or not—were regarded as something less than human. Young soldiers, I think, are incredibly impressionable, and if they're not given guidance about the preservation of human rights, and about the protocol when, say, kicking in the doors of Iraqi civilians, then things can devolve quickly and irrevocably. As they did at Abu Ghraib. Zimbardo is saying that there's a bit of the devil in all of us, and that complicity and silence might be the greatest enemy to human rights. And his thesis with the Stanford experiment and Abu Ghraib is that in both cases it's not that there are bad apples in the barrel, but that the barrel itself is bad. And for eight years under Bush, we were living in a very bad barrel. Zimbardo seems like an optimist, though, and I am, too. I believe that with good leadership, with role models showing us how to behave, there can be very positive and tangible trickle-down. That is, if you have a Bush-Cheney administration that is openly disdainful of the concept of human rights, the guards who were running Camp Greyhound, for example, have no incentive to act humanely. Unenlightened leadership can quickly grease the wheels of oppression at the lowest levels. On the other hand, Zimbardo talks about the importance of heroism on the individual level. His wife, actually, was the one who shut down the Stanford Prison Experiment. She walked in, saw that everything was horribly wrong, and she insisted that it be shut down. Zimbardo himself was too close to it, perhaps; so this outsider, his wife, had to call bullshit on what was happening. With Zeitoun, it took the apathy or complicity of hundreds of people to collaborate on this injustice. If one person stood up and questioned what was happening—one person with either courage or imagination or both—then his and other injustices would have been avoided or curtailed.

Shivani: How can the Zeitouns of the world be compensated? Their lives have been shattered, their psyches broken, the pieces impossible to put together again. In a country that places itself above human rights account-ability (unlike any other country), how does accountability begin?

Eggers: I think we have to do a certain amount of it ourselves, as indi-viduals. Zeitoun has basically no chance of receiving restitution from any governmental body; that would set off a chain of events, most likely, that would bankrupt the state of Louisiana, given that there were hundreds if not thousands of men and women who were wrongfully arrested and incar-cerated. So the government, in this situation, isn't thinking of what's right; they're thinking of what's practical. This goes for the compensation of most wrongfully convicted Americans; some states have no laws about restitu-tion whatsoever, some states have certain rules and guidelines (including caps on compensation, like $15,000 for every year in prison), but overall there's a concerted effort by all states not to compensate anyone wrong-fully convicted or incarcerated. So we have to act as individuals. So the book's proceeds, in addition to going to the Zeitoun Foundation, are going to the Zeitoun family, and to Todd Gambino (who also did many months in prison). The Zeitouns and I thought Todd should get some money for the time he did, those months that were taken from him. And we're looking to do the same for the others arrested with Abdulrahman. It won't be any-where near what they deserve, but it's a start.

Shivani: How did you change as a person and as a writer during the com-position of *Zeitoun*?

Eggers: I have to admit that I never learn so well as I learn when I personally experience something. Nothing I read about Islam prepared me for the power and beauty of the actual text of the Qur'an, for example. And nothing I'd read about Syria prepared me for the incredible warmth of the people and the beauty of the coast in particular. I might have read about Islam or Muslim Americans or Camp Greyhound, but nothing could compare to becoming immersed. I just got off the phone with Abdulrahman a few minutes ago, and we were talking about reading the Qur'an, and how hearing about the Qur'an or getting it filtered through experts or whomever isn't quite the same thing. I've been urging people to pick up a recent translation by Laleh Bakhtiar, which is a very faithful but also very accessible English translation. After reading the text, and also the text of the Hadith, it made me more frustrated about how Islam is portrayed and interpreted in the mainstream media. The text itself is so focused on human rights, and on compassion, empathy, charity, and—this is so key—on the practical application of one's faith, that it becomes clear that those who distort Islam for their own purposes, whether they're Muslims or not, are going pretty far afield to do so. Reading the text, and having the Zeitouns discuss it and how it guides their lives, all that was life-changing.

Shivani: Tell us something about *Zeitoun*'s style. How did you keep the narrative focused so sharply on Abdulrahman and Kathy's point of view? There would have been a natural temptation to smuggle in more information than necessary for the emotional arc of the narrative, yet you overcame it. I particularly liked the buildup, which splits the narrative into schismatic halves, in the way that broken lives can never entirely be healed. Until Zeitoun is arrested, the reader is struck by the pastoral calmness that defines New Orleans for this hardworking immigrant. And then come aspects of Abu Ghraib and Guantánamo, realities that we have unfortunately accepted as part of our lives for as long as we can see into the future. How does your style disrupt our satiated consciousness of these enormous and ongoing rapes of human dignity?

Eggers: Well, I cut a lot of passages that I was tempted to include. There were long passages about the contracting business, long passages about the Iran-Iraq War, long passages about the history of FEMA and Homeland Security. But I was determined to keep the focus on Abdulrahman and Kathy, and to avoid inserting my own thoughts about New Orleans or FEMA or Bush. So I had to keep it focused on what they knew and what they saw and felt. And Kathy's role was a surprise. I went into the project not knowing how great a role Kathy would play. I knew that she was a strong personality and a great storyteller, but after a short while I was reminded of how much suffering is imposed on the family members of those wrongfully incarcerated. I edited a book a few years ago called *Surviving Justice: America's Wrongfully Convicted and Exonerated*, and one of the major themes in the book was just how great the pain is for the family of the wrongfully incarcerated. There's just such collateral damage when someone in a family, especially a parent, is disappeared into the American prison system. You're really condemning an entire family to years of chaos, and possibly to a lifetime of mistrust and confusion and emotional devastation. As a society, we're so ready to throw people away—fathers, mothers, sons— and usually without any regard for the consequences. So in *Zeitoun*, it was essential that we spend a good deal of time with Kathy, alone, as she deals with weeks of wondering if, and then assuming, her husband is dead.

Shivani: Please evaluate what writers in this country have attempted in response to the massive political upheaval in this country since the turn of the millennium in terms of what you would have hoped or expected. What stands out in this output to you? What gives you hope? What frightens you?

Eggers: I think this is a golden age not so much for American writers—though it is a very good time for them, too—but for American audiences and publishers discovering, and developing a greater appetite for, writers from non-American or English origins. Khaled Hosseini deserves a good deal of the credit for that, given his work on the page and as an ambassador. Rushdie and Achebe and countless others brought non-Western worlds to American audiences, but Hosseini brought these worlds to contemporary book clubs, which I think are vitally important. He and others, Roberto Bolaño most recently, have opened audiences up to work by Chimamanda Adichie, Etgar Keret, Chris Abani—the list goes on. When you have the book clubs listening to non-Western voices, then real understanding becomes more plausible. I think there's a growing willingness for readers to say, "Tell me something I don't already know."

Shivani: *Zeitoun* is a document of immense empathy, one of the boldest leaps of imagination I have encountered in response to the last decade of worldwide sadistic depravity. Did you accomplish in it everything you wanted to?

Eggers: Well, you're always left with the passages you didn't get into the book. Every day I think of another aspect to the Zeitouns that didn't make it into the text. When I got back from Syria, I had a hundred new pages in my head I thought should go into the book. But I wanted the book to be tight, as opposed to sprawling. I wanted the reader to feel the tension and the pain that the Zeitouns felt. And that meant keeping it lean and taut. And in the silences, the readers are allowed to insert themselves, their own thoughts and outrage.

Shivani: America ten years ago was a little boring, and very predictable. Uncertainty seems to be the defining characteristic now. Anyone might get pulled up on minor charges and enter a world of violent sadism from which there is no escape. This pervasive uncertainty was the most salient characteristic of the twentieth century's totalitarian regimes. The uncertainty is in some ways more frightening than wholesale violence. How did we end up this way?

Eggers: I think there are large segments of American society that have lived with this uncertainty since the country's inception. Native Americans certainly lived with the possibility of their extinction at any moment and with countless indignities and human rights violations that were visited upon them in the hundreds of years hence. And African Americans have lived with uncertainty in many guises for centuries and continue to live with uncertainty. And now it's Muslims, and immigrants, and gays. I'm really disappointed in our willingness at any given moment to find it acceptable to discriminate against a certain segment of our society. It's as if we say, "Okay, discrimination against women was wrong, of course it was, sorry, what a blight on our history! But discrimination against Blacks, well, that makes sense." Then twenty years later we say, "Wow, what were we thinking? Discrimination on the basis of skin color? That was crazy. Madness. No more of that. But immigrants, gays, Muslims? Those folks, they're a bit less than the rest of us, right?" We really have this odd amnesia about universal rights; we keep forgetting that equality must extend to everyone, not everyone except this one group.

Shivani: Abdulrahman is arrested at one of his own properties, with his identification on him. Recently, Harvard professor Henry Louis Gates Jr. was arrested in his own house. Does this point to a systematic rot to you, extending beyond the confluence of events in New Orleans?

Eggers: Professor Gates was arrested just around the time when *Zeitoun* was published, and the parallels hit me in the gut. Gates has been a hero of mine for a long time, and we're lucky enough to have him on the board of advisors for our educational nonprofit in Boston (826 Boston). If you had to conceive of a plotline in fiction to demonstrate just how screwy things are in our sense of the role of police and how far we have yet to go in race relations in America, you would not have a white Boston police officer arresting, in his home, the country's most famous and respected African American professor. In fiction, it wouldn't work—it's too unbelievable. But it happened, and then, impossibly, somehow the debate turned into a fifty-fifty thing, where instead of there being 90 percent outrage, you had 50 percent of Americans saying, "Well, Gates had it coming if he mouthed off to a police officer." I couldn't believe the debate took that turn, especially in a country so dedicated to property rights and the sanctity of a man's home. Gates was in his home! He has a right to yell or ask the cops to leave; he even has a right to kick the cops out the door. Once he proves he lives there, it's time for the police to go. He has a right to privacy. It's his home. But when the police feel that they have the power to arrest a man in the sanctity of his house because they don't like what he's saying, or they don't like his tone of voice, well, then things are upside down. Police who arrest people for hurting their feelings, for annoying them? It's ludicrous. What prevents two cops from showing up in my house tomorrow and, when I ask them to leave, accusing me of disorderly conduct? It's circular reasoning: they've caused the very problem they're arresting me for. But the thing is, I've personally had almost entirely positive experiences with police. I know the job is thankless and difficult. But we have got to get back to a place where we remember that the police work for us. These small abuses of power were what drove a good deal of the narrative of *Zeitoun* and make possible far larger ones.

Shivani: How do Abdulrahman and Kathy Zeitoun and their children feel about your book?

Eggers: It's been fun to talk to them every few days about it all. Every day New Orleanians come up to them, shake their hands, have them sign the book. We've had to ship them hundreds of copies because they keep giving them to their neighbors and relatives. Abdulrahman is heading back to Syria to visit his family there, and he'll bring a bunch of copies of the book with him. The family is really proud, especially now that we know the book will be translated into Arabic. There's so much happening, so many good things with the Zeitouns. I think I've met about twenty-five of the Zeitouns here and in Spain and Syria, and I've never known a greater family. They've taught me immeasurably about how to live, and they deserve all happiness that might head their way.

Dave Eggers:
The Heart of the Matter

Sam Cate-Gumpert / 2010

From *mono.kultur*, Autumn 2010. © by Sam Cate-Gumpert. Reprinted by permission.

Q: I want to read you the last line of *What Is the What.* Valentino says, "Whatever I do, however I find a way to live, I will tell these stories to people who will listen and to people who don't want to listen, to people who seek me out and those who run. All the while I will know that you are there. How can I pretend that you do not exist? It would be almost as impossible as you pretending that I do not exist." The thought to me here is that what Valentino is doing, and by extension you with your work, is telling a difficult story that people might not want to hear, that they want to run away from, that they have trouble grasping. With *What Is the What*, with *Zeitoun*, and even with *A Heartbreaking Work of Staggering Genius*, you're telling a story that people have trouble dealing with. With Voice of Witness, it's the same thing. Is that one of your goals?

A: I'm attracted to stories where something happens. And I don't know if I always was attracted to them. I grew up in a leafy, quiet suburb where nothing ever happened, so I really had no connection whatsoever to anything, to any part of the real world or any walk of life. I was at a remove from most of the world and reality. A lot of suburbs are a bubble. And I think when my parents passed away, that woke me up a little bit, and I entered into a different category, where suddenly I could empathize with all single parents and all people who have had loss, and all people who have to go to the social security office to deal with death benefits, and all that stuff. It gave me a sense of empathy, whereas had I had it easy, it would have been a little different . . . probably. Who knows?

At the same time, I studied journalism, and right away, the very first day, you go out and you're trying to learn something new about the world and communicate it effectively and compellingly to a readership that might not otherwise be listening. That's the whole idea, at least. So I guess there are parallel tracks. I can see that the stories I wrote when I was a kid and in high school were very much removed from . . . you know, I liked fantasy, I liked monsters—stories like that—I liked fairy tales. And I also was attracted to fiction where not a whole lot happened because, to me, I had no connection to real life-and-death issues. I think if you grow up in a suburb and you watch a cop show or something, it seems crazy, unrealistic. I remember watching cop shows and cynically thinking, "This is so fake. None of this ever happens." I mean, that is a strange perspective born of suburban living. Nothing happens in your town, so you assume nothing happens anywhere in the world.

But now, because writing a book is so difficult and takes so long, I like it if within that narrative something really important happens and you learn something about the world that you might not otherwise know. I have to learn something during the process, too. If at the end of four hundred pages somebody's just moved from one end of the room to the other . . . That's valid, but for me, when I think of four years of life, that's an epic amount of time to spend on something, so I would hope that there's an epic scope to the book itself. More and more, when you really feel the limitations of your own time on earth, you really do have to start thinking, "Wow, is this really gonna . . ."

Q: "Does this matter?"

A: "Does this matter?" and, "How much?" and, "Is this going to be worth the next four years of my life?" When I met Zeitoun, I knew that his story was interesting on a certain level—I knew from the five to ten pages of his story that were in *Voices from the Storm*—but it wasn't until I met him and he started talking about Syria and about his brother Mohammed and ocean swimming and his grandfather and his father spending time on the sea and the shipwreck his father was in during World War II . . . Then I knew this had an epic scope to it. Right away, in the first few hours, I thought, "Okay, well, I can probably sink my teeth into this. And maybe I would be useful in helping tell this." You start realizing that real things do happen in the world, that, for a lot of people, there are struggles that absolutely dwarf what most of us deal with in our lifetime. I mean, I just met a kid that spoke at this fundraiser who was a crack addict and a crack dealer, and then got kicked out of six different high schools, and then he found God and he became a spoken-word poet, and now he's about to finish college, and he speaks on behalf of other students and raises money for this organization called YouthSpeaks . . . And I just thought, "Well, you don't have to look far for stories that need to be told." This kid will write his story someday, and the world will benefit. I mean, I interview cabbies everywhere I go . . .

Q: When you're in the cabs?

A: Yeah, you know, I hear an accent and I see if I can guess it. I'm pretty good these days at guessing, especially if the cabbie is African—I can usually get it within a country. I can get West African, and I can get a Nigerian name down in a second, and Ethiopian, Eritrean, I know those guys. I had a Sudanese cabbie about a month ago in Austin, and I knew it right off—if they're of a certain generation, then you know that they came over from Kakuma with Valentino and the rest of the guys. I'll interview them, where they come from, what they do, and always these stories are fascinating and more interesting than my own life, and so when you come to the realization that there are four or five billion stories that are more interesting than your own, then it's really a matter of taking it in and listening.

Q: If there are four to five billion stories that are more interesting than yours, how do you narrow it down? Where do you start?

A: This is my life right now: trying to narrow it down. Because, at this point, I do get an email or so a week from somebody saying, "I know a story that must be told." Everyone I know has a friend or uncle who wants me to write their biography. It's tough because, again, that's a few years at least out of our lives to get it done. There's just not enough time. But at this point I know what the next few books I'm going to work on are. Sometimes it's just like a visceral connection that you feel with some story or some person, and sometimes there are other things where you hope that one particular personal narrative can illuminate something universal. Zeitoun's story spoke about so many different things I was interested in, like wrongful conviction and the Bush-era misappropriation of national focus and resources. But there was also this fascinating life on the sea in Syria and elsewhere, and family issues, and Kathy's conversion to Islam, the seeking or perfecting of faith, all of these things . . . So a story really has to hit you on a lot of different levels, and sometimes you find a story that might work on three levels, and that's not enough. It really has to be ten, twelve, twenty different things that interest you about it. And you have to think you're uniquely qualified or able to tell it. Sometimes there's somebody better out there who is probably going to do it or has done it. But when it hits that spot where it hasn't been told, and you think you could do it, and it has the depth that will keep you interested for a number of years, then you take the plunge. But even then, I take it very slowly. I have one story in my head, that's been in my head for about five months now, something I read about. And I'm still taking it slowly. I haven't committed. You have to be sure, because it's a big commitment on everyone's part. It's too bad, because I do think that there are so many stories out there, and I feel like had I gotten started sooner—because I was thirty before I really got serious about writing—I wouldn't feel quite as careful and precious with my time. But at this point, with kids, you really have to pick your battles.

Q: One of the things I found interesting about *Zeitoun*, that I loved, really, was that, while addressing all these issues—Bush and FEMA and wrongful conviction or incarceration—it's not explicit. It isn't indicting Bush in an obvious way.

A: Not overtly. No one needs me to be another voice hating Bush. I mean, it's probably implicit that had I been the biggest fan of Bush, I wouldn't necessarily have written that book. At one point, I wanted to go into op-ed writing. I did write a lot of opinion pieces when I was younger, but I was one of many voices there, and I wasn't the most eloquent. But I think that if you can illuminate the effects of the government's policies on individuals and families, individual stories can be a lot more powerful in terms of moving the debate or moving people toward action. The first book we did in the Voice of Witness series was *Surviving Justice*, and it was about the wrongfully convicted and exonerated here in the US. When I was much younger, I thought the death penalty was justified, and I felt that the criminal justice system, if it was flawed, it was just by a tiny bit, you know? I had very little idea about the workings of it, or when it could go wrong, or how it could go wrong. And then meeting all of these exonerees, spending a whole weekend together with all of them in a room, and hearing them tell their stories, and also realizing all the ripple effects of their convictions on their families, and realizing just how many different ways the judicial system can go wrong, all these things, they personalized it in a way it hadn't been personal before. You know, the difference between a Republican and a Democrat, a lot of the times, is that Democrats know people that have been affected by policy and Republicans either don't or don't choose to listen to them. That's an oversimplification, but I'm really more interested in history and policy on the ground level, and in finding practical solutions to those issues or problems, than I am in just commenting on something.

Q: The *Times* Op-Ed page . . .

A: Well, look, the *Times* Op-Ed page is super valuable, and I've contributed to it, but at the same time I try to always come up with a practical solution. If I have a voice in something, I'm not just going to blabber on; I would prefer to come up with a tool to address it with rather than just complain. I'm really not a big fan of idle chatter and complaint.

Q: You quite obviously consider *Zeitoun* nonfiction, as opposed to *What Is the What*. Is there something that *What Is the What*, as fiction, can offer that "polemic journalism," as you say, can't?

A: Well, in both cases, you're trying to see history through one man's eyes. And in both cases, I was trying to bring a novelistic level of detail to the story, to better put the reader in that person's shoes, to see the world through their eyes. *What Is the What* started out as nonfiction, and it would have been nonfiction had we had more information at our disposal, which we just didn't. We didn't have the level of memory and detail to do it adequately, so I had to breathe life into some of these skeletal scenes. But with *Zeitoun* it was so recent. We started a year after it happened, so he remembered everything, and I could go visit the prison he stayed in . . .

Q: The prison was still there when you went back?

A: Well, not Camp Greyhound—the Greyhound station was there, but the prison wasn't there anymore. I could go to Hunt Correctional, though, where Zeitoun had gone after, and I could go to every location where he spent time and see videotapes of every flooded street he paddled through. The evidence was so extensive that I could get that level of detail that I needed. So with Zeitoun's story, nonfiction was the appropriate tool.

Q: Is that why there is a difference in tone between the two books?

A: Yeah, because if I had been free to write fiction with *Zeitoun*, it would have been a lot richer or thicker; the language wouldn't have been quite so plain. One of my favorite books is a Norman Mailer book called *The Executioner's Song*. He generally had a very strong prose style, unmistakable, but then suddenly that book was stripped completely clean of his presence and his voice, and the book was reduced to just the facts. And it was powerful for that reason. I've borrowed that style, in having the episodes in *Zeitoun* separated by spaces, by these pauses. It gives it kind of a rhythm that way. But that style was forced upon me because I actually didn't necessarily know what happened between eight and noon on a given day. You're tempted to fill it in, "Well, and then he did this and that," but you can't; you don't know "that." Sometimes Zeitoun would say, "Well, I paddled around Broadmoor, and later on I saw some horses at this intersection that were just roaming free." I'd ask, "What happened in between?" And he'd say, "I don't know." So one episode was there and then you'd jump ahead to the next one. But there's something about the style that actually worked, because the nature of memory, it's episodic like that, and so much of what he experienced was really quiet and meditative and apocalyptic and eerie. The structure, then, gives you that hypnotic kind of feel, at least when he's paddling around. So it actually worked. But it's tough. That's the part that's not quite as fun about journalism, when you're constructing something that you weren't there to see. The writing is not always really enjoyable because you're so constrained. The next thing I'm working on is a novel, so I can work with a richer prose style, which I haven't been able to do for a while.

Q: Did you ever think of serializing Zeitoun's story?

A: No. I don't write beginning to end, so I could never write a coherent serial. I tend to write chapter 34, then chapter 12, then 22. I circle in on a book, and I tend not to tighten all the language until I get to the end of a book. I recently did an event with this older novelist, a famous dude, who says he writes straight through, beginning to end, one draft. He starts at the beginning and he just writes one sentence after another, and if he doesn't get that one sentence, he'll sit there and just look at the screen until he gets it. I can't do that at all. It does limit my ability to excerpt or serialize because I'm never done with a part of it . . .

Q: . . . at the right time.

A: Yeah. Why?

Q: Well, David Simon is doing *Treme* now, and he's less didactic than he was in *The Wire*, much more focused on the individual relationships. You get this criticism emerging out of smaller things. That kind of storytelling I think of as analogous to what you did with *Zeitoun* in that it's episodic, but you get these kernels of stories hinting at a larger picture.

A: Yeah, well, Simon is the closest thing to Dickens we have right now in terms of just saying, "I'm going to take a whole city and populate it with all these characters and follow them." Had Dickens been writing today, he very well might be writing for HBO, because those shows are such a writer's medium now, and you can go so deep with your characters. But it's also tough because you never really know where to end. I don't even know if they know where that series is going to end. I love to know the ending before I start.

I've had people say that *Zeitoun* should be a TV show. Somebody suggested a sitcom with the whole family. That would be horrible, of course, but there would be value in having a Muslim American family on TV. I mean, Kathy is hilarious. She could be a stand-up comic herself. And it would be really nice if there were a mainstream depiction of a regular Muslim American family. All of these weird misperceptions would fall away almost immediately.

Q: With *Modern Family*, you've got a gay family on TV.

A: Yeah, no doubt, I think it won't be long before you do see that, but it's weird that it's been so slow in coming. There is a Muslim public affairs council that does a media image awards ceremony I was at, and there was an episode of *Grey's Anatomy* that was being honored, to say, "Here's a depiction of Muslims in pop culture that is fair." It was nice, of course, but then it's a bit sad that these awards need to exist, because I wish it wasn't so rare that they felt like somebody got it right. But unfortunately it is rare. You know, it's always the religion that's the foremost thing. That's what Muslims are dealing with right now. They can't walk into a room without their religion being an issue, or people wanting their opinion about some political event. But they were honoring this episode just for having a regular patient on *Grey's Anatomy* who was Muslim, and that it was extraordinary that they depicted him praying. That alone, without it going in any other direction. He doesn't have a friend who's in the Taliban or anything like that, they didn't write his faith into it, they didn't have to go any of those places. And that was considered such a rarity that they celebrated it. So this all means that we have a long way to go.

Q: Now *Zeitoun* might not turn into a sitcom, but Jonathan Demme picked it up as a movie. Are you going to be involved with that?

A: I've been a little bit involved. I would prefer not to be that involved because, for one thing, I can't tell Jonathan Demme how to make a movie: he knows better than I do. I think it's rare that the writer of the book is the best adapter, because it's frustrating as a writer. You have other people who want to shape it in different ways, and that's fine, but . . . Also once you write the book, the last thing you want to do is spend another few years rewriting the same story for another medium. I don't know how anyone does it because, for me, to some extent, you've got to move on. But it's exciting about Demme. I think he knows how to make a movie that can appeal to a pretty broad spectrum of people, and maybe, again, that will take it a little further, where you have the first Muslim American hero on screen. And I think that that community is kind of excited about that prospect. It's one thing to have a fairly depicted American Muslim, and it's another thing to have a hero, somebody who is really heroic—and old-school, a guy from Syria, and where it's not an issue that he's from Syria, and it's not all about the Syrian government and whether or not they were complicit in this or that. He's an immigrant who's built a successful life for himself. So the movie moves the ball forward a little bit. I mean, if you're going to spend millions of dollars on a movie, or years on a book, why not move the ball forward a bit? I think that's always a final deciding factor for me to get involved in anything: "Is this moving anything? Are we changing minds a little bit? Are we making anything just a little better?" And to try to do that without it becoming pedantic or didactic.

Q: Where are the Zeitouns now?

A: They're in the same house. I mean, they rebuilt their house.

Q: Is he still working as a contractor?

A: Same thing, exactly the same thing! They came out here about a month ago, and then I was over there in New Orleans, so we saw each other twice in one week. Their house is a lot bigger now, and the kids are bigger—but otherwise everything is exactly the same. He even has the same van with the broken window in the back. The only thing that's any different now is that they know a lot more of their neighbors that they didn't know before. People have written very nice letters to them, and people constantly apologize on behalf of all of America to them. They've been really embraced by a lot of people that feel terrible about what happened to them. But also, they've been recognized as heroes to the Muslim and Arab American communities, and that's good. And Zeitoun's business is doing okay, even though he wishes it were doing better. He complains that his one worry now is that he fears that people think him to be too much of a big shot to paint their back deck. But otherwise, they're doing well; they're exactly the same. And that's nice to see.

Q: You've written for other films, *Where the Wild Things Are* and *Away We Go*. How do you feel about film as a narrative vehicle versus fiction or nonfiction, as you've done it so far?

A: It's such a funny medium, because as a screenwriter, it's the easiest thing to at least get a screenplay written in one draft. It's easier than writing a novel: it's a lot shorter and sparser, and you don't have to fill everything in. You have to just sort of give an outline and a general set of directions to people. And it's really fun to write in that form, too, given it's mostly dialogue and you don't have to create all the scaffolding and fill everything in. I think of a screenplay as being the first step, and the director, the actors, the production designer—they'll all take it the remaining legs of the relay. But as fast and easy as it is on the one end, it's infinitely slower and more frustrating on the back end—although *Away We Go* was incredibly easy the whole time, and fun. *Where the Wild Things Are* was very hard. It took five, six years in production. It's hard to see all of those clichés about studio involvement and money problems, to see all that unfold in slow motion. It's true that too many cooks in the kitchen do spoil the broth. And just to see a friend like Spike struggle with a lot of those forces . . . It was not ideal.

There's a reason why McSweeney's is how it is: small and nimble, and there aren't a whole lot of people that are paid to say no, and there are no lawyers vetting projects. We try to keep the runway between where something starts and where it gets to take off very uncluttered, and that's why we can publish books quickly and publish them the way we want to, the way the authors want us to. McSweeney's exists for a lot of reasons, but one of them is I'd rather not argue about my intentions, or argue about how I want the cover to look. I mean, I have great publishers all over the world that I work with; in Germany they're great, but here in the US is the one place where I'd like to control the entry of the book into the world. I just don't want to get into debates about things. Obviously we don't make nearly as much money as a big company like Random House would with some of my books, but just to save one argument or just one back and forth . . . Life is just way, way, way, way, way too short. And it's a lot quicker and purer to just do it the way you imagine it should be done, and you don't have to go to a committee on everything, and so everybody has a lot of autonomy to do whatever they want to do. As long as *The Believer* and the *Quarterly* come out on time, we don't need to have a whole lot of control over every little thing. But I'll readily admit that early on in my life, with *Might* and when I went to work at *Esquire* for a year, I did flirt with the idea of mass media. And then my first book was more popular than was comfortable for me, and I just realized that kind of scale makes me . . .

Q: . . . nervous?

A: Nervous, and tense, unhappy. And that's why a lot of these media just won't really ever be for me. Mainstream TV is too big for me, so I won't do that anymore, and the internet sometimes gets intense . . .

Q: I think it stresses most people out, even if they don't admit it.

A: Yeah! You know, when we worked on *Zeitoun*, I told Kathy and Zeitoun and the family, "Your lives will change somewhat, and I think that you'll have a lot of people that really learn about your lives and appreciate what you've done, and what you've been through, but your lives won't change much unless you do TV. If you appear on TV, then it's different." The book world is a very polite and rational world, and made up of really good people. You go around to a book festival, it's just good people. There's something about that scale, and the same with the nonprofit world: you feel really lucky just to be around a lot of good people all the time. I think that's a little bit different than some other media, where there are more questionable motives and personalities.

But still, screenwriting, it was fun. In a lot of ways, the film world was too big for me, and the movies we wrote were ultimately marketed in ways I wouldn't have done myself. But you have to let go of those things, and it creates a weird kind of dissonance within. Some writers and directors compare their films and books to children, as in: making a movie is like giving birth. And to carry that metaphor way too far, having that movie marketed is like having someone else dressing your child. Suddenly you see your child leaving the house in lederhosen and a felt cap, and you think, "Hmm. I would have dressed him differently." And when the child is made fun of for dressing like that, it gets to you.

But, again, you have to let go. I learned a while back not to take myself too seriously. I mean, if I were to go to my grave never having written a screenplay, I don't think I would have regretted it. But at the same time, to have it as something you experimented with and tried out, I like that I have at least done it; it was something I was interested in. I feel like I've dabbled in a lot of things at some point or another, and I've realized there are people that are better suited to that form, so now I know I'm not the greatest screenwriter. I don't know if it's a form I'll ever go back to again, but it was good to try it out. And it made me realize, again, the many advantages to books. The book world is still the best of all media, for me. It suits me the best. That's not something I would have predicted when I was twenty; this was not the road I thought I was on necessarily. But having touched on these other areas or, to continue the road metaphor, having veered off onto some of these side roads, I do come back knowing that this feels like home.

Q: It seems like the characters that populate *Away We Go* and *Where the Wild Things Are* and also some of the other stories you've told, they're in these in-between periods. Max is eight or nine and he's on the brink of self-awareness: he almost knows who he is, and I've always thought of the Wild Things as parts of his personality that are in conflict with one another. The same thing can be said of *Away We Go*: these two people are finally realizing that they are adults, and that they have to make adult decisions. It's also something you confront pretty explicitly in *A Heartbreaking Work*, where you've been thrust into this position. Are you attracted to stories like that?

A: Well, who isn't? There's not a whole lot of narrative thrust in those who live lives of perfect contentment. But I can't be credited too much with the story line of *Away We Go*, which is something that Vendela and I did when we were expecting our first baby. I think that there are stories that come from your subconscious and things that are really crucial to your core, questions that you are trying to figure out through whatever medium, that you don't even necessarily know that you are asking yourself. That's the purest form of art, I think, and sometimes I'll look at some of the stories from my story collections, and I only now know what I was getting at, what questions I was asking. But *Away We Go* was coming from a different place, a lighter place, I guess. Less of a molten-core kind of place and a more "Wouldn't it be funny if . . . ?" kind of place. I don't mean to stratify different works, but then again, I think you can, and I think you have to. At least with me, there's the core stuff that you write because you have to—like my first book I really had to write, I couldn't get past it, and I probably would have collapsed had I not gotten that out of my system. Even the couple of books after that were coming from a core place, a place where I was just like, "I've got to express this somehow, now." And you sublimate that through whatever narrative forms you can create. And then there's *Zeitoun* and *What Is the What*, which were coming from a place of feeling like I really knew how to tell a story at that point, and knew enough about craft to make it make sense, and trying to work more from a sense of journalistic duty . . . I'm not sure if that's the right word. But then, a number of the things that you do you're doing because every so often it's okay to have fun writing. I can't say I've had a ton of fun over the years writing . . . I mean, I have fun when I write very short stories and I have fun when I write those screenplays, for the most part, and I had fun writing the novel based on *Where the Wild Things Are*, and I had fun doing those drawings of animals with slogans, but these other books aren't necessarily fun. *Zeitoun* was work, hard work, and *What Is the What* almost killed me. You feel duty to a real person and a sense of obligation to do right by not only them, but by their constituency. For Valentino, it's three thousand, four thousand Lost Boys and Girls, and two million dead in South Sudan, and four million displaced, and you just feel like you've got to get it right for all of those people. And then with *Zeitoun*, there's the family that you care about, and then there's the people of New Orleans you care about, and Muslim Americans, Arab Americans. It's a type of pressure I don't relish. I'm trying not to take on another story like that, where you feel obligated to so many constituencies, to at least get it right.

Q: I want to go back to something you just said about McSweeney's, and how you've cleared the runway. Do you think that that can serve as a model for struggling publishing houses, or even larger publishing houses?

A: I actually think that a lot of them have already done this; they've had to trim a little bit . . . I don't think that everyone needs to gut their staff, and I don't like anybody losing their job; so many people I know have, because they've cut the staff. But I do like small. I like small businesses and I like small organizations and I like fewer obstacles toward making anything, toward bringing anything into the world. I think the best artwork generally comes out of small groups or individuals acting more or less untethered. So, when you have companies getting bigger and bigger, and more layers and more bureaucracy, and more people that are fearful, or people that are paid to say no or to question every last move, you do lose quite a bit of the ability to react and to do things well. I think if you spread around that responsibility to too many people and give too many people reasons to act out of fear, to get in the way of things, it doesn't serve anybody, and you end up with this huge, unwieldy machine.

Q: And then they can't make money . . .

A: They can't make money, so it doesn't work either way. And that's why we're doing fine, and we grow just a little bit every year. In our organization, we grow on average one person a year. We've been around eleven years, and we have eight people working here. I mean, that's some glacial growth. But we exist. We can get the books out that we want to get out. It's not an incredibly complicated business. That's why I'm in it. I'm not good at math, but I can figure out the split on a book. I know where all the dollars on a given cover price go. It's not that hard to break down, and there's not that many people involved in it. There's us, there's a printer, a distributor, there's a bookstore, and there's a reader, and there's not much else. It's a pretty simple and very gentlemanly and elegant business, and I think that when you overcomplicate, that's when there are problems. When anything grows too big—and the publishing business grew a little bit too big for its britches in the eighties and nineties—it can't last. I don't think that books will have any problem surviving, but I think that the companies that publish them have to continue to be nimble. If you build any business model on giant hits, on giant returns on investments, then it's not sustainable. But with a book or with newspapers or magazines or anything, if you keep the staff reasonable and the scale rational, you can exist without a problem. When we built *The Believer*, I knew that it was never going to be some giant thing, so we built it in a way that one person could maintain it. That's Andrew Leland, the managing editor. I built the magazine's original template so that one guy could maintain it every month, and I knew we could pay at least one salary. And that's where we're at. We pay the contributors and pay the other editors a part-time wage. That's it. And it exists! It's influential to those who read it—it means a lot to a lot of people. And that's fine. It doesn't have to have a circulation of five hundred thousand. A small, loyal readership is better than a massive, diluted, and passive readership.

Q: I think you make this point with the *San Francisco Panorama*, that there's this magic number that corporations look for, that 12 percent profit margin . . .

A: I know, it's terrible.

Q: . . . and if something is not above that margin, then it's not worth it. One of the things I was thinking about, and I've heard this argument made other places, is that you also have to change the individuals that want to go into this profession. They have this vision of journalism or book editing as something glamorous, theoretically high-paid, when really, if it's going to survive, it can't be that, and it wasn't that before.

A: Yeah, it never used to be. I think if you go back to early in the century, or hundreds of years ago, there's a certain breed of person who wanted to go into publishing. They loved books and they wanted to get good books published and put them into people's hands, and it didn't get much more complicated than that. I was in New York in the late nineties, and I saw the town cars that would pick up editors, drive them to work and back home, with the expense accounts and lunches. I remember being taken out to lunch. I mean, every week there was some lunch at some place in Midtown that must have cost $200 or something, and I was coming from the small magazine world in San Francisco, where to spend over, like, eight dollars for lunch was a big deal, like, "Fuck, man, we're going to spend eight dollars for lunch?!" I just thought there was a lot of waste in New York. I don't like spending. I'm not a restaurant guy. I don't recognize most of the food on these menus. I admit to being a total caveman when it comes to food and things like that. So in New York, there was this unsustainable model. People were going into books and magazines for some glamorous lifestyle, and it didn't make sense. It would be like going into basket weaving for the glamour. It doesn't make sense. The numbers don't support it.

If the goal is "I want to run a gallery," you've got to work backward from how you're going to run that gallery sustainably, not "I want to run a gallery *and* I want to be rich." You've got to ask, "If I like to do this, how do I build a model that will allow me to be around doing this in ten years?" Well, put the gallery in a space where the rent is rational. That's why we're in the Mission and not downtown. Our revenues have grown every year. We've done fine. We just don't take any risks. We never suddenly say, "Now it's time for us to borrow $6 million and get a big office or buy a building." Maybe I'm just risk-averse when it comes to things like that, but I want to ensure that we're around in five years. I think that part of it is having a DIY model, and another part of it is just a slow-and-steady-wins-the-race kind of model.

I've learned from a lot of mistakes on my own, and also mistakes I've seen around me, because when I was publishing *Might* magazine way back in the early nineties, we tried to get up to a hundred thousand circulation, and get advertising and all that stuff, and I could see that we didn't build the machine the right way. None of us got paid; we were counting on our success, and our success depended on advertisers. If we didn't have the advertisers, then nobody got paid. Or sometimes we had to wait to go to press until we got the ads. And meanwhile I had to do meetings with advertisers, with ad agencies, and it was absolutely soul-sucking. It was the most depressing stuff I'd ever done, trying to prove the worth of this magazine.

And I thought, "Never again will we depend on the few to determine whether or not we get to publish." So that's why, when we did *McSweeney's*, we did it without ads. We decided to be small, and to stay small. So originally we printed twenty-five hundred copies, and I knew if we sold those, we could print five thousand of the next one, which we did. If we sold those, we could print seventy-five hundred copies the next time. But again, with no advertisers, with nobody else saying yes or no, the readers alone determine whether or not it is worth continuing. And if they say yes, then we'll keep doing it. Running the risk and the investment around that, it's five thousand readers, not five junior media planners at McCann-Erickson, who decide whether or not what you do is valid. And that's partly why I left painting. I studied painting all the way through college, and I worked at galleries. But most of the art world wasn't attractive to me.

Q: It's still like that.

A: I know! You depend on galleries to show your stuff, and even then, maybe five people go into the gallery in any given month, and then, if you're lucky, a couple of rich people will buy your work and put it in their bathroom in Palm Beach, and then, if you're really lucky, twenty years down the road you can get a retrospective, and *then* people on a mass scale get to see your work. Or at least that's how it used to be. The internet and lots of other things have improved it. That's why I really like Banksy, because he brings it straight to the people, and that's why a lot of the artists I like do books, and put it out there in a more democratic way. And there's a great gallery out here called Electric Works, and the gallery across the street from our office, the co-op, who do it differently. But with the fancier galleries or any of those things that depend on too few, it seems very fraught. Any medium that's inherently undemocratic isn't very interesting to me, and that's why books are ideal. There's nothing more affordable and easier to get out there, except music, I guess. That's what we're always trying to do: just get things out there. We're always asking, "How can we do it? How do we make it affordable? How can we make this work?"

Q: What do you think about the internet, then, supposedly the most democratizing medium of them all?

A: I think it's great. We exist in part because of the internet. We have our store, which does well, and the daily updated website brings people to us all the time. It's been a great tool. But, that said, I don't spend a lot of time on the internet. I'm an old dog and the internet is new tricks.

Q: Is your site still designed on the old Mac?

A: We started the website back in 1998, and I didn't have high-speed internet, and I never had a really fast computer, so the design had to be super basic to load. So Elizabeth Kairys and I designed the site in this insanely simple way. It was at a point where I was reacting against overblown New York glossy magazine design. I thought, "How funny would it be if there were no images whatsoever, and no flashing, and no hyperlinks and all that stuff." And so it went up that way, and all these years later, we haven't seen a reason to change it. It's still the same, and I think it's been really helpful to us. I use the internet as a tool; I think it's a nice place to visit, but I wouldn't want to live there. A lot of people are making the mistake of living there. It has diminishing returns.

Q: It's not the solution to all our problems.

A: Right now, that's the conventional wisdom, and you have to fight against that assumption every time. In the education debate, it starts with, "Now, I assume that the internet is going to solve this, but . . ." And with the book debate, it's, "Let's assume that the internet will kill books dead within five years." It's just a very strange time. But it was the same thing with radio, and the same thing with TV. They assume that any new medium is going to kill everything sacred within a few years. And it's never happened. I do think that the real culprits in terms of overglorifying the internet as the solution to everything are people my age. It's not the kids. You'll see these kids that come here, they'll just be sitting reading short stories from the *Kenyon Review* and they'll be very happy to do it. And none of them will be on their phones or missing the internet.

Q: I've never seen a young person with a Kindle, ever.

A: Oh, you won't. You write them an email and you won't get a reply from them in eight days, because it's just not on their mind at all times. The wealthier kids, for sure, but not necessarily our students at 826 Valencia. Some of the discussion is very classist, very disturbing that way, because e-readers are just not affordable or practical for working-class families. How can a family struggling to get by afford a $400 device to read a $10 book? It's an insane system right now. Meanwhile, the family can check out an actual paper-and-board book for free. Or they can buy a used book for a dollar. And they can share that book with the whole family. With e-readers, how does a family share it? They need five e-readers. It's not tenable. But for business travelers, fine. I just want the e-readers to stay out of kids' lives, because the last thing kids need is more time looking at screens.

The internet is a really good tool, but when everything has to be channeled through that medium, I think it's a shame. I saw a friend of mine the other day—we used to go see a lot of bands together, and we had a very, we thought, cultivated taste in music in high school. We knew Echo and the Bunnymen before anyone else did, and we would go to see Sonic Youth and Public Enemy downtown. That was actually only one show, in 1990. And we thought we were really cool to do all that stuff. And then he got into the Grateful Dead one day, and it was like the Grateful Dead had to obliterate all other music that he listened to; he threw everything else out and it was only bootlegs and that kind of thing. There are some people who feel that the internet has to obliterate all other media by its very existence. It's just a very strange logical fallacy to think that it's this zero-sum thing. I do think that there's a certain amount of diminishing returns when you're reading shorter arguments online, and then you're commenting on those articles, and those are even shorter and less meaningful, and then you're Twittering about the comments, and that's only 140 characters . . . I'm not sure if we're getting any closer to understanding life on earth that way, and I don't know if we're getting any closer to alleviating the suffering we see around us, or understanding ourselves better. We're *commenting* a lot; there's a lot more commenting than there used to be.

Q: Anonymous, at that, too.

A: Yeah, so . . . I don't know. But I always vowed never to be the grump that believes that everything was better when he was younger, because I don't. And I actually do think that, through desktop publishing and the software that we use and the internet, it makes what we do possible. I never take that for granted. Because of these new media and more egalitarian forms of distribution and the democratization of the whole process, it's the best time in the history of the printed word to be a publisher or to be a writer. I could prove it to anybody; I've never lost a debate on this, no matter how full of malaise anybody is about the medium or books in general. It's so easy to prove that this is the best time. In the next issue of *McSweeney's*, we'll publish proof of why this is the best era ever with a bunch of aspects of the issue, lots of data. The numbers are hard to deny, there being more readers on the planet than there ever have been before, far greater overall literacy than ever before, easier access overall. There was a time when only 10 percent of the population could read, you know. Being a writer or publisher in, say, medieval England wasn't some golden age. It's just an inherent tendency of humans to assume that things were better at some other time, some fictional halcyon era, and if you put it to anybody as, "When was this golden age of publishing? When people were walking around talking about Proust and everyone had read the new book by Philip Roth?" Nobody can pinpoint this, and if they did, they would be completely wrong. It's a funny thing. But again, the fact that a company like ours, where none of us really knew what we were doing—I mean, we were all self-taught, and everyone came through as an intern—and that we're growing and that we can get by, that means that it's a pretty good time.

Q: I'd like to talk about design, since you mentioned desktop publishing. You come from a fine arts background, and almost all of your endeavors— *McSweeney's*, *The Believer*, the covers to your books—have a pretty strong and shared graphic sensibility. Where does that come from? There's a strength to the designs you choose that you don't really see in other books.

A: I learned graphic design in high school, with the predecessor to desktop publishing now, a design program called Ready, Set, Go. So I started setting type and laying out stories, and I did it in college and then with *Might* magazine. But I can't look at many of those designs with pride. I was learning slowly, very slowly, to have any kind of distinct sensibility, and a lot of times I was beholden to clients, so I didn't do any really good design until *McSweeney's*—I mean, outside of a few pages of *Might* here and there. I had no training in it whatsoever. I've never taken a design class, though I wish I had. With *McSweeney's*, I limited myself to one font, Garamond 3. I think that those constraints are sometimes the best thing for any kind of artist, whether it's using two colors to paint something or only one font to design with, and I just struck upon a model that was based on old Bibles and pamphlets that had that center-justified layout with the same font in different forms. It felt to me like the right marriage between the content, which was offbeat, and the personal nature of publishing. We were publishing a very small thing, this small journal for the castaways, the people screaming from the woods, and that's why it had a much more pure feel to it, I guess. With *Might*, we were always designing in the hopes that we would break big like *Rolling Stone*; you know, we were going to be the *Rolling Stone* of the nineties. It was aimed at a bigger group of people. With *McSweeney's*, we just never had that illusion at all, nor did we ever want it. We were working in a smaller format and away from the potential of a mass audience. So I just kept on trying to get weirder and weirder, and I hadn't gone in that direction since I was a painting student. It was so nice just to explore the logical extreme of something. Issue 1 was weird, and issue 2 was weirder, and 3 was the real end point.

Q: The circular one.

A: Yeah, where I thought, "Okay, that's going as far down that road as you can get." And then we broke open and I painted that bird for issue 4, the boxed issue. And from there, we decided to change the format more or less every issue. And I think that because it looked a little bit unlike other things, a lot of designers liked it. And that was really new to me, to have any validation from the design community, because I had been doing hackwork for so many years. So that validation meant a lot to me. I started realizing that there were people out there who really wanted us to keep pushing things in new directions, so we'd commission stuff from other designers and illustrators, and we became a place where you could really experiment with the form of the book. We just became convinced because we saw all these people collecting issues of *McSweeney's*.

Q: So having magnets or other oddities makes people want to keep them?

A: All that stuff ensures that it's really hard to throw away a *McSweeney's*. People always have a group of them on a shelf, and subscribers subscribe because they want to know what we're going to do next. If you keep the object, you keep the words within. It becomes an insurance policy, or some kind of armor for these delicate words and stories inside, that they might survive a little bit longer. And if you see it there, ten years down the road, and you still have it, you might be more likely to read it. I buy old books all the time—I'll buy them just for the craft of the cover and the book—but I'll end up reading them, too. I think that you've got to put an equal amount of craft into the book itself. If we just said, "Eh, here's this book. They worked five years on it. Let's slap some cover on it and throw it to the wind," it would be a shame. Any book needs to be celebrated with an appropriately new and memorable package. It ensures that people won't gravitate inexorably toward the Kindle or other electronic media, because if you give them a distinct choice between that tactile experience and this electronic and sterile experience, then I do think people are always attracted, ultimately, to the tactile. People like to be delighted—they just do, and they always will. So if you can find ways to achieve that, like, "No one's done magnets before, so let's try magnets!" Or, "No one's done . . ."

Q: . . . glass?

A: Glass is always something we're talking about. We're still trying to figure out glass. I mean, you could, you really could. You'd want it to be very thick, that's the problem, but it can be done. But then that becomes an object in itself. As a designer, that's why you're in design: to do something new, to push the form in new directions. And if it's just a matter of playing with the same five elements, that's not quite as much fun on the design side. Our subscribers are subscribers, in part, because they want something different every issue, and that ensures that we continue to survive. Their need or hunger to be surprised ensures that we can publish new work. And if we were just straightforward or if it was a very cheap object, then we probably wouldn't have survived. So it actually serves both purposes, and it keeps us entertained, too.

Q: Is that the same impulse that was behind the *San Francisco Panorama*, the idea that it was a newspaper, which you traditionally read and then recycle?

A: I don't know. I wonder if people are keeping that or recycling it, or part of it. But yeah, it was the same thing. I was a newspaper fan and I still am, and I think it's such a great medium that in some cases is underutilized. We're trying to remind people of the beauty of the form, and also try to remind editors and designers and publishers of newspapers that they have to differentiate themselves from the internet version of news.

Q: They can't become more like the internet.

A: Which they were, for a long time. Everything got shorter. But it's like that with anything, I'm sure. Again, when TV came out, everyone assumed newspapers would die because they had news on TV. And I think for a while newspapers tried to be more like TV, and that's when articles got shorter and graphics got brighter. Some of that is fine, but it's a lesson that's had to be relearned, over and over, that you don't need to imitate your supposed competitor; you need to differentiate from them, and zig when they're zagging. And celebrate and emphasize the strengths of whatever form you're working in. We just decided to take that form to its logical extreme. And we only got about halfway through everything we wanted to do; there were about a thousand ideas left on the table. But I'm just always going to prefer paper. I have to look at the screen eight hours a day anyway, because it's the best form for me to write and design. So I love the tool, but I don't want to wake up and look at the screen, and go to bed and look at the screen, and live on the screen, and have all my photos on the screen, and have all my contacts be on the screen. The fact that we willingly go in this direction is strange to me. Our complicity in that seems really kind of more gung ho than I would have expected—there's not a whole lot of resistance, which surprises me.

Q: Who knows, maybe at some point diseases will emerge from staring at the screen.

A: Listen, you said it: this is usually how it goes. We like something so much that it makes us sick, and it has happened many times. Cell phones are supposedly giving us giant tumors, and maybe in ten years we'll all be blind from the screen. I do think that it's too much of a good thing. It's just a matter of balance and moderation and diversifying our own intake. But, yeah, that's the beauty of our subscriber base and this model—that we could just decide to put out a newspaper, and just do it.

Q: You don't want to continue? I'm sure a lot of people are clamoring.

A: Yeah, yeah! We got a lot of eccentric millionaires come through and ask us if we would continue putting out a newspaper, and they'd fund it and all that stuff. In another life, it would be what we would be doing. But it would be impossible to do anything else. It would take the whole staff, maybe three times the current size, to really do it and make a go of it, to put out a daily paper and make a living doing it. It would mean all hands on deck and everything else would fall away. And that would mean I wouldn't have time for writing or 826 or anything else. So to just maintain our own equilibrium and everything else we do, we could just do it once. But it is a shame. You do realize that there are a lot of things you wish you could do in life. I wish I could move to Sudan and help Valentino build more schools, but I can't do that. I can't put out a daily newspaper. I barely approach the writing of the books I want to write. There just isn't enough time. And so you just have to wait and encourage and help when you can. There are a million of those things. That's what's very hard about being made of decaying flesh. There's only so much you can do.

Q: Do you think that the programs at 826 are a success for some of the same reasons *McSweeney's* is a success?

A: Yeah, they're built on the exact same model, which is: small. Each 826 center has been built by a dedicated group of people who are invested in the idea and don't expect to make a lot of money doing it. I mean, if there's one thing I've learned the hard way many times, it's just to listen first, and to always be in tune with the community you're serving or representing. With 826 Valencia, we just opened a building here in the Mission. All we knew was that we could probably help with tutoring; we didn't have any other plans beyond that. And, at that point, I had learned enough humility to know that I don't know education any better than even one teacher alive, so we'll open this building and we'll let the parents and teachers help us define how we're going to be useful.

Q: You give them the space.

A: It's a space, that's all it was at first. And they helped shape it. Teachers said, "Let's do field trips," so we said, "Okay, then we'll do field trips." Teachers said, "Well, why don't you come into our school with certain kids we wouldn't otherwise see," so we said, "Oh, okay, we'll do that." Teachers said, "Well, how about a workshop about radio production?" And we said, "Okay." "How about a workshop about comics?" "Okay." And it's been nice. My favorite thing is just to open a building and then let other people take it in a million different directions. I can just watch, and support. I can walk across the street right now and see things that have grown in the last two days. Ideas that I didn't know anything about but are brilliant ideas—ideas maybe some young staffer or one of the tutors came up with. I just came back from a tour of all the other 826s, and they're all different—they're all totally, drastically different in a lot of different ways. They do share some things and some core values and services, but they're all geared to their local communities and to the personalities of their staffs. So they're similar in that they start small, they grow rationally, but it's never some overarching design where everything's got to be uniform. A lot is about picking or working with people that you respect, and empowering them to do whatever they think is right. We have very little oversight with the other 826s; I don't know the first thing about what the kids of Ypsilanti, Michigan, need, so I leave it to the educators there to decide. I was in schools recently in Ypsilanti with some of our tutors, just watching and listening, and I saw some things that seemed familiar to me and other things that I learned. And then the same thing with Seattle: a totally different population there. There's something very true about wisdom with age, and especially the wisdom that the older you get, the less you know. And I know that I know very little, so I live the rule. I don't pretend at knowing that much anymore. And once you realize and admit that, you can spend most of the time listening and learning. Listening first and asking questions second, and then speaking third.

It's nice, being able to walk into these centers anywhere and meet some of the students and all the people working there. It makes you very optimistic. It confirms your most idealistic notions, and inclinations and hopes, because you know that real change is happening. When I used to be more of an opinion writer, in my twenties, I used to think that if I could just wave my hand at a problem or talk about a problem, then naturally it would change.

This was what *Might* magazine tried to do. Change would come because we mentioned it, change would come because we had recognized it, or had written a pithy article about something. And it was frustrating to realize that none of that change that we thought was needed came to pass because we thought about it, or mentioned it, or commented on it. We didn't really do anything. You realize that the real work is brick by brick.

For example, we have a new website called ScholarMatch. It's a site that connects individual donors with kids that need money for college. We have no control over the budget process in California. We have no control over the fact that tens of millions of dollars are lost in the University of California system, and in the Cal State system, and that a lot of the kids that could barely scrape that tuition money together last year won't be able to get it together next year, and so they're not going to college. All this promise of higher education in California is a farce right now. We have no control over that, and I could protest from here until 2020, and hold a picket and complain about it, but it's not going to change it. And so we just created a tool that right now will get, I think, a few dozen of these kids off to college by August. It's not millions of this and millions of that, but it's practical, and a few dozen is a scale that seems rational. Like *McSweeney's* at seventeen thousand or *The Believer* at twelve thousand, or a given book at four thousand, that's significant; it means something, and it moves the ball forward a little bit. A lot of life is managing expectations and setting things on a rational scale, and within that rational scale you can do it the way that you feel like it needs to be done, without a whole lot of compromise. And you might be able to actually get something done, as opposed to spending ten years trying to raise money, or spending ten years complaining about something. Trying to achieve change on a smaller scale is more realistic and more satisfying. For me, at least.

Q: Belief as an idea runs through a lot of your work; it's a theme that's picked up on with Kathy's search and her belief that her husband was still alive. It's in Valentino's search for epistemological solid ground on which to stand. And your magazine is called *The Believer* for a reason. What does belief mean to you? Why *The Believer*?

A: Well, there very well might be a tie between those three. What's funny is that I'm a lapsed Catholic, but I have ended up writing books about people of great and unwavering faith. And I have great respect for their faith. I just tried to depict it as it was. But I don't know how related that is to the title of the magazine, *The Believer*, because the other title for it was *The Optimist*. There were two parts of the newspaper I was always confused about: that there could be genocide going on the front page, but the strongest language and the most vitriol in the newspaper would be reserved for baseball players, basketball players, or something like that. And I felt like that's so strange! I read sports, I like baseball, and I just can't believe how upset some people get about somebody not running fast enough, or whatever else it is. It just seems like a very strange place to focus one's anger. You find a little bit of that with book coverage, too. So, at the time, we were sort of creating a space and a cultural magazine that chose to really celebrate the things that we liked and books that we found were important. We thought of *The Believer* as a place where, since there's so much to love in all these different modes of culture, we could accentuate those things that hadn't gotten enough attention but that we felt strongly about. So we decided to focus on a lot of things, like interviews with philosophers, and people that were really doing bedrock inquiry into the nature of life, and why and how we exist, and how best we might live, and how that was channeled through art in any kind of form. And the philosophical take on a lot of this informed the title, too. A lot of those early interviews were about the nature of belief, or the nature of existence, or can we believe that we have purpose? That's a kind of faith, too. It's really strange and hard to justify in itself. If you don't believe in God but you believe in purpose, that's a difficult thing to square, you know. So all of those things got tied up in it. I also just liked the title, and I pushed for it because I thought that that would be fairly radical, to give all art and all artists the benefit of the doubt, and to proceed from a point of view that to make art or to write or to make music or whatever was probably an inherent good. We might split hairs after that about how good, but let's assume it's an inherent good, and people are proceeding out of a place of purity in their hearts, and then we'll go from there. And I still love the title. I like it mainly because it's just so . . . odd. It's just such an uncool word, to be a believer . . . At the time, Garth Brooks had a magazine called *The Believer*, which was a Christian magazine, so we got confused with them a lot, and had to disabuse a few people of thinking that they were subscribing to the Christian magazine when they wrote us a check. I love that.

Q: My last question: Why San Francisco and not New York? Why make here your personal home and your publishing home?

A: Well, I lived in New York for a while and I love going back there, but, really, for me it started on a purely aesthetic level, from the first minute I got here. I had only been here once before, when I was a kid, so I didn't know San Francisco from my ass. But when I graduated and I moved here to be with my brother and sister, I knew right away that I was going to stay.

I know it's weird, but colors are important to me, growing up as a painter; so on a pure color level, it's the yellows and blues and greens that you see in incredible vividness all year round. And being surrounded by water on three or more sides, and then the hills—even if you're driving to Walgreens, you're going to crest a few hills and see some breathtaking views. It's such a startlingly beautiful place, and beauty is really important to me. It informs my daily happiness to such an extent. Whereas New York . . . I lived in Brooklyn and I really liked that. Manhattan just wasn't really my palette. Just too big. I felt a little overwhelmed in Manhattan.

On a people level, it's the sense of goofy idealism in San Francisco, because no one here will ever say no to you, no idea will ever get anyone doubting. It's so rare that you have anybody putting up any resistance to anything. For better or for worse, that's why you also have people dressed as giraffes and tap dancing. That's why you have the Bay to Breakers, and the Folsom Street Fair, and why Halloween is so big here . . . I mean, this is a place where some of the strangest and goofiest people in the country find a home. I also think that there is this sense of possibility that felt right to me. There's a sense that you're around a bunch of people that are here to think of new ways to do things, tied to a sense of social justice that becomes very addictive. Like recently, I had to do a fundraiser for YouthSpeaks, which is like a sister organization to 826, and then I had my Best American Nonrequired class meeting here in this room, and then there was a friend of mine who was doing a fundraiser for Mapendo International—they help refugees from around the world find new lives, usually here in the US; they help get them resettled. That's three equally powerful and odd things in one day, but there were probably a hundred other similar fundraisers happening the same day. And it's a small city.

Then the last thing is the literary tradition here. Literary culture here is so supportive and so one-for-all-and-all-for-one. It makes it a comfortable place to live as a writer. But, I have to say, it really did start on a purely aesthetic level. Even if there wasn't a reader within ten miles of this city I still might live here, because it's so beautiful. So this is where I'm stuck. I would never leave here—there's nowhere else I would rather go, unless I left the country altogether and moved to Costa Rica or Iceland or something like that. But it is weird to know that I've been here since I was twenty-two and I'll never leave.

Dave Eggers Talks with *Buzz* about His U of I Memories, *Zeitoun*, and His Many Writing Projects

Joe Lewis / 2010

From *Buzz* magazine (the *Daily Illini*), November 17, 2010. © 2010 by Illini Media. Reprinted by permission.

Buzz: You were an Illini Media alumnus. What department did you work for? Any special Illini Media memories?

Dave Eggers: I started out my freshman year as a photographer, shooting during the day and developing in an actual darkroom at night. It was a pretty great gig, actually. One of my jobs was to go to Illini basketball games—this was the year we went to the Final Four—and sit under the basket and get dunk shots. I don't know if I ever got anything published, but it was a nice place to watch the games. From there I did illustrations for the Op-Ed page for a while, then I went into feature writing, record reviews, art reviews. My junior year I edited the section called "Directory" (that's what *Buzz* used to be called), and my senior year I edited the monthly magazine, *InPrint*, that featured long-form journalism. I think I did just about every job at the DI, short of ad sales.

Buzz: Did you live in Champaign or Urbana? Where did you hang out?

DE: The DI was at First Street and Green at that time, and I lived about four blocks away on First Street. I slept at the DI a lot, too, in the old *Illio* offices. They never knew that, though. Not until now, at least.

Buzz: On *Zeitoun*: I noticed you were able to ask a lot of intimate, personal questions, like on page 40 when Kathy describes her weight troubles. How long did it take to develop relationships with this sort of confiding to develop?

DE: It was different for the two of them. Kathy is very quick to warm up to people—she's very talkative and unguarded. So with Kathy, the relationship was almost immediately very open. She's also a great storyteller with an incredible eye for detail, so she really made the book possible. With Zeitoun, it took a little longer for that same rapport to develop. But after we had shared a number of meals together it felt very familial, very trusting. Pretty early on he started telling me things he hadn't even told Kathy. This happens a lot when someone decides to tell their story: they tend to open up and go into far greater detail to the reporter than anyone else. But it takes time. Many of the most crucial parts of the book came out of times we just spent driving around together, rather than in formal interviews.

Buzz: When did you decide to incorporate the extended Zeitoun family (Kathy, as well as Zeitoun's family in Syria) into the book? It worked nicely thematically. How did you realize that you wanted to extend the story?

DE: The very first time I met the Zeitouns, we spent most of the time talking about Abdulrahman's life in Syria. Even in that first meeting it was obvious his upbringing and extended family would play a large role in the story. And then when I went to Syria and Spain, the role of his family grew even more. I was able to see the effect of Abdulrahman's disappearance on his brothers and sisters and cousins, and see their side of it. It was important to be able to show the impact of this kind of injustice on not just the man victimized but on all those who care about him.

Buzz: Without spoiling the end, the book details American government officials in an embarrassing and controversial light. Have you personally received any feedback about this from any government officials?

DE: There's been no official response, and I didn't expect anything like that. There's no chance of any official representing New Orleans or FEMA commenting or apologizing without risking liability. Then again, it's hard to find any officials associated with the response to Katrina that felt like they did a good job, or who deny their many failures and missteps. Even Bush, in his new autobiography, admits that the response was deeply flawed.

Buzz: It seems lately you've been writing a lot of nonfiction books, yet your prose style is still very lyrical. How did you progress from fiction to nonfiction?

DE: I spent my twenties writing almost exclusively nonfiction: features, travel writing, criticism, op-eds. I was probably about thirty before I got serious about fiction. These last few books are really just going back into my journalistic training.

Buzz: How is the 826 Valencia project going? Any new updates or features?

DE: We just opened a new center in Washington, DC, and that's been pretty incredible to see grow from an idea, a few years ago, to a thriving center with a pretty great storefront. So we have eight centers now, and I'm not entirely sure how many more we'll add. There are a lot of centers based on our model that are popping up, in places like Alabama and London and Dublin, and that's good to see. They don't have to be affiliated with us directly to do the same kind of work.

Buzz: After writing two movies, do you feel famous? Do people recognize you on the street any more frequently?

DE: Very few people know much about the people who write movies. I don't think I knew what the word *screenwriter* meant until I was in my mid-twenties. So no, it hasn't changed anything. The guy at the video store once thought he'd heard my name somewhere, but he couldn't place it. That's as close as I've come.

Buzz: What's your next project?

DE: The Voice of Witness series has been really active this fall—we have two books coming out very soon: one called *Hope Deferred: Narratives of Zimbabwe Lives,* and one called *Nowhere to Be Home: Narratives from Survivors of Burma's Military Regime.* Otherwise, I'm working very slowly on a novel and enjoying the freedom that comes with writing fiction.

The Rumpus Interview with Dave Eggers

Stephen Elliott / 2012

From *The Rumpus*, June 4, 2012. © 2012 by Stephen Elliott. Reprinted by permission.

The Rumpus: *A Hologram for the King* is your first imagined-from-scratch book in a while. In a lot of ways it seems like a real departure from the last book we talked about, *Zeitoun*. So I guess the question would be, Why a novel set in Saudi Arabia?

Dave Eggers: Well, about four years ago I had one of those moments where you think, Huh, that's an interesting framework for a novel. My brother-in-law had just been to Saudi Arabia with his company, and he told me about these cities that King Abdullah is trying to construct from scratch, these centers of education and manufacturing and other catalysts for a post-oil economy. I was fascinated by the idea of American businesspeople coming to these nascent cities in the desert, trying to get in on the ground floor. That was the start of it at least, and it gelled with some ideas I was having about this aging businessman who's painted himself into a corner.

Rumpus: That's your protagonist, Alan Clay. He's middle-aged, with a background in sales, management, and cost cutting, but he's been downsized himself and is having a hard time getting work. He's fifty-four years old and believes that no one is interested in his services anymore. Though he also presents himself as an optimist.

Eggers: I think he presents himself as an optimist because optimism is the necessary veneer of a salesman, right? Alan started out as a Fuller Brush salesman, going door to door selling household products, and when he did that, he had to act like he was selling happiness, security, possibility—and he was good at it.

Rumpus: He's a joke teller still. He knows how to charm people. You have jokes in there that I've never heard, but must be old standards.

Eggers: It's strange that the telling of those types of jokes has gone away, because they're still funny. You set up a funny situation, you deliver a surprising punchline. Alan knows a million of them and uses them effectively to break the ice. It was one of the tools of a salesman like Alan.

Rumpus: Alan spent a bunch of years at Schwinn, which I didn't realize was based in Chicago.

Eggers: That's a fascinating thing, right? They made Schwinn bikes on the West Side of Chicago till the mideighties. Millions of bikes were built there, but then they started outsourcing to Taiwan and China, and eventually the brand lost its way. Alan looks back on the days when he could believe in what he was selling, and he wants that feeling back.

Rumpus: But he was complicit in the downfall of Schwinn.

Eggers: Sure, but he doesn't quite understand that or own it. The hollowing out of the American manufacturing sector was a death by a thousand cuts—not strictly a top-down product of, say, the Bain Capitals of the world. Guys like Alan, who just were trying to cut costs, found offshore production irresistible, and they handed more and more of the supply chain over to these cheaper overseas factories. But Alan and others didn't foresee the day when their own jobs were more or less superfluous.

Rumpus: So now he's in a tent in Saudi Arabia, trying to sell something he knows almost nothing about.

Eggers: He's trying to sell IT to the king of Saudi Arabia, with telepresence technology as a lure. It's basically a way to have long-distance meetings using holograms. And Alan really doesn't know what he's doing. He's like a lot of men of his generation, who were trained to sell *things*, to make deals over dinner, golf courses, all that. But now things are very different, and he's adrift. I have a lot of friends who work in management and consulting and manufacturing, and they talk a lot about men like Alan, and what to do with them. Their modes of working are sometimes outdated, and they're hard to hire because they're very expensive. Alan's surrounded by young people who know more about IT than he does, who work cheaper, and who assume all things are made in China. They would never see it as fiscally plausible to hire someone like Alan. He costs too much and, in Alan's case, comes with a lot of baggage.

Rumpus: Alan's kind of Beckettian; he's waiting for the king. He keeps worrying that he can't go on, but he does always go on. Is his persistence existential or peculiarly American?

Eggers: I don't think it's particularly American, but Alan's predicament is unique, to some extent, to this particular moment. He's a guy who knows manufacturing, the making and selling of actual objects by actual people, but now he's in the middle of the desert trying to sell a hologram to a man who may or may not ever appear. He has no choice, though. Alan's at a point in his life where he's hoping that this one deal can solve a lot of his problems. He's deeply in debt and has all kinds of pressures on him, but if he can just get a meeting with King Abdullah, he might be able to get back on his feet.

Rumpus: When we first meet Alan he's just arrived to Saudi Arabia on behalf of Reliant, a large IT corporation. He once knew the king's nephew, and so Reliant thought he would be able to sell the king their services for the King Abdullah Economic City. Is that how business works there?

Eggers: The people I know in Saudi Arabia all say it's difficult to get any business off the ground without some connection to the royal family. And the funny thing is if you *do* get something off the ground without the royals, and it's successful, some royal will swoop in and, you know, strongly suggest he become your business partner. So Reliant thinks Alan will be useful, even though on the surface of things he's not the most natural choice to send to Jeddah.

Rumpus: How particular do you feel this book is to Saudi Arabia? Or is it more about Alan? Could this story have been set anywhere?

Eggers: The book really isn't about Saudi Arabia. It takes place there, but it could be any place where American multinationals might be doing business like this. I spent some time in Saudi and wanted to describe it accurately, even if most of the things that happen in the novel, at KAEC, are fictional. Of course, there's some appeal to a character like Alan, who's in a place of existential uncertainty, being placed in a blank landscape, with relatively few buildings and characters—in a city that may or may not come to be.

Rumpus: Alan has been trying to get back into manufacturing but is finding it difficult. He's been bogged down by bureaucracy, unable to build a simple yard wall at home, his credit ruined by a Banana Republic charge card. Are you trying to say something about obstacles thwarting innovation or the entrepreneurial spirit?

Eggers: I think Alan is like a lot of people who rightly or wrongly feel the current system is suffocating a lot of nondigital business ideas. A guy like Alan has knowledge and experience and maybe even a good idea, but can't get a loan to save his life. He proposes making bikes in the US again, but he gets laughed out of every bank, every venture capital firm. That's a reality for a lot of guys like him, especially if they're trying to do small-to-midscale manufacturing in the US—meanwhile, some very dubious digital ideas have money thrown at them without hesitation.

Rumpus: And Alan's got bad credit.

Eggers: Yeah, there's the tyrannical rule of credit reports, which is really one of the more comically absurd elements of Alan's life and modern life. These credit agencies wield incredible and absolute power, but their methods are highly questionable and often illogical. But whatever random score they post next to Alan's name determines his fate for home ownership, loans, everything. It's a terrifying, Orwellian thing that we came up with ourselves and we obey without question. I mean, a mysterious algorithm concocted by shadowy companies with no accountability or transparency that produces a single all-powerful number that no one questions but determines your economic fate? It's maniacal.

Rumpus: Alan becomes fairly close friends with his guide and driver, Yousef. I'm really fond of the story of their friendship, but it's fraught. For starters, Yousef's father doesn't approve of Americans. When Yousef brings Alan to his family home, some of the neighbors are suspicious. How much does their friendship mean?

Eggers: Saudi Arabia isn't a country overrun with American tourists, so the Americans that do make it over there are seen with some skepticism. Yousef wants to like Alan, though. He presumes the best of him. Still, it's clear that young Saudis are a lot like young Americans—they're from a wealthy country, they're ready to start their lives, but the opportunities aren't there like they should be.

Rumpus: Sometimes I feel I can learn more from novels than from nonfiction. Fiction presents a more accessible window onto something that is true. It's not an exact situation, it's not journalism, but there's a deeper truth, I think. I feel that way about this book. I feel like I learned something about Saudi Arabia and Saudi/American relations. Which leads me to two questions: Are you comfortable with that? And do you think it's important that a novel teach something?

Eggers: I don't think novels need to be instructive, but ideally you come away knowing something more about the world. That's how I think about the writing of books, too. If I haven't learned something in the process, then it's not quite as inspiring.

Rumpus: There's a beautiful romance between Alan and his Saudi doctor, Zahra. Could something like that happen in Saudi Arabia?

Eggers: A romance like that is eminently possible. The Saudi women I know are incredibly adept at navigating the byzantine rules governing their behavior and movements in their country. For a long time now, the more educated and wealthy women were already coming up with all kinds of ways to circumvent the rules and live semi-normal lives, and then cable and the internet really opened younger women up to what they were missing. So things are changing, even if slowly. And at Zahra's level—she's got a varied family ancestry, she's a doctor and has traveled extensively—there are myriad ways of moving within and outside the system. Like anywhere, factors like wealth and education and status create opportunities and exceptions. But the younger women of Saudi Arabia I met, who were uniformly well educated and ready to start their lives—they were exasperated by some of the limitations on their opportunities. They were all ready to bolt, go somewhere else.

Rumpus: And that comes up in your book. Someone says that Saudi Arabia is going to "pop." Alan is surprised to hear that what they mean is that people think the women are going to revolt and demand more rights.

Eggers: Well, I don't know if it's just the women who want more. The young men, too, are frustrated. A place like the King Abdullah Economic City, though, is there to present the younger people with an oasis of opportunity, openness, education, employment, all that. But whether all that actually happens is a big question.

Rumpus: Do you show people your books while you're writing them? This one touches on so many different topics, I wonder about their responses.

Eggers: I always want a book like this to seem at least plausible. In terms of Saudi Arabia, I wanted to be sure that there were no errors of culture or language, so I made sure my Saudi friends found the book to be plausible and truthful. I didn't have to make any major changes after showing it to them, but they definitely corrected some terminology, a few matters of custom, some names.

Rumpus: The style of this book is very different from your other fiction. It's stripped down, meditative, carefully sculpted.

Eggers: When I got back from Saudi Arabia and started writing the book, it just seemed like the right form. I'm convinced that every story has its appropriate form, and that you really can't fight it.

Rumpus: You try new things with your work. First memoir, then novel, then a novel based on journalism, then nonfiction. And I love that because it keeps it interesting, but it's also got to be a little scary. Do you get nervous each time you publish a book?

Eggers: Definitely. It never really gets any easier. Going into this one, I thought it would be far easier than *What Is the What* or *Zeitoun*, which both required so much research. But *Hologram* took three or so years, just like the last two did. I guess a book needs the time it needs. If there's one thing I've learned over the years, it's that. You have to wait for the fruit to fall from the tree.

Beyond the Lattice: Dave Eggers

D'Arcy Doran / 2013

From *Huck*, no. 38. © 2013 by TCOLondon. Reprinted by permission.

Dave Eggers came to us as an orphan, baring himself to the world in his heartfelt memoir, *A Heartbreaking Work of Staggering Genius*. At twenty-one, he was left to raise his eight-year-old brother after their parents died of cancer in a span of five weeks. But that was only the beginning. Since then, Eggers has re-energized America's lit scene with *McSweeney's*, his quarterly-turned-publishing-house, founded a national network of tutoring centers tucked behind fantastical shops, and collaborated in books, film, and music with the likes of Spike Jonze, Judd Apatow, and Beck. Eggers spoke to *Huck* about the need to explore, live a creative life, and do some good along the way.

"We have more time than you think," Dave Eggers says as he settles into the red sofa that serves as his desk in the corner of McSweeney's office in San Francisco's Mission District—also home to *The Believer* magazine and a growing array of other publications. All at once, his words are an apology, an assurance, and, just maybe, he is letting us in on a secret. Stretching and slowing time is a power Eggers, now forty-three, possesses both on the page and in real life. Moments earlier he was working out details for an album of songs written by Beck and performed by several bands to raise money for 826 Valencia, his pirate store–fronted tutoring center across the street and its seven sister centers. In just over an hour, he'll huddle with teens in McSweeney's basement for their weekly class to compile his offbeat annual, the *Best American Nonrequired Reading* anthology. Then he will disappear into his garage for the rest of the week to finish his next book, *The Visitants*, which collects more than a decade of travels around the world. As he talks about *Visitants*, the office walls seem to fade, and it's easy to picture Eggers in a stranger's car barreling across the desert at "900 mph."

He was in Jeddah on his last day in Saudi Arabia researching his latest novel, *A Hologram for a King*—a tale about a struggling American businessman whose last-ditch attempt to stave off foreclosure leads him to a rising Saudi city—when Eggers realized his flight home was actually leaving from Riyadh, more than one thousand kilometers away. He flagged down a stranger, not a cabbie or even a professional driver, and hired him to speed across the desert. Thirty minutes into the seven-hour drive, as all traces of human settlement vanished, the driver phoned a friend, chatted in Arabic, then glanced at Eggers and said into the phone in English: "Yeah, American. Boom-boom."

Eggers picks up the story:

Eggers: I don't know what that means. It doesn't sound good, you know? We have complicated relations with some young Saudi men. Although everyone I met when I was in Saudi Arabia I had a great time with. I met a lot of friends. But this guy? You start letting your brain go and you start getting a little paranoid. Could this be bad? I've always assumed the best of anyone I've met, and I've always had faith in everybody because I want them to have faith in me. I've trusted them because I want them to trust me.

But this was right after a friend of mine, Shane Bauer, had been arrested and imprisoned in Iran. He was in for almost a year. He was a translator who did a lot of work here, he did Arabic translation for us for *Zeitoun* and for the book we did in Sudan. So here I was thinking, "Well nothing ever bad has ever happened to me so I have to believe this is going to be fine." But in the back of my mind I actually know a guy in an Iranian prison, who was picked up for hiking over the border. Your mind starts running.

[The episode opens *The Visitants*, his first book written in the first person since his debut. It tells the stories behind the books, including journeys to Saudi Arabia and China for *Hologram*, trips to Syria for *Zeitoun*—the true story of Abdulrahman Zeitoun, a Syrian American who remains in New Orleans after Hurricane Katrina, distributing supplies from a canoe, but then disappears—and Eggers's venture into South Sudan for *What Is the What* and his Voice of Witness series, which highlights social injustices around the world.]

Eggers: The rest of the book follows the same arc, which is going in as a blank and completely open mind and then letting yourself be informed, or made concerned, or even paranoid, by things that you hear outside. And then realizing the dangers of that secondhand knowledge and making assumptions, and then finding common humanity.

At a certain point, I pulled out photos of my family and I was like, "Hey, you have kids too?" You're trying to find some common connection. By the end of it you end up being as friendly as you can be with a guy you've barely met and you're paying to drive you.

One of the impetuses [for *Visitants*] is just hearing that travel rates are down among younger people. Fewer passports are being issued, and fewer people in their twenties leave their state and have their driver's license. They attribute all this to online time and people feeling like they've seen things because they have access to it all. There's a little bit of me that's wanting to say, "Really, you don't know anything until you've been there, or until you've met somebody." You don't know the first thing about a young Saudi unless you've met a young Saudi. You can't make an assumption about the lives of Saudi women unless you've met them and really listened and really gone somewhere. It's the value of real-world, tangible experiences, person-to-person contact.

Q: Your first book was extremely close to home, but ever since your second, *You Shall Know Our Velocity!*—about two friends traveling the world in one week to give away $80,000, a sum they feel was undeservedly inherited—you shot off, telling stories that span continents. Is something pulling you out into the world?

Eggers: A lot of writers will spend their careers plumbing their lives in different ways or sublimating their experience through fiction. But if you start with a memoir, you've sort of blown that. From the beginning, I couldn't find anything left to write about. And you also get a taste of that and it's enough.

But ultimately my training was in journalism, and that was my background for a long time. So I just developed an interest. I got hooked on the process of feeling like I could communicate a good story to an audience to maybe have an impact.

I'm always trying to educate the person I was too. I was just talking to a friend who grew up in the Bay Area and was saying, "You don't understand the bubble we're in sometimes." A lot of people like me in Illinois, or Wisconsin, we're well-meaning people, but you would be surprised how "in the middle of nowhere" we are in terms of our awareness. I didn't have a passport until I was twenty-six. There's a lot of people like us, and you've got to be forgiving of people like that. They have good hearts.

Especially with *What Is the What* and *Zeitoun*, I'm speaking to those people I grew up with. We're all incredibly nice people who might not be aware of what happened in New Orleans after Katrina, or might not be aware of human rights crises that Voice of Witness tries to illuminate. I do try to remember who I was and where I came from. There's still many other millions of people in a country as big as the US that want to learn about these things, and if you can start from a place of, "Hey, I was there too. I couldn't have placed Sudan on a map when I was twenty-five, but I'm going to walk you through it."

The Revolution

When Eggers, with his little brother in tow, and a few high school friends, left the suburbs of Chicago for San Francisco in the early nineties, they set out to start a revolution. Their call to arms would be an indie magazine. The plan was that *Might* magazine would "force, at least urge, millions to live more exceptional lives, to do extraordinary things, to travel the world, to help people and start things and end things and build things," as he explained in a manic moment in his memoir. But they soon learned that simply writing about a problem didn't solve it. Frustration fueled cynicism, he says, which increasingly crept in over *Might*'s three-and-a-half-year run. After the magazine's demise, Eggers moved to New York to become an editor at *Esquire*. But the glossy magazine world disillusioned him. He left to write his first book, and on his kitchen table in an act of procrastination created *McSweeney's Quarterly Concern*, initially a home for stories rejected by glossies.

He returned to San Francisco as a best-selling author to set up the *McSweeney's* office. Inspired by friends who, like his mother, were teachers, he decided to put a classroom at the center of the office at 826 Valencia. In contrast to *Might*, Eggers says, 826 had immediate impact from the very first student. He had stumbled on a model for sustainable, effective, community-level change. The center's success inspired *McSweeney's* collaborators Nick Hornby and Roddy Doyle to set up transatlantic cousins, the Ministry of Stories in London and Fighting Words in Dublin.

With each book, Eggers finds a new microproject. *What Is the What*—which tells the real story of Valentino Achak Deng, one of Sudan's Lost Boys, who fled civil war by crossing the desert on foot, eventually finding his way to America—inspired a foundation that built and operates a school in Deng's home village. His travels in South Sudan for the book also led to Voice of Witness, a nonprofit series that aims to empower victims of human rights abuses by sharing their personal narratives. *Zeitoun* spawned the Zeitoun Foundation, which funds reconstruction projects in New Orleans and promotes understanding between Muslims and non-Muslims. *Hologram*, a book about outsourcing the American Dream, inspired his latest initiative, the Mid-Market Makers' Mart. It's a proposal to set up a market/workshop space in San Francisco's long-depressed Mid-Market neighborhood where artisans can make and sell goods ranging from surfboards to stuffed animals. "I would like to bring my kids to a place where you can see things being made and in a couple of hours you might be able to see fifty different makers and buy something original," he says.

Q: How do these projects come about? Is it that after writing the book you feel there's something left to address?

Eggers: It always comes out at about the same time, and it's something I'm trying to cure myself of. I always thought there had to be some real-world application. So when I wrote about Valentino's life [in *What Is the What*], we thought of a school in his hometown and then the Valentino Achak Deng Foundation. We built this school, and all of these buildings happened from Valentino's story. Now they've graduated their first class. Then it was the same thing with the Zeitoun Foundation. Although it was a little different—all those funds went to existing nonprofits, so we didn't have to start anything from scratch. But again it's trying to make something tangibly impactful out of a story. But I really don't have all the time and energy that I used to. It's a lot of work because these continue to exist. They need my help every so often. These things start adding up. So to do any of them well I have to stop doing new things. I've come to grips with that recently.

Q: Is it that the idea builds inside as you're writing, because writing alone isn't enough?

Eggers: There's a lot of different reasons. But one is that writing is incredibly solitary and sedentary. I sit on a couch just like this that's in my garage. It's filthy. I sit there eight hours a day to get any kind of work done. It took me a really long time to get used to all that time alone. I've always been part of a group like a magazine or a newspaper or whatever. One, you feel incredibly guilty about your parents having actually worked for a living and you get to sit on a couch in your garage and think of stuff. That doesn't seem like real work to me. So you try to alleviate a little bit of that guilt by trying to make something impactful in the actual world. That's the truth, just as a lapsed Catholic.

Then there's the idea, "Wouldn't it be fun to get a group of people together and let's open a center and let's have a publishing company?" because it addresses your social needs. Then, "Boy, it's not that hard to put a book together, and I've got a buddy, he just sent me his book that he can't get published. How hard would it be to publish that book?" You publish one magazine and it's not so hard, so you think, "What would it cost to put out a different one?" It starts adding up, and before you know it, you have a habit.

And you don't want people to tell you no. So if I want to publish a book, I would like to publish it. I don't want somebody to tell me that I can't. So you create a situation where you continue to publish your own work, or the work of people that you like. It's worth it to not be told no.

The Artisan

Dave Eggers can confirm he is not Banksy. But had he known earlier that such a gig existed, life could have turned out differently.

Instead, Eggers's artistic impulses have focused mostly on the book world. His early innovations included planting friends to heckle him during bookstore readings to distract from his lack of flair as a reader. He had to defend one heckler from fans at a San Francisco event. Then with McSweeney's, he started experimenting with books themselves: abandoning dust jackets, starting the first chapter on the cover. Cutting covers, painting covers, carving covers. Changing the way books were made.

Q: You're a big Banksy fan. Is there a connection between his work and what you do with McSweeney's?

Eggers: He did a mural—you don't call it a mural. He did an artwork, a tag—what do you call it?—on the roof here.

Q: So you met Banksy?

Eggers: Nuh-uh. But another guy on staff here, Chris Ying—he started [McSweeney's food magazine] *Lucky Peach*—did. Ying let him in one night. He needed to come at 11:00 p.m. or something. I wasn't around, and it all happened at the last minute. So he did this beautiful piece on the wall of that building [he points left and upward]. So it wasn't actually owned by our landlord, who would gladly let it stay. But that owner didn't like it so much. It stayed for about a week. All these people came by and took pictures, and then it was painted over. It was very sad.

I was a painting major. That's what I studied in college. I wanted to be a painter all my life, but I always had a problem with that knowledge that if I were successful, there was the chance most of my work would be in somebody's bathroom and never be seen again—by me or anybody. That's very hard for me, especially because I'd started working at newspapers in high school and college and really liked the democratic access. I didn't have it figured out, but later I saw what Banksy was doing and what [Barry] McGee was doing here in the city when he was Twist (his graff name). If I had known back then in east central Illinois when I was studying painting that was a route, that would have felt right to me. My paintings were political and narrative, but I was loathed and discouraged by the faculty.

So when Banksy started coming up, I was a big admirer. Then somehow, I never had any contact, but one day he was doing some exhibit in London and asked to use some text I'd written—not about him but about something corollary—in some way. I said, "Of course." Then a year later, he came here and did that. But I've never had any real contact.

Q: Did your painting background shape your attitude toward book design?

Eggers: When I first started building canvases in high school, our art teacher made sure we knew every rebar, every part of the canvas-supporting brackets. Everything was part of the artwork. Even the stuff on the back. He had us paint on every piece of wood one time just to say that it all mattered. I guess that got into my bones a little bit. So now I'm not so interested in this [points toward a plain mass-market paperback on the table]. This is artifice in a way, which is fine, but I really prefer addressing the actual board and the materials and having that tactile sensation because that's an object. Just working on the paper alone is fine, and sometimes we do that. But it feels like you're missing a lot of opportunities.

We used to print all our books outside of Reykjavik. I was on the printing floor seeing all the other stuff they printed and saw their bibles. Iceland only has one printer, so they print all the bibles in Iceland. I was like, "What is that?" It was beautiful. It made the other books with their dust jackets look very paltry and meek and pedestrian by comparison. That's when I started studying old printing techniques.

It got us really hooked on the partnership with the printers. Because we collaborate pretty closely with the printers, the possibilities open up so much. I feel like we've seen a lot more books in the last ten years that have aspired to a higher level of craft. A lot of that is because of the same thing we're doing—trying to give people a more clear choice between a physical book and an e-book. In order to survive as a physical book publisher, you have to make the books more wantable as objects.

[A few days earlier, Eggers sat on a panel on "the future of the book" in Germany. He mentioned "how nice it is to hold and keep a book and maybe pass it on to your grandkids," at which point one of his copanelists, a young woman, called it "a horror," the idea that a book should be something that lasts forever. But in a way, he says, her comments echoed his younger yearnings in *A Heartbreaking Work of Staggering Genius*.]

Eggers: It reminded me of that stage where you are ready to just erase everything and replace it with something new at any moment. That's fine. I've seen it in cities, or whatever it is, "Let's erase it and start over," and that sort of impatience with either a lack of progress, or a disinterest, or frustration in everything that's there and won't get out of your way—all the people and buildings that are there. You want it to be different, you want progress, or replacement, overnight, and you don't want to wait for it. A lot of it's idealism, or hubris, or madness.

The Lattice

I see us as one, as a vast matrix, an army, a whole, each one of us is responsible to one another, because no one else is. I mean, every person that walks through the door to help us with Might *becomes part of our lattice.*
–Dave Eggers, *A Heartbreaking Work of Staggering Genius* (2000)

The lattice began with Eggers's siblings, his friends, and then grew. Friends of friends entered, and then other orphans, like the Sudanese Lost Boy Valentino Deng, were drawn in. Soon legends like Talking Heads' David Byrne came knocking too. ("It's incredibly strange," Eggers says. "But it's inevitable as you get older, sooner or later you're going to bump into some of these people that you admired when you were younger.") Spike Jonze, Judd Apatow, Miranda July, Zadie Smith, Sam Mendes, David Foster Wallace, and many others have joined over the years as the lattice expanded further and further out.

Q: Has your thinking on the lattice evolved since you first wrote about it?
Eggers: No, not a bit really. I haven't read that passage since 2001 probably. I think I know what it says. I like that word so much still. I feel like it's been proven a lot more than it had even then. Back then, it was a latticework of friends. It felt like we were all our only family, the bunch of us that moved out from Chicago at the same time and the people that you meet along the way. In a way, in your twenties in a new city when no one's from here, we're all sort of orphans. The only people that you can count on are a bunch of people that you work with and that you know. You're only as

good as the reliability of that latticework. If it holds it can feel very good. And if there are any weak links it can be very heartbreaking, and definitely I had both experiences back then.

But my conception of it has grown to the latticework of a neighborhood, or a city. Like at 826, I use the word *fabric* more than *latticework* these days, but when you have a couple thousand tutors that are signed up and weaving themselves into the schools and helping at 826 and after school and during field trips, you are tightening the fabric of that neighborhood.

[As if on cue, Eggers calls to a teen in the hall: "Hey!"]

That's Marco, who I've known since he was eight. Now he's fourteen and he's in the high school class. He knows I'm looking out for him. His siblings recognize me. This goes on with all the tutors.

I feel like knowing that you're part of that latticework and knowing that you have a role to play, it's both very inspiring—"I'm part of this fabric, I help keep things together"—and it can be very validating. But it's also very humbling; you're just part of that fabric. There's a lot of threads that matter, that have to interconnect.

If you're one of the threads, you have to do your part and help hold it together.

Q & A with Dave Eggers

Tom Gresham / 2014

From *VCU News*, August 11, 2014. © 2014 by Virginia Commonwealth University. Reprinted by permission.

The Circle, Eggers's latest novel, is a provocative thriller about a massive technology corporation called the Circle, which has become the world's most powerful company while promoting apparently benevolent messages of transparency and sharing. The last vestiges of personal privacy are rapidly being swallowed into the digital realm as the Circle's technological breakthroughs prove too appealing and sweeping for consumers to turn down.

Mae Holland, the novel's protagonist, starts her employment at the Circle as a fairly average user of the internet and social media. In the novel's opening sentences, she arrives on her first day of work and is immediately besotted with the company's remarkable campus: "My God, Mae thought. It's heaven."

In the ensuing pages, Mae becomes an increasingly central figure in the Circle and its pursuit of a utopian future constructed with the company's products—products that are ostensibly designed to make the world a more friendly and secure place. In the *New York Review of Books*, author Margaret Atwood wrote that one of the most compelling effects of the novel is "to remind us that we can be led down the primrose path much more blindly by our good intentions than by our bad ones."

Virginia Commonwealth University chose *The Circle* as its 2014 Summer Reading Program selection. This is the first work of fiction that has been chosen by the selection committee in the nine-year history of the program. Eggers will visit campus on August 19 to discuss the novel with students and to serve as the featured speaker at New Student Convocation.

Daphne Rankin, PhD, associate vice provost for strategic enrollment management, said *The Circle* was an ideal fit for the Summer Reading

Program because of its exploration of a topic sure to inspire debate among students, faculty, and staff. The selection committee felt that *The Circle* could be referenced and discussed in a number of first-year classes.

Eggers answered some questions from *VCU News* in anticipation of his visit.

Q: How possible do you view the events that transpire in the novel?

A: There are a few things, like the transparent all-consuming shark, that might not be so likely. But otherwise most of the technologies and company policies are within the realm of possibility. A few of them have actually transpired since the book came out.

Q: Part of what makes *The Circle* unsettling is how the company's leaders and advocates seem to believe that what is essentially the Circle's creeping global domination will lead to a more just and safe world. And their arguments can sound convincing. Many of the less powerful characters in *The Circle*—with some notable exceptions—seem either oblivious to their loss of privacy or to welcome it. How closely do you think that approximates the way we are now?

A: *The Circle* is of course an extreme example of groupthink and of a situation where utopianism outstrips rationality, individuality, common sense, and any respect for privacy. But at the same time, most of the Circle's creators are absolutely sure that their efforts are improving—perfecting, really—the world. But with perfection usually comes a certain suffocating control, and that kind of control is sometimes hard to see when you're in the thick of it. There's also a funny tendency with some of the companies extant today to ask for forgiveness, not permission, which means that most of the time, the control or surveillance we know about is only revealed after the fact. The recent Facebook experiment in manipulating the emotions of its users is one of the creepier examples.

Q: Do you have a particular hope or expectation about how younger readers—such as VCU students—who are coming of age with social media as a natural extension of themselves and with the ubiquity of the internet as a given will engage with this novel?

A: The book isn't meant to be proscriptive in any way, but I do hope it stimulates discussion, and maybe even awareness, of the potential overreach, and diminution of certain rights, in a highly connected but ultimately profit-driven world. A good college education should instill a healthy skepticism—without dampening one's optimism—and the digital world, more so than any other I can think of, needs plenty of both.

Q: *The Circle* is filled with internet products and services that are somehow both attractive and sinister. What was your approach to coming up with . these ideas?

A: I've been living in the San Francisco Bay Area for about twenty years, and it's impossible not to absorb, or somehow be connected to, dozens of startups and digital visionaries, successful or otherwise. Over the years I've heard a lot of ideas and pitches, and so it wasn't a stretch to imagine what sorts of ideas might be percolating in a place like the Circle. In most cases, I wanted technologies or applications that were, like you said, both attractive on one level but highly sinister if misused.

Q: You are a cofounder of 826 National, a nonprofit network of writing and tutoring centers for kids. Can you talk about the 826 mission, its impact, and why you are devoted to it?

A: My mom was a teacher, and many of my friends became teachers, and back in 2001 a small group of us had the thought that we could raise an army of tutors who could help public school teachers in whatever ways they found useful. 826 Valencia, our first center in San Francisco, served mostly students from Spanish-speaking homes, many of them new Americans. So from a concentration on English and writing help, 826 grew into creative writing, publishing programs, field trips, college access, and too many other areas to name. But we've always been driven by the hope that volunteers can help level the playing field for inner-city students in public schools, who often don't have anywhere near the advantages of students from better-funded districts. I just made 826 National sound a little drier than it actually is. The one thing we're dedicated to is making writing fun—allowing for the inherent wildness and weirdness of young people's imaginations. So the eight centers we have around the country are all tasked with keeping it weird, so learning doesn't have to be something formal or dusty.

Q: How important a role do you believe service plays in a college education?

A: I'm a fan of service being part of the college experience. Four years is a long time to be rattling inside your own skull, and getting out of the classroom and putting your brain or skills to work in the community can only lead to a better-balanced human. I think service is habit-forming, too, so it's good when we make a permanent habit of fitting some volunteering into our lives.

Q: What do you wish you'd known when you were a college freshman?

A: For some reason, I signed up to be in the dorm set aside for students who wanted to cook for themselves—as opposed to being on the meal plan.

I have no idea why I did this. It meant I lived in a very funky-smelling all-male dorm.

Q: Is there anything in particular that you're looking forward to about your visit to VCU?

A: I'm really honored and humbled that VCU saw fit to choose *The Circle* for their common read, and I'm really looking forward to hearing the students' thoughts on the book's themes and ideas. And, as a failed cartoonist, I'm also hoping to get a peek at VCU's comics archive, which is one of the best in the world.

Dave Eggers on Working for Justice through Oral History: "There Wasn't Much That Allowed Those People to Seem Fully Human"

Scott Timberg / 2015

From *Salon*, June 13, 2015. © 2015 by *Salon*. An online version remains in the *Salon* archives. Reprinted by permission.

Some were mysteriously scooped up for crimes they had supposedly committed. Others lived in the ruins of post-Katrina New Orleans. Still others—like the teenager in East Harlem who woke up to find FBI agents with loaded guns in her family's apartment—saw parents or spouses dragged away with little explanation. There are confounding and engaging stories from all over the world in the Voice of Witness oral history series McSweeney's puts out, all of which try to give the rest of us a fuller and more human sense of what's going on in the world. "To read a Voice of Witness book," short story master George Saunders says, "is to feel one's habitual sense of disconnection begin to fall away."

San Francisco–based McSweeney's has just put out a selection of its previous books—which include *Surviving Justice* and *High Rise Stories*—called *The Voice of Witness Reader*. We spoke to executive editor Mimi Lok and Dave Eggers, McSweeney's founder and editor of the new volume.

Scott Timberg: For people who don't know, what is the Voice of Witness project about? What does it aim to do? And how does this collection fit into the larger mission?

Mimi Lok: Voice of Witness is a nonprofit based in San Francisco. We've been going for about six years as a nonprofit. The mission, because every nonprofit has to have a mission, is to foster a more empathy-based, more nuanced understanding of human rights crises. Basically, we want to change the way people think about human rights crises. We do this through providing a platform for people who have been most impacted by some of the most crucial human rights crises of our time to have a voice and to share their stories and experiences. It's often left out of the mainstream narrative around these issues. We also do this through our education program. The books themselves have covered a wide range of issues, everything from wrongful conviction to undocumented immigration and Chicago public housing. And internationally we've interviewed people from Burma, Sudan, Colombia, Zimbabwe, and Palestine.

The book series started ten years ago, with the first book being *Surviving Justice: America's Wrongfully Convicted and Exonerated. The Voice of Witness Reader* is basically a greatest hits of the last ten years of the book series. But it also features some of the most powerful narratives, these edited oral histories of these people from the last ten years. Each book is represented, and we had the hardest time choosing stories from hundreds in the series. The selection that is in the *Reader* is people whose narratives are somewhat—in some cases just one narrative from a book, in some cases there are a couple of shorter ones—but we wanted to include stories that reflect experiences and issues that are still ongoing, stories that are emblematic of an issue.

A good example is Beverly Monroe and Chris Ochoa. And Chris Ochoa is not an unusual person, profile-wise. Prison, wrongfully convicted, a man of color. With Beverly Monroe, she is this soft-spoken woman from the South with a degree in organic chemistry, the epitome of Southern gentility, and suddenly she gets wrongfully accused of the murder of her longtime partner. So we wanted to also include these more unusual stories to say that this shit can happen to anyone.

Most of the narrators in this book are people who we get updates from. We wanted to share with readers where are they now and what have they gone on to do. In some cases they are simply just living, struggling. Or maybe their cases have improved. In cases like Beverly Monroe or Ashley Jacobson or Theresa Martinez, from our women's prisons, they have become quite powerful and active spokespeople for either justice reform or reproductive rights in prison. There is a range.

Timberg: Dave, you say in your introduction, "A human is more than his or her trauma." Tell me what you mean by that, and why that idea is important.

Dave Eggers: Well, I think that that notion or that idea maybe was first formed when we did the interviews for *Surviving Justice*. We heard again and again from the narrators that they felt even when they were written about in media articles and newspapers that it was so brief sometimes and so focused on what had happened to them, that moment when they were arrested or jailed, and there wasn't much follow-up in terms of their life before or after.

Timberg: They exist as an anecdote in our minds.

Eggers: They exist as an anecdote or a statistic. I noticed it again when reading what little literature or information there was out there about women and children who have been abducted during the Sudanese Civil War. There was so little out there, and there was maybe a name here or there in a few sentences and a statistic or some estimates. There wasn't much that allowed those people to seem fully human. That guided our approach to oral history, which is really trying to expand the scope of what a narrator was allowed to tell us about their lives and give them more space and more room and start at the start so that we could better know them, empathize with them, walk many miles in their shoes, and could know how they arrived at this place where their rights were compromised, and what happened afterward. With *Surviving Justice*, it was one of the primary goals to find out what had happened and what the lives were like for these narrators after they had been freed, after exoneration, after freedom. Most of the time, their lives were still exceedingly difficult, with very few or no services for exonerees. That story became an essential part of it, not just to say, "Here's when they were convicted. Here's when they were freed," and to end it there, which was the tradition: to end when they got out of prison. To keep going for the years afterward and to give us the full consequences of that.

Timberg: Right, so we can't really understand this stuff if we just see it as a snapshot.

Eggers: Well, I think that snapshots are sometimes part of it. The media has no choice but to sometimes give us a snapshot. It's a rough draft of history, newspapers and media and the news where you have to react on a day-to-day basis. But I think that that's the first draft, and then, ideally, if you wanted to know about one of the issues talked about in one of the Voice of Witness books, I think oral history is just a really central part of that issue, whether it's public housing, whether it's the situation in Colombia, in Zimbabwe, in South Sudan, or understanding an issue like the rights of workers in the global economy. What we find again and again is people that feel like they—even people who work for NGOs and that field—find that they learn new things. Because even if you do have clients, and I have a lot of friends who are asylum lawyers, for example, there's a certain limit for how well you get to know a client and how well you get to know people who are in the sphere of your interest or influence. Oral history provides this long, elastic arena where the interviewer can ask questions that the narrators are rarely asked by anyone, including people that are close to them. Let's start from the start. So, that's rare for anybody.

Timberg: Mimi, In your opening note to the book you say you want these stories to have what you call a "novelistic level of detail rather than just the case studies." What do you mean by that?

Lok: If you only see someone as a case study then it normally homes in on that instance or instances of where they had their human rights violated. It's reducing that person to that moment of injustice. You are reducing that person's whole experience. We want to do the opposite. I think that most people are, the most that they hear from someone who has been directly impacted by human rights crises or social injustice, is maybe a quote in an article. It's really rare that we actually get to hear more than a few sentences from them. The limitation of that is that your understanding of that issue isn't wrong, but it's not complete. You are not getting the full picture. Seeing that human rights violation in the context of a life. And in describing that life in the context of the society of that person makes their life. It's really all about context and seeing how these aren't just violations that occur out of the blue, in isolation, they are part of some form of systemic injustice. The other side of that is at the core of what Voice of Witness is. It's having more empathy-based understanding of human rights issues so that you as the reader, as the listener, you identify and empathize with that person's experiences. You root for them more.

You might have a certain idea or views on immigration or illegal immigration. You sit down with someone who is actually an undocumented immigrant and you hear their whole life story, and I'm sure you are going to walk away with some of your preconceptions complicated. It's really wanting people to have their thinking complicated in a good way. Even if they hear just one story, to think, "I had this idea about what was going on in Sudan or in the West Bank with undocumented immigrants, but I see that it is a lot more complicated than that." It sounds so obvious saying that, but people don't often have the opportunity to spend that much time hearing that perspective. It makes for a much richer and much more textured and nuanced understanding of these issues.

The last part is that this approach, this sort of more literary approach, is our way of making the stories more engaging and compelling for their own sake. You don't have to necessarily have a preexisting relationship or engagement with this or that issue or this or that country, but you just know that if you pick up this narrative you are going to get a really engaging story, a compelling human story.

Timberg: You've been a fairly busy as a writer, Dave, and McSweeney's has a lot going on. What made you want to devote all the time and resources to this project that you have? Did you see something traveling abroad that showed you how messy the world was and how we weren't hearing about it? What was the straw on the camel's back?

Eggers: The real impetus was when Valentino Deng and I were in his hometown of Marial Bai in South Sudan back in 2003. He was reuniting with his family that he hadn't seen in seventeen years. We thought we were doing research for what became *What Is the What?* Meanwhile, we got to meet three young women who had been returned to the village by Save the Children, and all three of them had horrific stories of abduction and enslavement. I had only read the briefest anecdotes about this practice that been reinstituted during the civil war. As a journalist, I just thought the story had to be out there, and people had to know. We just tried to think of what would be an efficient way to tell that story and to allow the narrators to tell their narratives. We thought oral history would be that way. That was what drove it initially. It overlapped with the work at 826 Valencia.

Timberg: I hadn't thought of that, but it makes sense.

Eggers: Yeah, over the years we find that oral history is incredibly teachable, that readers really respond to first-person narratives. An issue that seems very abstract and complex becomes approachable and more immediate when told through the eyes of one narrator. We found that again and again with 826. It's become a major part of Voice of Witness to make sure the narratives are available to teachers and students, that the books are available, that oral history as a practice is available to educators. That's where they've got this really strong education program to make sure that, as a tool for a teacher of English or history or political science or anything, I think there's nothing more powerful than oral history.

Timberg: Mimi, how did you get involved personally in this? Why did this seem important and worth throwing everything else aside to concentrate on?

Lok: I did throw a lot of things aside actually. My background is in fiction writing and teaching, and a little bit of journalism in Hong Kong. I came to San Francisco to do my MFA in creative writing, and I worked with the writer Peter Orner. About a year after I finished, basically my last year in the country, I was doing a bit of freelance, but I finished up with school and he got back in touch and said, "I'm working on this book on undocumented workers in the US; would you be interested in helping out?" Turns out he was assembling this A-team of documentary filmmakers, attorneys, fiction writers, and journalists. Maybe fifteen or twenty. I hadn't heard of Voice of Witness as a book project. I was a fan of Dave's writing, but I had no idea they were doing this book project that was human rights and oral history. That seemed so outside of what I knew that they published. I was really intrigued, and as a first-generation British Chinese immigrant I was obviously very interested, so I volunteered to join the team.

I spent about a year doing the Chinese immigration beat, interviewing all these Chinese immigrants in New York and in the Bay Area, and it was just a fantastic experience. When I worked as a journalist I was really craving a chance to spend more time with people, but also to have the chance to craft the final piece a little more. But as a fiction writer I always felt a little bit guilty about not having any social contribution to society. This seemed like such an amazing nexus of those two forms of storytelling.

The other thing that struck me about Voice of Witness when it was still in that early incarnation as a side book project was that it is such an important project, and there are fifteen, sometimes twenty of us, working on this project, and there are like three functioning tape recorders that we are all fighting over. And there was no money. If we had to travel to an interview we'd use air miles or crash on people's couches. I just thought, this is something that is really important, it needs dedicated staff, it needs dedicated funding, it's providing a public service. Fortunately, Dave was thinking the same thing. Lola Vollen, the physician who did *Surviving Justice* with Dave and helped conceive of the book series, was thinking the same thing as well.

Timberg: What kind of larger impact or effect would you like this book or the others to have? You're getting these stories out to children. You're spreading the word in all kinds of ways, in which this book is the latest example. What are you hoping for in the long term about this project?

Eggers: I should emphasize: they're not going to children. I would say the youngest readers are seventeen or eighteen. The teacher in me is just making sure that we don't share books that are inappropriate for children.

This is understanding [how to see] the world through another's eyes. Being able to live and breathe another person's life through their narratives. This is the key to empathy, and I think ultimately, what great books do is they expand our capacity for and practice of empathy. I think that we want to engender that as much as we can, but also bear witness. The two overlap. In a lot of cases, the narrators have not been heard from. They have not been given the opportunity to tell their stories and to make permanent their narratives and to reclaim their narratives.

The goals and effects of oral history and Voice of Witness are many. On the one hand, we want to educate any readers, not just in schools, but the general reader, whether they're new to an issue and pick up a book like *High Rise Stories* the same way that they would pick up a novel. We hope that those readers come to these stories and their understanding of an issue is deepened and complicated.

On another level, the narrators, we want to give them the right to be heard, and for so many of them whose narratives have been taken from them in a way—if somebody has been called a refugee or if somebody has been called a criminal or if somebody has been called a terrorist—we can allow them to tell their story, to reclaim their narrative, to self-define themselves, and that can be a process of real healing. If somebody's feeling like they've told their story, they've been heard, and they have been—and sometimes being heard can be very healing and can make somebody feel a little bit more part of society. Somebody that's been on the outskirts can feel again heard and that their story is told and printed and is being talked about and used to educate people about a given issue. We've found so many of our narrators have become activists, have become very vocal, have sort of become emboldened or strengthened by the process of being heard and having their narratives published. It's kind of been great on that level, something that we didn't necessarily anticipate. It's now a big part of Voice of Witness: making sure that the narrators have all the tools that we can provide for them to become more vocal advocates for themselves and also for the issues raised in the book.

Voice of Witness is a small nonprofit, and we're trying to plug away and put out a few books per year. We respond to a lot of great proposals and try to advance the cause of oral history for general readers and for educators and students and to just continue to get these stories told.

Oral history has never been an easy sell, to general readers, but I think it's a shame because books are so readable. We always try to make sure they're very accessible. It doesn't have to feel like you're doing a graduate thesis reading one of these books. They're very approachable. My hero Studs Terkel made oral history popular and approachable, and we're trying to remind general readers of what he did and that it can be accessible. We try to do the same thing, and I guarantee you'll learn something through any of the books.

Dave Eggers Interview

Andrew Bablo / 2015

From *Steez* magazine, July 7, 2015. © by *Steez* magazine. Reprinted by permission.

Q: You're at a party, social event, etc. Someone you've never met approaches you and introduces himself or herself. They have no idea who you are, so they ask, "What do you do for a living?" What do you say?

A: I just say I write books. It's not a very interesting answer. It's always tempting to fib and say I'm a stuntman, but I never have the sack to lie.

Q: Can you give me the process of writing a novel from start to finish? I know it's not as easy as having an idea, sitting down, and writing fifty thousand words over the course of a month, and then having it edited and published. What's the whole process and timeline, if you don't mind? Maybe we can use one of your past works as an example?

A: In the past, every time I've written a book it's been radically different. *What Is the What* and *Zeitoun* were very protracted processes involving a lot of interviews, travel, research, fact-checking, on and on. *The Circle*, because it was the most recent, was a relatively quicker process. I'd been taking notes for years, thinking I might someday write something involving technology and privacy and democracy, but it wasn't really coming together until 2012, when I wrote a scene involving a woman being scolded for spending a weekend without documenting it on social media. It was just a satirical scene, but it made me laugh, and out of that the novel grew. Usually a book starts with a passage, a scene, that clicks. Once something clicks, the rest comes in a rush. Once I had the tone and the protagonist for *The Circle*, that book was written in a shorter span of time than anything else I've done. Still, there are multiple steps: revising repeatedly, then showing the book to ten or twelve other trusted readers, sending it to Knopf, revising various parts up to a dozen times, copyediting, proofing, then finally publishing. In this case I think the whole process was one year, which is about as fast as it can happen for me.

Q: In *The Circle*, the main character becomes overconsumed in a near future world of technology, consumption, and overbearing social media. How closely do you believe this mimics our future society? Why did you choose to make the book take place in in the next decade as opposed to forty years from now, and did you base *The Circle* off of any specific company, like Google or Apple?

A: *The Circle* is a fictional company that's subsumed all the existing companies and combined all their services into one unified operating system. To some extent it's what every existing company would want most—to have most or all of a person's life channeled through their portal. It would make them insanely powerful and incredibly dangerous. So I just imagined what would happen if a company like that existed, and if the company was run by dangerous people without much regard for freedom, privacy, or human rights. I think much of the book's predictions have already happened to some extent or another. We do live in a world where increasingly everything is measured, and data drives an incredible amount of decision-making, rightly or wrongly. And in general we're blind to the terrifying amount of data that's accumulated about us, and how it's commodified. But then again, it hasn't gotten as dark as *The Circle* depicts.

Q: I want to talk about your artwork. I came across it at Art Basel and was surprised to see so much work. I know you studied illustration in college and used to draw and paint. Writing is obviously an art form, but what made you get back into drawing and painting recently?

A: In college I studied painting for a few years, and once took an illustration course, at a different school. Growing up, I more or less assumed art would be the way I made a living later on. In high school and later at the University of Illinois, I worked at the school newspaper, and that got me more interested in journalism. I was really drawn in by the immediacy of the form, and the impact you could have. I also had a strange experience as a summer intern at a Chicago gallery. There was this incredible apparatus set up to show and sell contemporary work, but only about ten people a month would visit the gallery. It seemed really sterile and elitist and sad. So that turned me off painting for a long while. But recently, I got involved with Electric Works, a great gallery in San Francisco; they do a lot of very street-level and hands-on events and outreach. And best of all, when we sell a painting, all the proceeds go to ScholarMatch, our college-access nonprofit. It gives me an excuse to do these paintings, which are usually ridiculous.

Q: Most of your artwork consists of animals, sometimes people, paired with a proverb or biblical quote that you choose after the character is finished. How do you choose the text for your piece, and why use biblical references?

A: Sometimes the text is from the Bible—which is full of incredible poetry—and more often it's some rejoinder that occurs to me. I just painted a dachsund with the words "Probably Not a Factor in 2016" around it. It made me laugh, but I do sometimes wonder about what my kids are seeing: a forty-five-year-old man painting dachsunds on the dining room table, chuckling to himself.

Q: I noticed you don't feature a lot of your artwork in your own books, either on the cover or as editorial illustration. Why is that? Humility?

A: I was considering putting some drawings in a new book, oddly enough. But usually there's an artist more suited to the subject than I am. I recently wrote an all-ages picture book about the Golden Gate Bridge, and I wanted Tucker Nichols, one of my favorite artists, to illustrate it. His work was just better for the subject matter. I've been an art director and designer for so long at McSweeney's that I usually can admit when there's someone more suited for certain material than I am.

Q: What's next for your art career? Do you plan to devote more time to drawing than writing, or will the two complement each other for future projects?

A: Painting gives me a level of in-the-moment joy that I can't quite describe. And I can do it side by side with my kids, and that's such a trip. So I think it'll always be a part of my life now. And when Noah at Electric Works says there's a show coming up, and can I paint some more mammals, I have an excuse.

Q: Working with Maurice Sendak and Spike Jonze on *Where the Wild Things Are* must have been a dream come true for a writer/illustrator. How did that project come to fruition, and were there any memorable stories that came out if it?

A: Maurice was everything you'd want him to be, and a lot more. He was brilliant, and bold, and opinionated, and he swore a lot, and laughed a big sinister laugh, and at the same time he was very gentle and very vulnerable. I loved him and will always be grateful to Spike Jonze for bringing me into that project.

Q: Are you still in touch with Valentino from *What Is the What*?

A: He's the godfather to my son! And he runs the Valentino Achak Deng Foundation, which the book helped get going. The foundation operates a secondary school in South Sudan—Valentino is the visionary behind it—so we have to be in touch about that periodically, too. Given the success of his school—it's rated one of the very best in the whole country—he was recently named minister of education for his whole region.

Q: What are some upcoming projects at McSweeney's that you're excited about?

A: There are always great books in the works. We just published *The Voice of Witness Reader*, a collection of oral histories from that series, and that book I'm really proud of. McSweeney's went nonprofit recently and is finishing a really nice Kickstarter campaign, so we'll have more freedom to do the stuff we always have wanted to do.

Q: A lot of students are scared to get into journalism or writing currently. They fear that there's no career in the writing fields, as everything online is published for free. How do you combat that through 826 National and your own personal advocacy?

A: I taught a high school class for eleven years called the Best American Nonrequired Reading. I stay in touch with a lot of the students, and a bunch have found writing gigs after college. There aren't as many print journalism jobs as twenty years ago, but there are some opportunities. One former student writes for an education-related website. Another writes for the *Baltimore Sun*; another for *San Francisco* magazine. A bunch have gone into the nonprofit world. One works at a bookstore. But that's all to say that there are a lot of ways to make a living as a full- or part-time writer. I didn't make a living writing until I was about twenty-eight or so. Before that, I temped, and illustrated, and did graphic design . . . a dozen jobs, and I didn't mind it. I knew I was learning. Young writers have to know that their twenties are a period of soaking things in, traveling, learning, seeing things, getting out of your personal bubble, having your presumptions upended. If you get right out of college and expect (or want) to get a job as a writer, you might be making a mistake. You might be better off working on a merchant ship or a cannery or a hospital—something new, something where you might learn a thing or two.

Q: Lastly, how often do you get tired of writing?

A: I don't. I might dread a deadline or get stuck for an hour or a day, but I never get tired of it.

An Interview with Dave Eggers and Mimi Lok

Sean Bex and Stef Craps / 2015

From *Contemporary Literature* 56, no. 4, Winter 2015. © 2015 by University of Wisconsin Press. Reprinted by permission.

The interview below consists of two parts. The first part deals with Eggers's literary work, homing in on *The Circle* in particular, while the second part focuses on Voice of Witness. For this part of the conversation we were joined by Lok, who has served as the book series' executive director and executive editor since 2008. Before that, she worked as a freelance reporter for the Asia bureaus of the *Washington Post*, the *Chicago Sun-Times*, and *USA Today*, and taught creative writing at San Francisco State University and in schools in Hong Kong and China. What Eggers and Lok clearly share is a passion for human rights storytelling. We kicked off the interview, though, with a few questions about Eggers's identity as a writer, his writing process, and the evolution of his literary work.

Q: Do you consider yourself a writer first and foremost? Is that the core of your professional identity, from which everything else flows, or do you see writing as on a par with your work as an editor, publisher, and activist?

Dave Eggers: When we started up *McSweeney's* in San Francisco and 826 Valencia, I can honestly say that that year I probably did not write a whole lot. Overall, though, it changes month to month. Sometimes I have a project that I want to dedicate time to, and I have to set aside writing for a while, but as I've gotten older, all of these foundations that we have started have matured. They are all in good hands, and so they do not need my help on a day-to-day management basis. As a result, I've been able to return to more full-time writing. When I enter a country and they ask me what my occupation is, I write "writer." However, this feels strange, because

I think it's a ridiculous luxury to be able to write for a living. I feel it's always very pretentious to say that; I've never quite gotten used to it. It's something that I feel very grateful for every day. I don't take it for granted: I feel like I'm still earning it every day, largely because my parents really worked for a living. My mother was a teacher, and my father worked hard as a lawyer. They had regular nine-to-five jobs that were hard, and I have the ability to choose my hours and wake up late if I want to. But because I feel so grateful or lucky, I tend to keep the same regular office hours these days. I don't always have a chance to write those eight hours, but at least I'm in the writing position. I feel so lucky that I have to put in the time, at least. Otherwise I have this crushing sense of shame that comes from my Catholic upbringing, which says, "Hey, what are you doing? You've been given this chance; other people really have to work for a living, so get back to work!" So I do feel an obligation to work as hard as the people, like my parents, who were not always doing something day to day that they loved. My mother loved teaching, but my father did not always get to take on cases that he loved. I think any of us who have the ability to do something we love tend to work twice as hard, to compensate for the luck that we have had.

Q: How do you usually begin a book? Do you start with a character, a plot, a setting, or an issue that you want to explore? Could you perhaps walk us through your writing process?

Eggers: I usually write one scene and one chapter first where I lock in the tone, the style, and the characters. It has to be something that you are interested in, that comes naturally, and that you feel passionate about. You can build the rest of the work around it once you've solved that case on the micro-level.

For *The Circle*, I'd been thinking about this issue for around ten years, because I've been in Northern California for twenty-two years and I saw the rise of the internet. I remember the first collapse of the dot-com bubble as well as its subsequent boom. Many of my friends are now in positions of power in some of these companies, while others have startups or develop apps, websites, and so on. I've been immersed in it for so long. I had been trying to synthesize ideas about it, about what exactly I find concerning about it. A lot of times I will take notes for years and years on something that might not come to fruition. But in this case I had two or three feet of notes, just stacks of paper, and I didn't know what to do with them until I had the idea of Mae, the protagonist, starting on her first day at one of the companies—the idea that somebody is given this great opportunity, leaving a terrible job to come to a utopia, a dream job, and that this slowly devolves so that the more nefarious aspects of this company would become clear as the novel went along.

The first scene I wrote for *The Circle* was the one about the Portugal lunch. I thought I'd write this scene, and then the rest of the book would build out from that. Mae is fairly new at this company, and she is in trouble because somebody sent her an email informing her that there was a lunch for people interested in Portugal and she didn't attend the lunch. The scene scared me because it was something that has happened in my life, too. You get thousands of email notices, and you cannot respond to all of them. You get this constant feeling that people around you are offended by your silence or your indifference to their invitations or their asking you to like or dislike something. There is an overwhelming deluge of stimuli that we are supposed to respond to.

Q: Do you start at the beginning and write until you reach the end, or do you skip around, writing scenes as you see fit and filling in the gaps later?

Eggers: I'm definitely an obsessive rewriter. I went to journalism school, so I was taught by old Chicago newspapermen. It's like going through boot camp for journalism, where they beat you down, tell you that you are terrible. You have to strip down your style. Any adjective that you cannot absolutely justify gets thrown away. It's constant revising and revising, and then after ten revisions you're lucky to get a C. That's the best grade we could get in school. It teaches humility, and it taught me, having worked with newspapers and journals for so long, that the revision process is endless. I learned that I could always learn something from an editor's input, and that I needed to vet my writing thoroughly myself and through other readers. So I would say that on average I do twenty drafts of anything I publish, even today. I also usually send it to at least fifteen different readers to get their notes before I feel comfortable.

This is also how we teach students at 826 Valencia. Of course, when I was in high school, I never revised anything. I would finish the draft the morning it was due and then turn it in, cross my fingers, and think that one draft was enough. The incredible hubris to think that your first draft is your best draft! So when we work with students who are reluctant writers, or who do not have a lot of one-on-one help that they can get, we teach them to revise. On the walls of 826 Valencia we have all these proofs and drafts. For example, we have Amy Tan's book *The Bonesetter's Daughter*, which is really popular in San Francisco. We have the twenty-eighth draft of that book on the wall, to show students that even Amy Tan—a professional writer who has written a dozen novels—is still revising and that she can still benefit from that. If you are humble about your writing and do not presume that any type of sentence is perfection, it actually opens up the process and makes it much more approachable and egalitarian. We can all reach a certain level of proficiency if we work at it.

I think being humble about it is key. You need to know that everything you do now is practice. You are not writing the best work that you will ever write at age eighteen or twenty. I don't think I wrote anything that I was proud of until I was thirty—or maybe twenty-eight. I think novelists get infinitely better into their thirties and forties, so it's a long game. You should not take yourself too seriously, even though you are serious about the work you are doing, of course. I was encouraged as a young writer to just submit to as many magazines as possible. Anything that you get published gets you to be part of a new community. You should not be precious about it. New readers and editors mean you get help with your work, causing it to advance. You get the benefit of reader response as well as the feeling of having your work out there. It really is a slow process of climbing a pyramid, where you are trying to get better.

Q: As is the case with *The Circle*'s Mae Holland, your protagonists tend to be hopeful and idealistic, bordering on naive at times. They seem to be almost willfully blind to the evil that surrounds them. Would you agree with this characterization of the "Eggersian hero," so to speak?

Eggers: I would not necessarily agree that there is any overarching trait. You will see connections in all of this that I will not necessarily see or endorse, but I understand that I'm not always the best expert. I'm not always the most knowledgeable at seeing connections between novels that I wrote fifteen years ago. You probably know them better than I do at this point. I never go back and reread some book I wrote thirteen years ago, because it's horrifying. You see all these mistakes, things you should have done differently. Eventually you simply have to let it go. You have to learn to see each book as a document of its time, a document of your mind, a place in your life, or a point you wanted to make in 2002 that you wouldn't necessarily make at all or in the same way now.

But I'll talk about the character Mae. I thought it was really important that Mae come from a point of relative disadvantage. She comes from what we call the Central Valley, which is ninety miles from San Francisco—lower middle class, a lot of farming, pickup trucks, not a whole lot of money. She feels like she has been given this incredible gift to work at the Circle. As a result, she is inclined to discount any hints that something is awry. So yes, I would say she is willfully blind. That's exactly what it is, and you find this again and again. Until recently, when Obama passed his health care act, anyone, any young person who could get a good health insurance plan was so grateful to their company. That's because it's rare, and if you don't have insurance, you're in trouble in the US. Mae has a sick parent, she came from nowhere, and she feels like she's been given this gift. She has to be naive, willfully naive, because even when there are little signs of trouble, she doesn't feel like she has a right to blow the whistle. She feels that no matter how bad it gets, it's never worse than where she came from, which makes it something of a perfect storm for turning or radicalizing someone.

Q: For a time, your books reflected a gradually broadening scope as far as subject matter is concerned. While *A Heartbreaking Work of Staggering Genius* dealt with personal family traumas, the books that followed it were set all around the world or featured non-American-born protagonists and addressed global problems and concerns. However, your two most recent novels, *The Circle* and *Your Fathers, Where Are They? And the Prophets, Do They Live Forever?*, are set entirely in the US, have American-born protagonists, and are primarily concerned with the American context, even if the issues they explore resonate beyond national boundaries. Was this refocusing on the US prompted by anything in particular?

Eggers: I think *The Circle* is—intends to be—a globally minded book, in the sense that the concerns it addresses profoundly affect everyone's life, across the globe, even though these companies are generally based in California. *Your Fathers* is definitely an American book, though. It takes place there, and it's very locally rooted. Ideally, though, there are universal things in all of my books, even though some are about someone coming to the US and adjusting to life there, like Valentino, and some are about an American going abroad. The American character in *A Hologram for the King*, for example, goes to Saudi Arabia, and the entire book is set in Jeddah. What I resist, and what I'm really not good at, is writing a book that takes place in one neighborhood or a single community. I wrote about my upbringing in Chicago in *A Heartbreaking Work of Staggering Genius*, and I felt like everything I could possibly say about the suburbs was said in that book. Now, when I take on a book, I want to be able to learn something. For example, *You Shall Know Our Velocity!* was set in Senegal, Morocco, Latvia, Estonia, etc., giving me an opportunity to visit all these places, too. As a journalist, with that training, you always want an excuse to go somewhere and have a reason to see something new, or learn something new, or interview people. All of my work has that in common. Other than that, I can't say that there is a master plan. The truth is I never know what is going to strike me next. Take *Your*

Fathers, for example: the fact that this book is all dialogue came out of nowhere. I actually wrote it before *The Circle* and put it aside because I thought it was too strange. Once I finished *The Circle*, I came back and read it again and found that it still resonated with me. I do have things that I've been taking notes on for years and that I'm trying to shape, but I have no idea what will emerge or crystallize next.

Q: Let's dig down a little into *The Circle*, which has been highly successful. Would it be fair to say that Mae Holland is not just a specific character but also something of an Everyman figure?

Eggers: Yes! There is not an incredible amount of background on Mae, so you could say that I tried to make her—not to say an empty vessel, but a pair of eyes that did not view things with too much baggage or skepticism. I think she is fundamentally optimistic and wants to believe in the advantages and ideals of the Circle as well as the campus at its center. There are two ways to see a campus like that. The founders and the staff of so many of these companies do so many things well; they take on a very active role in improving every part of the system, meaning that they aim to provide the best possible service to their employees in terms of food, exercise, relaxation, and accommodation. There are hundreds of campuses all around California that provide these kinds of things. But what is the trade-off? This is what I'm trying to get at in *The Circle*. What is the trade-off when everything is filtered through or being decided on by one central organization? The Circle would prefer that you interact only with other Circlers and that you stay on campus as much as possible. It can take a turn toward total control, and Mae is subject to the fact that the Circle knows all of her movements all of the time. I keep hearing from actual employees in these companies saying, "It's like you were in the room with us; this is exactly my life!" Not necessarily the evil side of it, but the day-to-day things. And this was the nicest person you will ever meet, which means that all of these companies are full of good, idealistic, bright people. These people struggle with the things that they need to be questioning or do not quite approve of. That's why I keep believing that everyone would welcome a conversation about ethics and boundaries. All of the people who work in these companies sometimes do stuff that goes beyond what they would approve of.

Q: *The Circle* is a satire on social networking and surveillance culture. It's a cautionary tale about threats to privacy, freedom, and democracy. I wonder, though, if you personally have any sympathy at all for the arguments of the company philosopher, Bailey, who sings the praises of radical transparency and total knowledge. He claims that we are at the dawn of a second

Enlightenment, and that absolute transparency will make human beings more moral. Does he have a point? Or are you completely on the side of Mae's ex-boyfriend Mercer and her lover Kalden, the two voices of opposition in the novel? They are convinced that the Circle is, or has become, utterly sinister, and that we are headed straight for a totalitarian nightmare. Where do you stand yourself?

Eggers: I'm very clearly a skeptic about a lot of these things. I think this has to do with the fact that I grew up before the internet revolution. I saw it rise, saw it come up all around me, and so saw it go from a pure, utopian idea to what it is now. I've talked to so many people who were there at the beginning of the internet and have read *The Circle*, and they say that they are horrified by some of the same things that I wanted to create horror about in the novel. That is, the conglomeration of power and wealth into a very few hands and the temptation toward submitting to this central funnel of all information where, in exchange for having all of your banking, your voting, and your social life in one place, you give up access to some third party, some capitalist company that uses it for means beyond your control and knowledge. That is where we are at right now. In exchange for "freedom," in exchange for "free things," we allow ourselves to be spied on. As such, I think the rise of the internet has turned out radically different from how the idealists originally thought it would; they imagined a much more egalitarian, democratic system, where the power was equally spread. No one predicted that it would end in an unprecedented concentration of power and wealth.

Q: In your novel, the culprit is a private company, and the government is cast as a potential savior, in principle if clearly not in practice. I wonder if you have reconsidered that position in light of the recent leak of classified NSA documents by Edward Snowden, which revealed the sweeping extent of the US government's surveillance and espionage activities. I believe your novel was released shortly after the first Snowden revelations. In a way, what these revelations suggest is that the completion of the circle, the attainment of absolute omniscience which is the company's ultimate goal, is already upon us, and that not only has it come even sooner than you expected but it's the government itself, rather than big business, that has pulled it off.

Eggers: The Snowden issue was unfolding when I was finishing the book. The really weird twist was that I finished the book in Ecuador—sometimes I go far away from everything to get work done—and I landed in Guayaquil the same day that Edward Snowden was meant to land there. This was before he went to Russia, when he was granted asylum by the Ecuadorian government. I was at the airport, and there were a great number of people looking for Edward Snowden. Then I went off to finish this book about some of the issues that had prompted this situation. It was an extraordinarily strange confluence of events.

I'm a massive critic of the NSA; I've come out on record many times to criticize their activities. I quite frankly think the NSA is completely out of control. It answers to no one, it seems; there is no transparency about what they do; it's not being regulated. I believe that all these internet companies do need to be regulated by the US government in the US, and there should be some sort of global response, too—some form of regulation by the UN that sets up a global framework that all of these companies would be required to operate under. We don't have a set of standards; we don't have a set of ethical guidelines.

Q: A digital Bill of Rights, as proposed by the character Kalden in *The Circle*?

Eggers: Yes, a UN declaration of digital rights with legal consequences. Think of Google, which is continually sued in European courts, especially in Germany, for violations of privacy. I think those lawsuits put a check on the power. Again, though, there is no framework that everyone operates under. I think that some of these companies would be reluctant to be outliers or outlaws in such a framework if it were created. They would try to operate within it to some extent. Any other industry—law, biology, medicine, food— has some form of global agreement about what is ethical, but there is no such thing when it comes to the digital world, and therefore that has to be the first step. We would hope that the NSA would be subject to that agreement, but the gathering of intelligence in the US has always happened to a large extent outside of all law.

Q: *The Circle* is often compared to George Orwell's classic dystopian novel *Nineteen Eighty-Four*. There are some unmistakable parallels between the two, not least the adaptation of Orwell's slogans "War Is Peace," "Freedom Is Slavery," and "Ignorance Is Strength" to "Secrets Are Lies," "Sharing Is Caring," and "Privacy Is Theft." Could you talk about the nature and extent of Orwell's influence on you?

Eggers: First of all, I think that any time you write a dystopian book, it's bound to be compared to *Nineteen Eighty-Four*. People compare *The Hunger Games* to *Nineteen Eighty-Four*, for example. I think it's something of a go-to corollary. That said, Orwell has been one of my favorite writers, his journalism as much as his fiction. When I started this novel, I made a point of not reading *Nineteen Eighty-Four* again, of not reading *Brave*

New World again. I deliberately steered clear of anything that might unintentionally trickle into me. However, once I had finished *The Circle*, I went back to Orwell's novel to make sure that I had not inadvertently borrowed from it. The only thing I did consciously was that nod to those three slogans: that was very much on purpose. Orwell's work reads just as freshly today as when it was written. One of the things I noticed was that on page 1 of *Nineteen Eighty-Four*, life is miserable. The apocalypse has already happened; everyone is subject to an all-powerful totalitarian regime; they have no rights or opportunities. The narrative is a matter of Winston Smith struggling within the narrow confines of that world, trying to break out, maybe having a chance at love, and then failing at that. I really wanted to have a much slower burn, where you slowly get to participate in the descent. I think that there are not a tremendous number of similarities in practice, outside of both being dystopian books. The other thing is that in *Nineteen Eighty-Four* you have submission to a totalitarian regime that you cannot resist or they will torture or kill you. I wanted *The Circle* to be pointedly such that everyone is participating, doing it willingly. Think of the younger engineers and developers who are pitching ideas to the powers that be at the Circle. All of their ideas take things so much further and make it so much worse than it already is. That's where it's going, and it's so hard to roll it back at this stage.

Q: *The Circle* reminded me in some ways of Gary Shteyngart's novel *Super Sad True Love Story*. Like you, Shteyngart conjured a dystopian vision of a near-future America characterized by pervasive surveillance and constant social networking. He has expressed his shock at the fact that many of the parodic, extreme predictions he made in *Super Sad True Love Story* back in 2010 have already come true. I wonder if that is also your experience with *The Circle*, in which you describe numerous new services and technologies that are being invented at this company. Weren't you at all worried about inadvertently giving the Mark Zuckerbergs of this world ideas?

Eggers: No, I think they've thought of everything. Honestly, nothing that came up had not already been thought up by someone in research and development. Some of it has even already happened. It's moving so fast, and there is so much money in it. These companies have so many billions of dollars for research and development that any notion that they have is looked into and potentially turned into reality. Google and Apple are both developing driverless cars. The US automobile industry is scared to death. They are not just developing the technology to drive the car, but the car itself. Apple has more cash than any company has ever had in the history of the world and can buy any company in any sector and make things. So again, I cannot imagine that something I thought of has not yet been thought of by some of these companies. You know, Google has this internal Project X, where all the new ideas are developed; all the campuses have secret research and development sites where they come up with whatever is going to happen next.

Q: Let's move on to talk about Voice of Witness. Ms. Lok, thanks for joining us. Could you start us off by explaining briefly the general idea behind Voice of Witness?

Mimi Lok: Voice of Witness is a nonprofit book series as well as an education program. The main idea is that we want to change the way people think about human rights crises. By that we mean that we want to engender a more nuanced, a more layered, a more empathy-based understanding and engagement with these issues, so that people become better informed and empathetic global citizens and more effective advocates for human rights and human dignity. The book series has covered a wide range of issues. We have interviewed wrongfully convicted Americans, people affected by Hurricane Katrina, undocumented workers in the US, and people in women's prisons. Internationally, we have interviewed people who escaped repressive regimes in places like Burma, Sudan, Zimbabwe, and Colombia. In addition to these collections of oral histories, we have produced a methodology book that comes out of our education program, *The Power of the Story: The Voice of Witness Teacher's Guide to Oral History*. It sets out how teachers can use the stories in the classroom but also describes a methodology for anyone who wants to do an oral history project.

Q: Could you tell us about the process of making a Voice of Witness book? How does it start, and how does it all come together?

Lok: It's quite an involved process. It normally starts with a conversation, someone with an idea for a collection. The criteria are straightforward: It has to be a contemporary human rights crisis, and it has to be underreported. We also want to know that the person who is proposing this project is not only qualified to undertake it—has a good track record in the field and experience with the communities where the interviews will take place— but also is not just interested in proving a specific hypothesis. They need to want to learn something and be genuinely curious. Once this has been established, we ask them to develop a proposal of around five pages, containing a budget, a timeline, and—most importantly—what their vision is for the project. I am usually the person who will help to refine the proposal by anticipating the questions the rest of the Voice of Witness team will have as we look at it and decide on whether or not to accept it. Generally, we want to stick to projects that we think will add something of value to the series. We want to keep the topics as fresh and diverse as possible. But there are certain things that we return to, like the justice system in the US, in *Surviving Justice, Inside This Place, Not of It,* and one other potential volume looking at solitary confinement. Someday we hope to do a book on the juvenile justice system. We have an extremely long list of topics we would like to address, but it's really about getting the right proposals from the right people at the right time.

Q: A question for Mr. Eggers in particular, as it follows on from something you mention in your introduction to *The Voice of Witness Reader* [2015]. You write about a Sudanese woman who had lost faith in media reporters coming to interview her, to cover her story, because she never heard from them again afterward. Is that something you often find, that fear that there won't be any follow-through, and a reluctance, therefore, to share one's story?

Eggers: I think a lot of people who've had their human rights compromised and then have had experience with the media are skeptical. They may feel as if somebody sticks a microphone in their face and gets a few quotes and leaves. Afterward, they're left worse off than they were before. It's a form of retraumatization. For example, you have the wrongfully convicted in America: they've had their names plastered all over headlines saying that they're convicted murderers. They sometimes have to wait eighteen to twenty years in prison to clear their names. Those people have had their narratives taken from them, their identities reshaped or misshaped. They are very skeptical, so we have to let them know from day one that we will give them control over the process. We explain that nothing will be published without their approval and that we want to get it right. Then we record their stories over the course of hours, days, and sometimes months or even years. Afterward, we order their story into a chronology, and we check with them, as well as conducting fact-checks at our end, in order to make sure that it is beyond debate whether it is the truth—the truth, that is, about the lives that they have lived. This process allows them to reclaim their narrative, in a way. I think that knowing that they're going to have control, that they can pull the plug at any time, gives them a sense of security. It means that they don't have to risk having another mistruth printed about them.

We do not interview people who we feel are at risk of retraumatization. Generally, with the books, we work with agencies that know people they have worked with who are comfortable talking. We don't necessarily go some-where and find somebody who has no record of speaking at all. Usually, it's a very gentle, careful process of vetting before we even begin an interview.

Q: How do the interviewers experience the process of collecting oral histories? How are they affected by listening to these testimonies?

Eggers: It varies. When you train as a journalist, you get used to hav-ing a defensive shield about these things. You need to put on a brave face and keep the tape recorder running while you keep asking questions. What was interesting when Valentino and I were in South Sudan, interviewing a woman who had been enslaved for sixteen years, was that she was very straightforward and could just tell her story. She was angry, and she wanted the world to hear. Valentino had to stop the tape a few times, however, because her story was overwhelming him. You never know how it will affect you. But we do allow our interviewers to be empathetic. They can stop the tape, touch somebody's arm; they can be human. People are both listen-ing as humans and have a tape recorder running. These two things happen concurrently. I'm not going to deny one or the other. It can be incredibly overwhelming for the interviewers; we hear that a lot. For example, when an interviewer in the US cannot believe that something is happening on our own soil.

Lok: We also realized the need to support our interviewers from the very start. There is a tendency for interviewers to think that even if they have a hard time dealing with what they are hearing, it doesn't compare to what the other person has been through, and it therefore doesn't matter. It does, though, because if you do not practice self-care, you cannot continue doing this job. We have guidelines that prioritize the needs of the person being interviewed but also acknowledge the interviewer's needs. We build the interview, in the sense that we do not go directly to the trauma. We will start off gently, talk about how your day is, what you are up to, how you are feeling, then talk about the trauma. This allows us to avoid unearthing the trauma and then just walking away, which would be jarring for the narrator and for the interviewer. Recently I've been having conversations with a clini-cal psychologist who has experience with vicarious trauma and compassion fatigue, which is something that human rights activists are often vulnerable to, even if it gets played down. You really do have to be strong and take care of yourself.

Q: You've mentioned that telling you their stories is a therapeutic and empowering experience for many narrators. Of course, Voice of Witness also seeks to create change in the wider society. Do you have any sense of the impact the series has made in that regard?

Lok: I think the impact shows up in the young. We try to make human rights activism accessible through the use of personal narratives, regardless of what your engagement with this issue is or is not. Our readers range from middle school–aged readers to policy-makers and activists. One of the major places we see an impact is among students. They are probably the leading examples of the type of reader who does not have prior knowledge of or a prior interest in what is happening in Burma, Sudan, or Colombia, or in public housing in Chicago. The series helps to bring these issues alive and helps students feel that they have a participatory relationship with contemporary history. The testimonies we get from young people who have read these stories are incredible.

In a wider sense, the stories have been used in case law in many instances. Additionally, testimonies that have been featured in our books have been used in advocacy campaigns. For example, Ashley Jacobs, whose narrative is in the book *Inside This Place, Not of It,* was six months pregnant when she was imprisoned, and in prison, women are shackled to the bed during childbirth—something that she did not talk about, even to her family, because she felt ashamed about it. The process of telling the story with one of our education team members over the course of a year and a half was healing, empowering, and restorative. It eventually made her want to share her story with the wider public. She ended up working with her local branch of the ACLU to end the practice of shackling in women's prisons. We have seen some changes being made now in several states in the US, but there is still a long way to go.

Eggers: I don't know what policies there are here in Belgium, but in the US, if a woman in prison goes to see the doctor, she has to be in chains or chained to the bed. This results in pregnant women giving birth with their legs chained to a steel bed—a barbaric and unconscionable practice, but nobody knew about it. By being told, this story became part of the public debate. Sometimes these first-person narratives can bring an issue to life in a way that a statistical approach could not.

Q: By focusing on the stories of individuals, though, don't you risk losing sight of the systemic nature of the injustices these people have suffered? How do you avoid individualizing and thereby depoliticizing social, collective suffering? How do you ensure that the bigger picture is not being missed?

Lok: I think you get at the universal through the particular. We make it so that each voice in a collection—there are usually around thirteen or fifteen voices per collection—highlights something different, a different side of the situation. Some stories can be taken as emblematic for a crisis; some are surprising in that this could have happened to this kind of person. Additionally, when someone mentions any kind of abuse or a specific situation, we'll contextualize that in a footnote. For example, if someone says that they were displaced from their farm in Colombia, we will show how tens of thousands of people experienced the same thing during that period. We also have appendices at the back of each book—a timeline, a glossary, mini-essays from reports—which provide background on the issues that are being discussed. Oftentimes, these are condensed reports from sources like Amnesty International or Human Rights Watch. We try to draw on a variety of sources to keep a somewhat objective and balanced overview of the situation.

Eggers: I would just add that you almost always have a better understanding of a situation through a first-person narrative—seeing what one person says and then seeing a broader view of it. I'd been reading about the conflict in Colombia for twenty years; it's very hard to unpack because it's so complicated and there are so many different players. But I remember reading the very first narrative in the Colombia book, and instantly all of it made much more sense. I saw it through one person's eyes, saw the devolution of the country happen piece by piece, year by year. Rather than causing you to lose sight of the political dimension, I would suggest, testimonies are actually the best method to illuminate the political context.

Q: I've looked at quite a few Voice of Witness books, and two of the things that struck me are that they are heavily edited—they're not simply collections of transcribed oral history interviews—and there is no fixed format: the structure and organization of each volume is unique. Could you talk about why it is that you go beyond simply collecting and transcribing interviews? And what determines the choice of a particular format for a particular book?

Eggers: There is a long tradition of oral history, and it's practiced in different ways by different people. There is a very strong academic tradition of collecting oral histories, and some that I've read were quite dry and hard to follow. Sometimes they are a series of questions and answers rather than a linear narrative. We decided that the Voice of Witness books would edit everyone's story—no matter how it was originally told over the course of days, weeks, or years—into a linear narrative, without changing words. That would be what the reader could rely on—that we would tell a compelling linear narrative with the narrator's original words and phrasings and idiosyncrasies of speech, which takes some editing. Once we have the tapes, we transcribe them and put them into a linear order for clarity. We then take the transcript back to the person who told us the story, the narrator, to make sure we got it right. More often than not they will say, "You got it exactly right: that's how I told it to you"—even though it took us one hundred hours to get it into that shape, where it's clear and linear.

Lok: I don't know if you've ever seen an oral transcript before, but it is like a big bowl of spaghetti thrown on the floor. Unless someone is a born storyteller, you calmly have to edit it all. Most people, myself included, jump around in time, misremember something, go back to correct something.

Eggers: We do a disservice to them if, after their bravery in telling their story, we do not put it into a form that readers can read. Readers will not read a seventy-page transcript, so it does need to be edited. We serve the narrators well only when the book itself is compelling and can be read by a broad audience. That is how we honor their stories and their courage.

Q: The slogan on the Voice of Witness website reads, "Illuminating Human Rights Crises through Oral History." Given that there are, sadly, so many human rights crises that deserve attention, how do you decide which crisis to tackle next? Are you at all concerned about balance or comprehensive coverage, especially now that the series has grown to such an extent that people might wonder why certain crises are not represented?

Eggers: There are still only six people who work at Voice of Witness, which means that if there are a hundred topics that could be approached tomorrow, and deserve to be, we're still limited by the tiny staff and tiny funding that we have. That's one key part. Thirteen books in ten years is something we're very proud of, but it's a struggle to make them and to continue to exist in terms of funding.

Lok: Another factor is the time it takes to create a book that we can be proud of and that does justice to the stories. Each book takes anywhere from one to four years to put together.

Eggers: What we also get are proposals from editors who have an idea, but when we ask whether they are in it for the long haul—up to four years— they back out. So it's a very intricate process, which needs commitment from the editors and the constituents they are serving, and, most of all, time.

Q: You do not shy away from controversial topics. A particularly good example is your recent volume on life under Israeli occupation in the Palestinian territories, but I'm also thinking of the volumes on undocumented immigrants in the US and on the plight of Muslim Americans in the wake of 9/11. What has the response been to these more politically sensitive collections? Do you deliberately try to redress the imbalances that you see in the dominant media and government narratives?

Lok: It's our ambition to amplify unheard voices—people whose experiences and expertise don't get into the mainstream narrative on an issue. It's not our explicit mission statement to think about how we can be controversial. It's more about whether there is something in a proposal that's going to help us learn something new, shed new light on something.

Q: Do you take any flak over covering controversial issues?

Eggers: Something that continues to amaze me is that nobody can argue with somebody's story. You simply cannot. They are not opinions or polemics. We make a point of that: even if the narrators want to offer hours and hours of their opinions, we still turn it into a narrative that answers the question, What happened? When *Palestine Speaks* came out, we did think we would get a lot of flak. The editors were nervous when they went out on tour that it was going to be controversial. It turns out that those fears were unfounded; it has not been very controversial at all, simply because you cannot argue with someone's story. The book does not take a political position. It does not have a prescriptive solution to the relationship between Palestine and Israel. The stories themselves are the stories of people who live in the West Bank and Gaza. This is what they see, what they have been through. You can form your opinions from there. Because of that, and because we stay neutral on those sorts of issues, I think everyone is willing to come into it with an open mind. We hope that is the case, at least.

Q: The Voice of Witness book series is victim-centered, in the sense that the narrators whose stories we get to read are all victims of human rights violations. It could be argued that in order to fully understand what happened and why it happened, we also need to know the stories of the perpetrators. Have you ever considered also interviewing the perpetrators, as Jean Hatzfeld, for example, did in his extraordinary trilogy about the genocide in Rwanda?

Lok: Yes, and we have in fact done that in some of our books. We've interviewed people who have been involved in committing crimes and become victims themselves, such as former child soldiers in Burma. The idea of working with a strict distinction between perpetrator and victim is reductive. There are different levels of perpetration. There is "dictator," and then there are child soldiers recruited to serve in an armed group for several years of their lives. So I think it's a lot more complex than victim versus perpetrator. But our mission is quite concise, quite focused: it is to amplify the voices of those most closely affected by human rights crises, and so we have to prioritize those.

Eggers: Our specific aim is to provide a platform for the powerless. Those in power have their platform, which they have used in various ways. We feel that if we're going to talk about women in US prisons, those women have to be heard first, because we've already heard the other side. We've heard that they are criminals, that they deserve this, that rape is a normal and natural part of going to prison, that they deserve that—in the US it's considered part of your punishment. We're trying to counteract that dominant narrative. As such, we're not aiming to compile comprehensive textbooks. Think of *Throwing Stones at the Moon: Colombians Displaced by Violence*. It's not everything you need to know about Colombia in one book. It is specifically a book about voices from everyday Colombians and how they've been affected by the drug wars and the chaos of the past twenty years.

Q: The focus in all of the volumes to date is on contemporary issues— ongoing human rights crises or very recent ones. Have you considered covering human rights violations that happened in the past yet might be instructive for the present?

Lok: There is incredible work being done in that field by countless other organizations. But our focus on the contemporary is also a result of the fact that our medium is oral history: we focus on the stories of those who are living. Witnesses have a particular power and relevance. Let's not forget either that victims of, for example, the prison system in the US are living now but that the systemic abuses to which they testify have been going on for decades.

Q: As a human rights activist, you see a lot of misery in the world that enrages you, but which you can often do very little about because of powerful interests stacked against you. How do you cope with that predicament?

Lok: We've had this conversation recently. It's so easy to feel over-whelmed and discouraged, to be thrown into a state of paralysis, because the problems are so huge. But I think it's about figuring out where you can be useful, where you can fit in. You can't do everything, but each person has unique strengths and passions that can help to move the needle along. It's also important to find other people who think the same thing and want to do the same thing.

Eggers: Also, if you focus on the micro-level and what you can actually change, then it's very rare to be discouraged. Think of 826 Valencia, for example. We could have said, "Let's try to change all American educational policy and make equal opportunities for all!" By now, we would have been very frustrated, because we can't do that at a national level. Instead, we started up this one center, in this one community. We focus on what we can do. We have two thousand volunteers in San Francisco who feel like they are changing something every day. They feel that electric charge when there is learning going on, and they focus on the difference they can make. That's always going to happen when you're engaged with real, hands-on work rather than engaging with something at the macro-level and thinking that just because you write an op-ed, it's all going to change. You have to focus on the day-to-day work as opposed to the theoretical and more frustrating work, where you know what needs to change but cannot effect that change.

Lok: I should mention that even though we've been saying that we are just six people, every book involves at least twenty to thirty people who help us—fact-checkers, translators, and so on—as well as dozens of volunteers. For them, it's the time they put into the one small piece of that picture that is meaningful.

Eggers: Whatever you do, though, don't accept any cynicism. Don't allow yourself to become cynical, especially before you've tried. The cynicism that I felt in my twenties, that nothing would have an impact—that was a terrible mistake. It's just a matter of finding something where you can make a difference. The cynics usually are not directly engaged in anything. They're floating above, saying, "I sent an email, it didn't have any effect, so I quit." I did that in my twenties: I wrote an article, and it didn't have any effect. Never let yourself descend into that. You can have a profound impact, but it's about where and how and when. It's about being serious and putting in the time, staying, and being courageous and fierce and true about it.

Student Stories: Youth Advisory Board Interviews Dave Eggers at Tell Me a Story

826LA / 2017

From 826LA Blog, July 5, 2017. © 2017 by 826LA. Reprinted by permission.

From the time-travel carpet at Tell Me a Story—826LA Youth Advisory Board students Ciro and Christopher interview Dave Eggers about his very first book and his advice to young writers.

Ciro: Why is writing important to you?

Dave Eggers: I feel imbalanced actually, if I don't write every day—even if it's something in a journal or expressing how I feel about the political climate or starting a novel. To me, writing is something very necessary. Otherwise, pressure builds up. Writing allows the pressure to escape and you feel at home again—centered. You become an owner to all of those thoughts. Do you agree?

Ciro: Yes. Definitely.

DE: Writing is therapeutic. Writing at your age is just as important, if not more important. You have homework that is sometimes so rigid and constrained with so many tests. Writing is the place where you can just put it all on the page—what you're thinking about, feeling about. It helps with your equilibrium.

What do you write? Fiction? Nonfiction? Poetry?

Christopher: Right now actually I'm writing just pieces about my own life. They are exciting because they incite emotion in me. I write to enhance my understanding of human emotion. Writing helps me understand how I'm different from the rest or similar to the rest.

DE: You said it so much better than I did. Because don't you understand yourself and other humans when you write?

Christopher: Yes. Yes!

DE: And when you read. Because reading is the key to empathy and putting yourself in someone else's skin for a day. The value the reading and writing have for understanding is underestimated because our feelings are so often kept inside, but when we write we can contain chaos and reshape our own personal narratives and own them. It's like, "Here is my narrative." What do you like write about?

Ciro: I'm starting to transition from nonfiction to more like romance and adventure. Right now I have this romance story in my head that I want to make into a book and then a movie.

DE: Have you heard of National Novel Writing Month? It's this one month out of the year where people dedicate themselves to writing one novel in one month. You should write your novel then.

You're the first high schooler I've met who's writing a novel and a romantic one at that. So you are doing something very unique and mature. Just get to the end! Not a lot of people get to the end. Don't overthink it. Don't get stuck on one sentence. If you have an idea, just get it out there. And then revise and revise and revise.

Ciro: When did you start writing and why?

DE: First grade. My first-grade teacher made us write a book. It's eighteen pages and I still have it. It's bound with yarn, but I still have it. I just was just encouraged by a succession of phenomenal teachers that kept on giving us that opportunity. Do you feel like you get a lot of help at 826LA? People who expect that absolute best from you?

Christopher: Absolutely. It's why I keep on going. I get to communicate my stories.

DE: And keep them! Those stories you write now will live forever. They're a documentation of your brain right now. If you don't write it now, you won't ever write it again. You'll never remember what you thought about at this age, but if you write it down you have this invaluable document of your mind. You'll treasure it like I used to treasure my old books. And the books that really mean a lot to me are the ones that are bound. Even if you use the tape binder, when you create something—when you hone and polish it—you honor your own work by publishing it. It deserves to be kept and studied and read.

Ciro: What advice would you give to aspiring young writers? Doesn't matter what age, but they just want to write.

DE: One: Once you got the writing part down, it's all about practice. And it's going to be a lot of practice for a lot of years. Be humble about it—you're still learning. Put all the hard work in year after year and know that you'll get there.

Two: Read voraciously. Ask, "Why is this book that I love so much working?" Study a book in the same way you take apart a car; put all the components on the garage floor and see what makes it hum. Not to take the enjoyment and imagination out of reading, but to look and study closely.

And lastly, use as much peer editing as you can. Show your writing to people you trust. Know that every time you show your work and people give you input, it makes you better. If you're willing to revise and edit and be humble and practice, you'll get there. You'll get there. And you both are infinitely farther than I was at your age.

You're on a very important path.

A Conversation with Dave Eggers and Mokhtar Alkhanshali about His New Nonfiction Book, *The Monk of Mokha*

Jordan Rodman / 2018

From Alfred A. Knopf, January 2018. © 2018 by McSweeney's. Reprinted by permission.

Question: This book is about coffee, but I understand that neither of you were longtime coffee drinkers.

Dave Eggers: I had my first cup of coffee when I was thirty-five. My wife and I were new parents and sleep was elusive, so to stay awake and have even a little acuity, I needed a new source of caffeine—Diet Mountain Dew wasn't working anymore. I will say that when you come to coffee relatively late in life, it has an otherworldly kick. But Mokhtar taught me how to appreciate coffee as more than a caffeine-delivery tool.

Mokhtar Alkhanshali: I didn't drink coffee much, mainly because the only coffee I was exposed to was cheap diner coffee that tasted like burnt popcorn. I thought coffee was too dark and bitter. One day I walked into a specialty coffee shop and had a cup of naturally processed coffee from Ethiopia's Yirgacheffe region. I tasted blueberries, honeysuckle, and it had a sweet lingering aftertaste. The barista spoke to me about where it was grown, the elevation, varietal, how it was processed—but most of all, how their direct relationship to these growers makes it possible for the farmers to make more money and live a better life. That part of it really became my entry point to the world of coffee.

Q: Mokhtar, you discovered your family's connection to coffee, and the Yemeni connection to coffee, when you were in your early twenties. What possessed you to actually go to Yemen and reinvent yourself as a coffee importer?

MA: That's a question that a lot of people ask me. In many ways I'm still trying to figure it out myself. To be honest, I didn't have a master plan; I just felt there was a disconnect between Yemen and the world of coffee, and I believed I could be that bridge. Looking back, I don't know if I would have gone on this journey knowing all of the things I'd have to learn and go through. I was naively arrogant.

Q: Dave, as a relative newcomer to the coffee world, what was the research like for *Monk of Mokha*?

DE: Mokhtar and I had met before, but the first time we saw each other after he returned from Yemen was at the Blue Bottle headquarters in Oakland. James Freeman, the founder, happened to be there that day, so between Mokhtar telling me much of his story, and the setting, it was a really immersive first step. But I was still skeptical. My impression was that there was a lot of pretension in the specialty coffee world. But I learned that the obsessive care that goes into one cup of coffee is coming from the same place much of the slow food movement is coming from. It's a reversal of the dehumanizing effects of industrial food consumption. When it comes to coffee, listening to Mokhtar's enthusiasm—and utter lack of pretension—really made me a convert. With any comestible, if you care about its quality, and if the people making it care, too, it will take longer and cost more.

Otherwise, the research took place on many levels, because the story has so many facets. There's Mokhtar's personal story—his upbringing and ambitions as a young man in San Francisco. There's the Tenderloin neighborhood and, in contrast, the high-rise world of the Infinity, where Mokhtar worked as a doorman. There's his extended family in the Central Valley, where we went early in the research process. Then there's the world of coffee, from plant to cup. There's Boot Coffee in Mill Valley, where Mokhtar learned about roasting and grading. I had to get familiar with all these worlds before we even went to Ethiopia, Djibouti, and Yemen.

Q: Mokhtar, you've done a fair amount of public speaking, and you'd given presentations many times to various audience before meeting Dave. How was that kind of storytelling different than what you did with Dave for the book?

MA: What I went through with Dave was a very intimate road trip. Dave was incredibly warm and someone I felt comfortable being vulnerable with. Some of those memories were hilarious, and others required lots of tissues. Dave's caring and loving personality were what made this book possible, because I know I wouldn't have been able to do this with anyone else.

Q: Dave, what drew you most to Mokhtar's story?

DE: For me it was first of all a story of towering will and imagination. For a guy as young as Mokhtar to simply reinvent himself, to risk so much to re-create his life, it's astonishing. The more I learned, the more remarkable his story became. I think it was about eighteen months into our interviews when he told me that he sometimes had to carry a grenade on his jacket in Yemen, just to imply he was not to be trifled with—in the pursuit of coffee beans. When I met Mokhtar, he was a doorman, so to see what he's built in these last five years is just awe-inspiring.

Q: One of the striking things about the book is how fraught things are for you, Mokhtar, when you're traveling through Yemen, simply trying to export coffee beans. You're held at gunpoint many times, you're kidnapped, you dodge bullets and bombs. And yet your attitude throughout is fairly positive. Are you just generally a fearless person, or does some absurdist side of you kick in during moments of grave danger?

MA: For most of my life I was terrified of small dogs, so no, I don't think of myself as a fearless person. People often ask how I managed living with violence and guns in Yemen. I grew up in Brooklyn and the Tenderloin; the first time a gun was put in my face was here in the US when I was eleven years old. There are only two countries in the world that own more guns per capita than Yemen, and one of those is the US. In those instances that you mentioned of extreme danger in Yemen, I was able to not react but to respond and figure out what I needed to do to survive, because I had already been equipped with that mechanism from an early age growing up in the inner city in the US.

With the comedy, I know it's hard for a lot of people to relate to in this day and age, but my faith in God is really a big part of my life. There's this idea in Islam called *tawakol*, putting your trust in God, and so, in those situations, I just had to rely on my faith, because logically there was no way for me to figure out how I would survive. That's the thing about faith: it's not based on facts and statistics, you just have to believe and let go, and that is a very liberating thing. Without that, I don't think I would have been able to laugh through those awful situations.

Q: Mokhtar, you come from a prominent Yemeni tribe, many of whom are still in Yemen. What are their lives like now, and what has it been like to see the country deteriorate over these last few years?

MA: The war doesn't care what tribe you're from, how old you are, or even what political affiliation you have. There isn't a family that I know in Yemen that hasn't been affected by this war. I have family members trying desperately to apply for their loved ones to come to the US, but because of the current administration's travel bans, they are stuck waiting for approvals at embassies in Cairo, Amman, Kuala Lumpur, and Djibouti. Eighty percent of Yemen is food insecure, 3.3 million people are displaced, and we're currently in the midst of a cholera outbreak that has affected a million people.

Q: Mokhtar, you still operate your company, Port of Mokha coffee, which continues to import coffee beans from war-torn Yemen. How much more difficult has the work become, and how are your workers and farmers faring amid the chaos?

MA: It's been challenging. Trying to run a business in the middle of an active war has its challenges. There are thousands of coffee farmers in Yemen whose sole livelihood is our work with them. Through our microloans we are paying for weddings, medical surgeries, and college tuitions, so for us it's a matter of being creative and persevering. Besides the material support that we send these farmers, there's an internal impact that happens. These farmers are pouring their hearts into the coffee they produce, and when they see it being showcased around the world in shops in Paris, Tokyo, Brooklyn, there's a deep sense of pride for them.

Q: Mokhtar and Dave, you two traveled to Ethiopia, Abu Dhabi, Djibouti, and Yemen together. Do you have favorite stories from your travels?

MA: Hmm, that's a hard one. Besides those international trips, the local ones here were a lot of fun. Going down to visit my grandmother in Southern California and hearing her tell her story, visiting my friend Jay Ruskey's farm in Santa Barbara (the only coffee farm in the US); probably the most impactful trip for me was Djibouti. I didn't tell Dave this, but at the time I was terrified about going. Part of my therapy was to go into these places where I had a negative association because of past trauma. I wanted to go to Djibouti and face my fears. Experiencing 130-degree weather and getting stuck in a sandstorm didn't help, but when I left I felt a huge weight lift off of my shoulders, and I'm always going to thank Dave for being there with me.

DE: I have a story. We spent a few years trying to get into Sana'a together, but when the war broke out, it was impossible for me to safely get into the capital. So we went to a more remote part of Yemen, and there we encountered an Italian man who was on a quest to visit every country on earth. He was very cynical, with a mordant humor that seemed at odds with a man so curious about the world. When he heard that Mokhtar imported high-end coffee from Yemen, and that Mokhtar was a Q grader—the equivalent of a sommelier in the wine world—he scoffed. He thought this was a pretentious affectation, a sign of the world's decadence. "A coffee sommelier? What's next?" he asked. But then, Mokhtar told his story and explained the world of coffee to this man—how Q graders can improve the lives of farmers, and how caring about where coffee, or any crop, comes from is actually a deeply humanistic thing. Mokhtar did all this while grinding and brewing fresh Yemeni coffee. By the time Mokhtar was pouring him a cup, the Italian wanted to know how he could invest in Mokhtar's company. No joke, that all happened in about fifteen minutes—this guy went from cynic to believer. The same thing happened to me, I guess.

The Monk of Mokha: An Interview with Dave Eggers and Mokhtar Alkhanshali

Jordan Michelman / 2018

From *Sprudge*, January 25, 2018. © 2018 by Sprudge. Reprinted by permission.

Jordan Michelman: Hello Dave Eggers, it's a pleasure to meet you, and hello Mokhtar, it's a pleasure to speak with you again. By way of starting, since this is how the book starts, Mr. Eggers—why did you choose that particular Saul Bellow quote to begin the book?

Dave Eggers: Oh, that's my favorite book, probably. I reread *Herzog* every year, and that's one of my favorite passages from my favorite book, and I think that there's something all-encompassing and yearning and big-hearted about that quote. It takes in all of the world and all its desires and ambitions and the political and the personal, all in one paragraph, and it just reminded me of the scope of Mokhtar's ambition and his worldview. For an epigraph, we needed something big to mirror the enormity of Mokhtar's vision and place in the world and what he achieved. It seems to, even though it's not a quote about coffee or San Francisco or Yemen, but it seemed to have a nice parallel in spirit to Mokhtar's story.

Michelman: Is that something you had in mind over the years rereading the book? Or was it something that came to you fresh as you were trying to think of what to put as an opening quote?

Eggers: It was rereading the book while working on Mokhtar's book, and when I came across that paragraph it just rang a bell. It just sometimes, something just hits you in the face. That's the right thing. And it's purely on a gut level, and I put it in and lived with it for the last year sort of feeling like it's the right thing. Readers seemed to respond—my early readers—to it, and feeling like it had a commonality with the spirit of Mokhtar's life.

Michelman: You mentioned early readers—I had the opportunity to read an advance copy of the book to prep for our interview today, and while

I don't want to rehash too much of what's in it or spoil the fun for people once they get a copy, I was wondering if, Mr. Eggers, you could tell us how you first came to be interested in telling this story?

Eggers: We had met from years before. We had a mutual friend in Wajahat Ali, a writer and commentator. Wajahat and I had worked on an HBO pilot about a Yemeni American police detective in San Francisco, and as part of our research, we met Mokhtar and he provided insight about what it was like to grow up as a Yemeni American man in the Bay Area. We got to know him that way, and then a few years later Wajahat wrote to me one day, saying, "Did you hear what happened to Mokhtar in Yemen?" And Mokhtar and I got together a few days later and began to talk. At first, it was just a casual couple hours' talk at Blue Bottle in Oakland, and without any goals or parameters, and just sort of a talk to see, out of curiosity.

And then it slowly, very slowly, grew out of that. We just kept getting together—we would do a little cupping and educational work, watch some roasting . . . this was out at Boot Coffee in San Rafael. I would sit in on some of the educational sessions there, and then afterward we would hang out in the back of Willem Boot's house and talk more about Mokhtar's recent time in Yemen. We just sort of went backward from there. It started with interviews about his most recent escape and the few months that led up to it, and then we just kept working backward and backward and backward all the way into childhood and earlier visits to Yemen. So it was a long and meandering process without a clear goal, until a little bit of the way in, when we realized that there really was a telling book in Mokhtar's story.

Michelman: How many total hours of interviews did you conduct for this book?

Eggers: I don't know. I guess in my mind it would be 100, 120 hours, or something like that. That would be recorded hours, and that's different than the countless amount of time that we spent just together and traveling and driving and visiting family and going to Djibouti and Ethiopia and Yemen and Santa Barbara and the Central Valley and visiting friends in the Tenderloin and family in Oakland and, you know. Over three years, it ends up really adding up, and I think that there's always two tracks for me as a writer/journalist. The on-record, recording, tape recorder between us times, and then there are the in-between times where we're just together and absorbing sometimes the atmosphere of a place like Boot or walking Mokhtar's old neighborhood in the Tenderloin.

Almost always when we were together, I had my tape recorder there, so a number of times when I would just turn it on when he was telling a story that I thought would be interesting. It wasn't part of an official interview, and it hadn't been prompted by a question I had written down, but suddenly we'd find ourselves in some very interesting and necessary territory and the tape recorder would come on.

I think to really do something like this right, it really does take quite a long time, because you really don't always know the questions you should ask until you get to know somebody pretty intimately. And even then, so many of the very most interesting and crucial parts of the story don't come out of an interview session. They come out of conversations and situations or being prompted by some place or memory that prompts another memory or a new story. A lot of that can only really happen over an open-ended long-term schedule.

Michelman: I'm curious, for fans of your previous work—is this book closer to something like *Zeitoun*, which is very much reported as nonfiction, or are there elements of the story that are dramatized as in your book *What Is the What?*

Eggers: It is not fiction. My training is as a journalist and my degree is in journalism, and this is what I did for a living and continue to do for *The Guardian* in London and other venues. I've been reporting on the Trump era, well, starting before he was elected and continuing. There's a piece I have to turn in in the next few days about the wall between San Diego and Mexico and how it affects the DACA recipients.

Because Mokhtar was such an incredibly detail-oriented and attentive interviewee and because the vast majority of the events depicted in the book had happened in the months before we met and began interviews, it was [reported as nonfiction]. All of the larger political context, whether it was a bombing in Ibb, or whether it was a Houthi takeover of Sa'dah, all of these other corollary political events took place parallel to his work.

All of these are part of the historical record. And so between the recentness of all the events and the incredible volume of other reporting done, it was relatively easy to confirm the veracity of all the events, the timing. And because Mokhtar is such an active documenter of his life, whether via Facebook, email, or WhatsApp, we were able to find and use countless pages and photos and entries—really everything from social media—and get events down to the minute in many cases. I was lucky to work with a really incredible amount of source material and ways to confirm all of the timings and dates and events to take.

Michelman: Mokhtar, I'm curious to ask you, once you knew that Dave had come on to the project and that it was happening, did you have to keep it quiet, or were able to talk about it with other people in your life? Were you able to tell people, you know, "Hey—Dave Eggers and I are hanging out and he's writing a book about me."

Mokhtar Alkhanshali: I mean, actually when the news finally came out, I felt bad because there were a few people I could only tell this to recently. And so I didn't tell anybody, I just kept it quiet. I'll give you an example. There was a Q course that Jodi [Wieser, of Gather Coffee Company] was taking at Boot. Dave was at that Q course with me, hanging out in the back, and Jodi had no idea he was there the whole time. She never knew until months later. She came to me and said, "Oh my God, I can't believe I just found out Dave Eggers wrote a book about you." And I'm like, "Gee, remember that time you were taking the Q course, that guy in the back taking notes?"

She's like, "Yeah."

"That was Dave Eggers."

She said, "Shut up" [*laughs*]. But in terms of telling people, I just didn't, really. For me I had a lot of things to work on—myself, my company—and I just didn't want to add to anything else besides that. Dave and I thought it would be best that way. Just keep things super quiet, especially as a journalist and a writer, be able to do things more effectively, and it was that way for a long time.

Eggers: It's important for me to always be as invisible as I possibly can. We had an understanding from the beginning that I would sort of, in many cases, follow him around without it being known that there might a book at the end of it. The last thing that's useful for me is sort of [to] walk straight into the door and announce to everybody that I'm going to be writing about their company or whatever it is. There were so many hours I spent at Boot and Blue Bottle and other places where I was just observing, sort of soaking things in.

Michelman: Mokhtar, for a nonfiction biography like this for which you are the subject, there are very real people in this book. There's your family, there's former employers, and there's even a pretty prominently featured old girlfriend. Have you gone back now and been like, "Hi, you're in this book about me"? How do you have that conversation with people? What is that like?

Alkhanshali: I was really lucky that Dave was the one writing this book. He is just incredibly great at making sure everybody involved is comfortable, and he's been through this a lot. So, for instance, Miriam, my ex-girlfriend—we're still great friends—he interviewed her and she knew what was happening. All the people in the book that I mentioned that way, they have all been a part of it, interviewed by Dave, and they had the option to like, change their name, and things like that. So it was important to myself also that this book was not just my story. It's a story about a lot of different people, about the Yemeni community, Yemeni scholars, and different people from the coffee community in Yemen. Making sure that it was an accurate portrayal was really important to both Dave and I. That was the case for the book and through the whole process.

Eggers: Yeah, there's no one depicted in the book and by name that was surprised to be depicted. I observed a thorough process of making sure everybody is aware and making sure that it's accurate from not just Mokhtar's point of view, but from their point of view, too. And so that's sort of the luxury of having so much time to do it is to make sure you can very soberly go through every word and make sure that every place where Miriam was mentioned, it's accurate, so that she doesn't wake up one day and is surprised to find herself in a book and feel like it wasn't the way she remembers.

Michelman: Dave, you talk about yourself, at the start of the book: you describe yourself as a coffee skeptic. And I'm curious to ask you now, What's changed about that? How has the process of writing this book changed how you feel about the wider take on coffee?

Dave Eggers: Well, I mean, I think I go through life skeptical about a lot of things. I'm a slow adopter when it comes to many things, especially things that, from a distance, seem trendy, for trendiness's sake, I guess. So I've been in San Francisco twenty-five years, and coming from Chicago, you come in with a cynic's eye, whether it's about yoga or legalized marijuana or coffee or nude beaches. It all seemed very exotic, very radical in a way, and I've grown to adopt everything, one by one. I grew to really appreciate the merits of yoga, for example, and I very much appreciate the slow food movement as I got to know it through publishing *Lucky Peach*. I got to know so many great food pioneers here through that, and publishing a lot of great food books through McSweeney's and becoming more and more familiar with where our food comes from.

You know, in the Bay Area, you can't help but absorb knowledge. There's so much awareness and so many enlightened people, and when it comes to food, so many great places to buy and experience it, and restaurants where you can trust that the food's been responsibly sourced. We are blessed by being surrounded by very enlightened food culture that you don't have to do all the work yourself. And for somebody like me, who is inherently lazy about this—I don't have necessarily all the time I want to do every bit of food research every day that I would like to—there are so many great, I don't know what to call them, go-betweens, whether it's your grocery store that you can trust that they have done the work and research for you, or whether it's a coffee shop that's done the work for you.

And so it's a long way of saying that I approach coffee the same way that I think the vast majority of people did even twenty years ago, thinking, my God, even I remember when I got to San Francisco and when I saw $1.75 for a cup of coffee or a latte, that just seemed extravagant and ludicrous. But slowly and surely, just as we realized we pay too little for most of our clothing and we pay too little for much of our food and we pay too little for a lot of goods that we buy, somebody along the supply chain is not being adequately compensated and corners are being cut.

And so it's the same way with coffee. And I've known this, intellectually, for many years about coffee, too; it's just that what I really didn't know was the level. I think it was the first day when we met at Blue Bottle that we popped in on a cupping and seeing that, and doing it at Boot Coffee many times, it was a whole other level. And even then the cupping aspect kicks in another skeptical impulse in me that says, "Oh my gosh, do we really have to go to this level of expertise and discernment when it comes to coffee?" And the answer is yes.

The way that Willem and Jodi and Mokhtar articulate the importance of cupping, the importance of the farmers who make the coffee having the same set of standards for those that are roasting and consuming, and how important that is to improving the prices paid and the lives of the farmers that are picking the crop, it was absolutely mind-blowing for me.

At a distance, a lot of people will look at this and see a level of erudition or pretentiousness, but if you really understand why this is all happening, and why there are cuppings and scorings and why people are using the vocabulary they are to describe certain varietals, it all comes back to actually caring about the farmers who are creating what's in your cup. And I think . . . That's what I was trying to get across in so much of the book, is coming at it from a skeptic's point of view and a generalist's point of view, I think I had a good position to explain it to other skeptics and other generalists and make it believable and credible, and maybe even convert a few people to understanding just how important it is to know the story behind how it all comes to your local café and into your cup.

That's a very long answer. Sorry, Jordan.

Michelman: No worries. I wanted to ask about a specific line in the text— there's this great beat in the book that I circled in my copy, where you're talking about Mokhtar and Willem Boot traveling together in Yemen. The line reads: "When Mokhtar and Willem met in the hotel lobby, something subtle shifted in their relationships. Willem was his teacher, but now Willem was in Yemen. He needed Mokhtar as much as Mokhtar needed him." And I wanted to ask you, Dave, did you ever feel like that as well, telling the story? Did you ever have your own moment, maybe traveling in Yemen or just in general, where you had that same thought to yourself as an author, as a journalist?

Eggers: Well, I was never in a position of expertise like Willem had been, so for me, the power, the knowledge balance was always that way, where I was always the student and Mokhtar was always the teacher. For Willem, being this world-renowned expert who had traveled the world and judged competitions and taught coffee cultivation and roasting and cupping for so many years, I think that was a new thing for him, to suddenly be on unfamiliar ground where Mokhtar had to be his guide and the noble expert. But for me, I was always learning. I was starting from scratch. I started from that place and I'm still in that place.

Michelman: There's all these different ways to unpack this story. It's an immigrant culture in America story, and it's also a really interesting class and money narrative—money serves as a kind of constant constraint throughout the book. But I'm curious if you thought of it at all generationally. Do you think of this as a millennial story?

Eggers: No, I don't think it's unique to Mokhtar's generation at all. I think it's a timeless story of the entrepreneurial zeal of somebody from an immigrant family. It's the story of this country. It's never been different. It's always been the same. Repeated every day in every city and every period. Our economy and the lifeblood of the nation is driven by the unfettered inspiration of young entrepreneurs, many of whom, an astonishingly high proportion of whom, have ties to other countries and might be first- or second-generation immigrants and who are seizing the American Dream with both hands.

But I do think that Mokhtar embodies that in a millennial way, interprets it or brings a millennial cast to it. Bones of Mokhtar's story are the same as so many stories throughout the last two hundred years. It's the same story of seeing the American Dream and reinventing oneself to seize it. But I don't know if you disagree, Mokhtar, if you think of it as a uniquely contemporary, millennial story.

Alkhanshali: That's an interesting question. You know, it's strange for me to see my name and the term *American Dream*, describing my journey that way, so it's hard for me to say. I will say that, yeah, that story that my grandparents heard when they came to this country—and my parents too, with their limited resource—well, we all hear stories of immigrants and what they were able to accomplish here. But it seems like that for my generation, as millennials, that upward mobility and opportunity has become very difficult to realize.

Eggers: Yes.

Alkhanshali: When I was growing up my ambition was just to get a job as a bus driver, so I could have health benefits. But I always read a lot of books, and always had this thing in the back of my head, this fantasy world I lived in. In many ways I probably fueled a lot of my ambition, and then, it's hard for me not to believe in this dream when I see where I am today. And I can talk to young people who maybe feel trapped in the system, in a box, and I was there, too. We do face difficulties, and there are systems that might be against you, but it doesn't mean you can just give up. Maybe you don't have to cross an ocean on a boat like me, but it's universal.

Michelman: That makes sense, and it feeds back into ways in which class and money are constraints in the book. No spoilers, but at one point in the book, you're trying to rent an apartment at a building you used to work in, and the person who is considering leasing it to you is attempting to figure out if you're a Saudi prince, or if you have a ton of money, which you do not. And ultimately it's your connection to coffee that impresses him enough to get the spot.

The narrative has to have that, you know? For it to be meaningful to get your dream apartment, you need to have been working there as a door guy in the first place. It wraps itself into the narrative.

Alkhanshali: That's my trick. You know, "started from the bottom, now I'm here." While I lived there I couldn't tell anyone because it was too fantastical. Who could believe I was a doorman there? I don't even tell people. It's hard to explain my life because it's just strange. That's one of the reasons I wanted to do this book. I'm not a Saudi prince. I am the opposite.

I think that in life, you have to experience bitter moments to be able to appreciate sweet moments, and there were moments in my book that are really hilarious. There are moments that are really not funny at all, and I have a hard time talking about that. I have never mentioned those, especially if you read the last third of the book, the last hundred pages, really, are just pretty intense, and it's hard for me to speak about that.

Again, like for me, I know I could not have done this journey with anyone else. Dave is really just a very caring and passionate person and was very endearing, and you have to feel comfortable being verbal with him, and I don't think I could have done that with anyone else.

Michelman: Thank you both very much, and best of luck on the book tour.

Eggers: Thank you.

Alkhanshali: Thank you.

Up Lifting: A Talk with Dave Eggers

Betsy Bird / 2018

From *A Fuse #8*, May 8, 2018. © 2018 by School Library Journal. Reprinted by permission.

Betsy Bird: We'll start with a generalization for kicks. At this point in time you've written three recent books for children in the last two years. The first two were picture books that examined those grandiose structures the Statue of Liberty (*Her Right Foot*) and the Golden Gate Bridge (*This Bridge Will Not Be Gray*). Your first middle-grade novel is about the very structure of a town collapsing into the earth. What is the benefit to asking kids to question and observe closely the seemingly safe and sturdy world that exists around them?

Dave Eggers: Wow, good question. Now that you put it that way, I do think there must be some subconscious thread between these three books. Well, there's the obvious thread involving iconic American structures in the first two, but I think you just deftly found the common thread with *The Lifters*, too. Maybe at a time when so many people live so much of their lives in the virtual world, it's important to continually remind young readers of the importance of—and the relentlessly fascinating stories of—the physical world. With *The Lifters*, much of it was written in uncertain times, so there's that jittery feeling throughout, that the ground beneath us might not be rock-solid. And that it might be up to kids to see it clearly and save all humans.

BB: Technically you've done work with kids for years, dating back to the creation of 826 Valencia with Nínive Calegari back in 2002. Since then it has become a national institution. I think we all thought you might start churning out the children's books then, but aside from the occasional short story in *McSweeney's* it was not forthcoming. Why have you chosen to write for kids now? And has your work with 826 influenced how you write for younger readers in any way?

DE: You know, I was always trying to get back to writing for young readers. We did an issue of *McSweeney's* dedicated to parables for kids; that was back in 2007, I think. In 2009 or 2010 I wrote *The Wild Things*, an all-ages chapter book based on Sendak's picture book, and that really whetted my appetite. Around then, Alessandro Baricco asked me to reimagine *20,000 Leagues Under the Sea*, and that was a blast. I'd never had more fun as a writer. Then, like many adults, I suppose, when I had kids and began reading to them, ideas for picture books started coming a bit faster, and there was that urgency to finish a story or two so I might be able to read my own picture books to my own kids before they grew up.

In terms of the influence of 826 National, in the last sixteen years I've learned so much from the kids in all the centers around the country. Mac Barnett and Jory John came through 826, too, and I think we all learned a lot about how kids read and what they respond to. I even had a committee of 826 students who read *The Lifters* in manuscript form to give me feedback. As editors, young people are very sincere, and they will not pull punches in telling you what's working and what's not. But they are also the purest and most patient readers. They want to love a book. I've seen this over the life of 826: kids truly want to love the books they pick up, and because they are so new to books, each one they get through leaves an indelible mark on their psyche.

BB: It's interesting to think about how an author shifts gears between writing for adults and writing for kids. Do you write for children and adults simultaneously, or do you compartmentalize, finishing one project first before proceeding on to another?

DE: I'm usually working on different things at the same time, in part because it's important to let a manuscript cool off a bit between drafts. I usually write a draft of a story or a novel and then let it sit for a few months, so I can get a cold read on it later. In the meantime, I might push forward on a different book. In the case of picture books, the process really is conducive to working on multiple stories at the same time. If I write the text to a picture book, it will take the illustrator upwards of a year to do the artwork—which is really an unfair advantage we writers have—and in the meantime I can get going on something else. So in a way, it involves compartmentalization, but the compartments are not airtight.

BB: I sometimes think that authors who have sacrificed the proper small animals to the illustration gods reap the rewards later. In your case it must have been quite the fine fat goose indeed to not only receive interior art from noted graphic novelist Aaron Renier, but also cover art from the Fan Brothers. Did you have any input on the art during the creation of this book? How did it line up with the images already in your head?

DE: In the case of *The Lifters*, I had a notion of what the cover might look like, so I did the crudest sketch imaginable, and the Fan Brothers took it from there and made the spectacular image on the cover. They really are extraordinary.

For the interior, I wanted the book to appeal to reluctant readers, like the reader I was as a kid, so I knew a certain frequency of images was crucial. I've seen so many readers, boys in particular, tune out if there's no imagery on a given spread. It's a weird phenomenon, but it's true, and I know that was essential for me when I was a young reader: If I flipped through a book and there wasn't the right ratio of text to pictures, I would put it down.

Because I wanted some kind of imagery on every spread, I asked Aaron Renier if he'd be willing. I knew he could create very mysterious and moody worlds like he did with *Walker Bean*, and I knew—because he illustrates for kids at 826 Chicago—that he was fast. Because we needed to do so many images on a somewhat tight schedule, the publisher let me and Aaron handle the process, communicating directly. The conversation was open and free and ridiculously fun all the way through.

BB: If *The Lifters* owes its style, pacing, or ideas to any other beloved children's books, what would those books be?

DE: I really set out to write an all-ages book that I would have wanted to read as a kid, but that wouldn't bore an adult who might be reading it aloud to a class or child at bedtime. So to that end I reread a bunch of classics from my own youth, but I can't say any of them helped me in this case. The one author who helped show me the way was Kate DiCamillo. Her book *The Tiger Rising* demonstrated the mix of naturalism and magical realism that I wanted to achieve. I wanted *The Lifters* to represent a world that was very familiar to a young reader, with schools and homes and streets and hills, but then it has this pulsing mystery just beneath the surface.

BB: Will we be seeing more children's books from you in the future?

DE: There are a bunch more in various stages of production. Shawn Harris is finishing the art for a book called *What Can a Citizen Do?*, and the great Laura Park is illustrating a silly picture book called *Abner and Ian Get Right-Side Up*.

I was able to do an event for *The Lifters* yesterday and met a bunch of young readers, a few of whom had already read it, even though it came out a week ago. That was really trippy, and led to a very great conversation with a nine-year-old named Rena. Every time I meet a young reader who's read something I wrote, it just knocks me flat.

As you probably know, I grew up down the road from Evanston and went to high school with Amy Krouse Rosenthal. We got to know each other as adults, and when she started writing for young people—and this has happened with Mac and Jory, too—I saw the profound effect their work had on kids in general, and on my kids in particular. Kids are so open and impressionable, and so appreciative of the goofy and absurd, that writing for them, trying to delight and edify them, is the most enjoyable thing I think a human can do. And these authors, starting with Amy, seemed just aglow at all times, surrounded and buoyed by the purest readers there are. Now I've been able to live in this world for a while, I can say there's no better place to be.

An Interview with Dave Eggers about New His Novel, *The Parade*

Knopf / 2019

From *McSweeney's Internet Tendency*, February 1, 2019. © 2019 by McSweeney's. Reprinted by permission.

Q: Tell us about the beginnings of *The Parade*—inspirations and catalysts.

A: The first inkling emerged in 2004, when Valentino Deng and I traveled back to what is now South Sudan. We flew from Nairobi to Lokichoggio, which was then the staging ground for international aid to the south. We were heading to Valentino's hometown, Marial Bai.

Q: You traveled by road, like the road in *The Parade*?

A: Well, no, there were no roads that could take you from Kenya all the way to Marial Bai. We had to fly, but there were no commercial flights at the time into South Sudan. The civil war was still going on, though there was a ceasefire in place. So we flew from Nairobi to Lokichoggio, and then Valentino negotiated with some people from a Norwegian aid agency to allow us to sit in the cargo hold of a flight bringing medicine and bicycles into the country.

Q: And you made it to Marial Bai?

A: We did, but first the plane made a bunch of stops, including one in the Nuba Mountains. There we got out for an hour or two, and some of the cargo was unloaded, and while that was happening, out of nowhere a Jeep sped onto the airstrip, full of four or five Western men and women in military gear. Our Russian pilots—at that time it seemed all the pilots going into South Sudan were Russian—told us that these were arms inspectors, there to make sure the plane wasn't bringing guns into the country. They took their work seriously, but there was a swagger about how they did it, too. They jumped off the Jeep like they were in a music video. That image stuck with me.

Q: The adventure-seeker in a war zone. Is that the model for the character named Nine? I should point out that the two main characters go by assumed names, Four and Nine, given they don't want to make themselves vulnerable to kidnapping. Four is nicknamed "The Clock" and is more responsible and businesslike, whereas Nine is flighty and unreliable.

A: There's some of those arms inspectors in Nine. He's the kind of guy who would leap from a Jeep wearing mirrored sunglasses.

Q: But Four and Nine aren't UN arms inspectors and aren't affiliated with any government.

A: No, they're just private contractors. They build roads anywhere they're paid to. On another trip to South Sudan, we saw the beginnings of a massive highway that was being built to connect parts of the south with the north. The way it cut through the forest looked like the path of a tornado. They had just removed every tree and every human dwelling. It was incredible. This was just after the civil war and was meant to symbolize the connecting of the two previously warring halves of the country.

Q: We would assume the road crews were American, given the US was involved in brokering the peace between the north and south?

A: Well, that's just the thing. The crew was Swedish. All of the equipment was Swedish. A Swedish crew was building a road through South Sudan.

Q: It would be easy to see this as a comment on American interventions, or Western colonialism. But it seems like you took pains to make sure that no countries were named—not the country the book is set in, and not the nationality of the contractors.

A: American readers are quick to assume the guilty party is always them. There's a huge swath of our people who assume everything our country does is noble and pure, and there's a smaller but very powerful segment of us who are guilt-ridden Americans, and who assume we're responsible for, or complicit with, every evil in the world. But both sides suffer from a national narcissism that's probably a bit unique to the US—good or bad, it's always about us.

Q: Right. But increasingly, this isn't true.

A: These contractors, Four and Nine, could be from any industrialized country. Now, for example, the roads in South Sudan, and in much of Africa, are being built by the Chinese. All over the world, for centuries, foreign contractors have built roads, ports, bridges, and dams. And often they do so without much concern for how these things aid the host country's autocratic regimes, or further the misery of the people of that country. Those are themes I'm interested in. I don't want *The Parade* to be read as a comment on American interventions, because that would limit its scope, just as it would limit its scope to think of the book as taking place in South Sudan. After seeing that highway being built in South Sudan fifteen years ago, I've seen similar infrastructure projects in places like Saudi Arabia and Bosnia, and always there are similarities in the interplay between the foreign workers and the locals.

Q: Such as?

A: There's an aloofness, for starters—an intentional distance kept, and sometimes with heavy security. I saw that in Papua New Guinea—incredible security there, and contractors being transported around in armed vehicles. And often there's a sense that the workers want nothing to do with whatever political implications there are to their work. They want to be left alone to do it, get paid, and go home. It's the same, in a way, with the contractors who built the samples at the Mexican-US border.

Q: The samples of Trump's prospective wall?

A: About a year ago, I went on a tour with some other journalists, led by Homeland Security and the Border Patrol. We went out to the desert at the border between San Diego and Mexico, and saw the wall samples, and it was profoundly surreal and disturbing. The border guards and the Homeland Security officers were very open and willing to answer any questions, but we weren't allowed to talk to, or photograph, any of the contractors who had built the wall samples. They disappeared from view pretty quickly. They wanted nothing to do with the controversy around the wall. They just wanted to collect the fees—the contracting companies were paid a significant fee for those samples, by the way—and go home. The role of engineers and laborers who built those samples was connected, in my mind at least, to Four and Nine building their road in *The Parade*.

Q: They're just following orders.

A: But maybe they're doing nothing wrong. It depends on how much we assume they know about the impact of their work. But I'm interested in what motivations and worldview Nine and Four would have brought with them to that work. Were they invested emotionally or intellectually in what was happening, or what had happened, during the civil war? They're paving a highway that cuts through former battlefields, and they no doubt had to move aside human and mechanical evidence of the war, and they're passing through all this war-ravaged land, and they have to either remain emotionally closed to it all, or, if they become involved at all, the project could unravel and they could expose themselves to significant danger. It's easier to remain quiet and do the work.

Q: It seems connected, in a way, to Ishiguro's butler in *The Remains of the Day*, who serves as a silent witness to history.

A: Right. I'm interested in characters who are close to the action but have no dog in the fight. Or they haven't deemed it necessary to pick a side.

Q: When I read *The Parade*, I thought of Coetzee's *Waiting for the Barbarians*, another novel where the author purposely doesn't name the country or time in which it takes place.

A: After I finished *The Parade*, one of the first people I sent it to was the writer and editor Nyuol Tong, and he mentioned *Waiting for the Barbarians* right away. I can't tell you how much I admire Coetzee, and how much his books have meant to me, but I hadn't read *Waiting for the Barbarians*. Then I did, and of course found that similar attempt to set the story apart from any one nation or specific period in time. But it's a story told within a deeply naturalistic setting. *Waiting for the Barbarians* isn't a fable, and I wouldn't call *The Parade* a fable, either. I'm not sure I could give it a label, but the story's been with me for a long time now, and it feels good to have exorcised it.

An Interview with Dave Eggers about His New Novel, *The Captain and the Glory*

Knopf / 2019

From *McSweeney's Internet Tendency*, October 10, 2019. © 2019 by McSweeney's. Reprinted by permission.

Q: When did you begin writing this book? Tell us about how it started.

A: I'd been covering the Trump era as a journalist since back in August of 2016, and I think like most writers, and most humans, trying to convey the madness of the time was hard to do in journalism. Or rather, in my reporting, when I met actual Trump supporters, they were always far more sane and reasonable than Trump himself, so it created this weird paradox, where at a Trump rally, for example, by far the craziest person in the stadium was Trump himself. So I'd get to know Trump supporters and go home and feel almost pacified by their reasonableness. I'd temporarily forget the towering crimes and cruelty perpetuated by the man. This book was the opposite of the kindly conversation with the reasonable Trump supporter. This was an attempt to understand this era by painting it in the gaudy and garish colors it really deserves.

Q: Careful readers will notice a resemblance to a certain sitting US president, but that person's name doesn't appear in the text. Why?

A: This is part farce, part parable, and I do hope, though the Captain bears more than a passing a resemblance to Trump, that the book will be readable when Trump is gone. That's part of the reason I called it *An Entertainment* on the title page. It's a nod to Graham Greene but also the way I hope people will read it. It was cathartic to write and I hope cathartic to read.

Q: Inevitably there will be more tragedy, more jaw-dropping incompetence and cruelty under our current leadership. Why publish it now?

A: I think we need satire in real time to help us deal with this moment. Otherwise the pain is too great.

Q: The subject matter is dire, but the book is laugh-out-loud funny throughout. How did you balance that? And how have readers responded to that aspect?

A: I had a blast writing it, because I abandoned logic and rationality, which is both part of the Trump era and crucial to comedy.

Q: Tell us about the illustrations—by Nathaniel Russell—and what they add to the text.

A: An editor I work with, Em-J Staples, knew Nat's work and connected us. When I was finishing the text, I ran across an edition of James Thurber's *The 13 Clocks*, with art by Marc Simont. It worked so well, and in color it added so much, so I asked Nat to imagine the characters any way he saw fit, so long as the tone was sinister. I wanted that juxtaposition of the text's manic energy with a kind of cool brutality to the artwork.

Q: During the course of writing it, did you do anything different than you usually do in terms of keeping up with current news events?

A: I keep up with the news far too much for a healthy life. But I did have to give up trying to include every last Trumpian crime in the book. The novel has a specific take on this moment, and it doesn't try to cover everything—that would be futile. Once the nature of the story was in place, that it involved a ship and its passengers and an unsteady captain, I let the narrative run its course without trying to mirror everything Trump has actually done. It's more a look at how someone like Trump would operate in such a situation, and what ultimately motivates him, which is really naked fear.

Q: *The Captain and the Glory* looks at the current US political situation a step or two removed from how we're experiencing it now, which essentially feels like an international perspective. Did you intentionally consider how other nations are viewing what's unfolding here as you were writing?

A: Weirdly, I finished writing the book in Idaho, which is about as American as you could get. But I do think we all need some remove from the day-to-day events to see clearly what's been happening. Setting the events on a ship gives the story some sense of containment, and giving this story an ending, I think, is comforting at a moment where we really don't know where we're heading.

Q: The book's youngest character is also the one who shows the most leadership and strength. Is that a reflection of how you view the world as it is now—or how you believe the world should be?

A: I do think young people have a moral clarity that we often lack as adults. They see through the bullshit and call a crime a crime. Yesterday Trump, in front of multiple cameras, asked China to investigate Joe Biden, his possible opponent in the next election. That's impeachable on its face, and yet the news coverage, and congressional reaction, has been muted and equivocal. We're either numb, or no longer able to tell the difference between surreal television and actual crimes against our democracy. Yesterday represented both. Ana, the young girl in the story, represents, I think, our better American selves, and she's just flat-out heartbroken by her compatriots' embrace of and fealty to the very worst human on the ship. In a way, this goes back to my journalism. I've been to a bunch of Trump rallies and have interviewed so many normal people who rationalize their support of him, and I always leave feeling almost calm, having met a startlingly diverse group of reasonable people who have in common their support of this man. That's the adult part of me, who sees all the nuances and can empathize with where these Trump voters are coming from. But then there's the Ana part of me, part of so many of us, that's screaming out, who just can't believe that we've lowered our standards so much that among 320 million people, we expect and embrace the most foul and cretinous lunatic of us all.

The Ship of State: A Conversation with Dave Eggers

Tom Lutz / 2019

From the *Los Angeles Review of Books*, November 22, 2019. © 2019 by the *Los Angeles Review of Books*. Reprinted by permission.

Tom Lutz: You write nonfiction, fiction, and now *The Captain and the Glory*, which is satirical fable. Or allegory? What do you call it, and why this form for this piece?

Dave Eggers: I think every story has its right form, and for this, for now, allegorical satire—if that is a thing, and maybe it is, because I say so—seemed like the right form.

Lutz: There has been a school of thought that this administration is so wacked in so many ways that it made satire impossible—it satirizes itself. I've seen this in academic novels, too, sometimes—the reality's distance from common ground can leave satire wanting. I remember reading one academic satire and thinking, "Wow, the reality is actually worse than this." Was the project daunting for this reason?

Eggers: Absolutely daunting. But I think that's where allegory comes in. Setting this in contemporary Washington, DC, with the actual president in the actual White House, would be impossible to satirize. But if you move the action to a ship, and reduce the cast of characters a bit, and introduce new ones and new themes, then it can have a new and different sort of life. This story is parallel to the one we're living, but it can be read, I think, without knowing the first thing about American politics. That was my hope, at least. You really only need to care about people, ships, maritime law, piracy, adult men who say they want to date their daughters, and maybe even human rights, too.

Lutz: But of course it is better if you do know something about our current ship of state, right?

Eggers: Sure. But the hope, my hope at least, is to give readers a bit of a respite, even while they know this story parallels our actual situation. Instead of, or in addition to, reading the transcripts from the impeachment hearings—which are phenomenally lucid and riveting, by the way—American citizens might also want to read about a very terrified man-baby who becomes the captain of a ship, even though he doesn't like boats or water.

Lutz: Forty percent of the US population that responds to surveys seems unshakable in its support for Trump. Do you have any sense that you are talking to them?

Eggers: A while back, I signed up for Trump's email list, to see what he sent his followers, and today I got an email that invited me to participate in a survey. That survey asked me who I'd be voting for in 2020, and it gave me two choices: one red button said Trump; the other red button said A Socialist Democrat. I did not make that up.

Then again, I've been to many Trump rallies as a journalist, and have interviewed so many attendees, and I have to say, uniformly, that the people I talked to were always willing to chat, ponder, consider, and reason. I'm absolutely sure there are some frothing caveman lunatic racists at these rallies, but the people I've met have been a startlingly diverse group of people who support Trump for a wide variety of reasons, some of them very narrow: they like his views on the military, for instance, or the police. Or they credit him with a strong economy. At the same time, they have reservations. They roll their eyes. But they have been extremely open and intellectually nimble with me, and I usually come away thinking that much of his support is less loony and unshakable than I feared. If, for example, the economy was not strong, he would be in deep trouble.

All that said, what's clear at every rally I've seen is that of the ten thousand or so people present, the weirdest, most brazenly demented person in the room is the one at the microphone. And that's a phenomenon that should puzzle anthropologists for centuries.

Lutz: I just wrote my first novel after a lot of nonfiction, and I was surprised to find myself feeling oddly exposed in the fiction—I had thought I would feel hidden, disguised, defended, but instead I felt like my Freudian slip was showing, and more exposed than I feel when I'm writing about my own travels or experience. You obviously move from genre to genre quite comfortably, but can you speak to the particular issues you faced as a writer taking on this new form?

Eggers: Well, back in the day, I wrote satire quite a bit. We even had a satirical magazine, *Might*, for many years, so I feel like much of my twenties was spent writing in a satirical voice. Returning to it felt very liberating and oddly cathartic. The writing in *Captain* flowed in a way that was weirdly jubilant at times, especially given the horror of much of the story.

Lutz: That makes me think that yes, there is a bit of satirical voice in *Heartbreaking Work* and elsewhere, like in *You Shall Know Our Velocity!*

Eggers: There's a through line there for sure, though it's different here of course. There wasn't the same kind of narrative distance in those books. Here I tried to give this story a blithe, omniscient narrator—a bit of Thackeray and some Fielding, and then again not much of either.

Lutz: I assume the subtitle, *An Entertainment*, is a reference to Graham Greene, who I love, and steal from quite a bit myself. Some of Greene's "entertainments" were screenplays first, and some were, like *The Captain and the Glory*, darkly humorous. How do you see the relation? And do you see a screenplay here?

Eggers: I don't see a screenplay, I don't think. But while finishing *Captain*, and just a few weeks before I had to turn it in, I was reading *The Comedians* and was reminded of Greene's sometime-subtitle, and it seemed perfectly appropriate for *The Captain*. I don't know of Greene's intentions when he added that moniker to certain books, but I like the way it sets the reader up to expect something light and airy, when in fact most of those books were anything but . . .

Lutz: It occurs to me that *The Parade* exists somewhere between Greene's work and the world of *The Captain and the Glory*.

Eggers: *The Parade* definitely exists in Greene's world, I think, though I hadn't had him in mind while writing it. (Conrad, yes.) Outside of the subtitle, *The Captain* doesn't really owe anything to Greene. It's much more insane and surreal than his work, which is—at least I see it as—more earthbound and true to the workings of the actual world. I wanted *Captain* to be heightened, to exist in its own world with its own rules and constraints, but with far less logic.

Lutz: Speaking of remaining true to the workings of the actual world: your nonfiction is quite varied, including the complex memoir *A Heartbreaking Work of Staggering Genius* and books like *Zeitoun* and *The Monk of Mokha*, which are other people's stories—novel-length profiles, would you call them? For my creative nonfiction students, can you say something about working in that form?

Eggers: I would just classify those books as nonfiction accounts of recent history, seen through the eyes of one or two protagonists, depending on the book. For whatever reason, we learn history better when our emotions are involved, when we can live that historical moment in a way only possible through the written word, and at a certain length. Novels and narrative nonfiction give us the chance to inhabit the mind—and see through the eyes of—another human and to experience that inimitable empathy transference.

Lutz: Both books do have a take on empathy and its lack. I don't want to provide any spoilers, but did you know when you started *The Captain and the Glory* that you wanted the ending to have the emotional resonance it does? It is very different than the way *The Parade* ends, for instance.

Eggers: I wrote most of the first draft about six months after Trump was elected. The first passage I wrote is the one where we witness the actual decision of the passengers of *The Glory* to entrust their lives to the ship's least trusted man. Then I put the book aside for a while, finished *The Parade*, and after a time came back to *Captain*. And I still liked it, and still thought it said something I wasn't seeing out there. So I dug in again and had that weirdly cathartic experience I described before—and an unexpected momentum in finishing the book. The ending, then, came almost as a surprise to myself. Very often, and definitely with *The Parade*, I know the general shape of the ending before I begin. In this case, I found myself writing something that was decidedly hopeful at the end, and I had to let that sit for a bit, to be sure it was earned and true. But it does reflect how I feel. I do think we're in a very anomalous, feverish time, where millions are dancing around a golden calf, without all their wits. I do think the fever will break, and we will, I believe, find ourselves returning to our better selves.

Nautical Disaster and the American Disconnect: An Interview with Author Dave Eggers

Brock Wilbur / 2020

From *The Pitch*, January 17, 2020. © Carey Media, LLC. Reprinted by permission.

Dave Eggers is an award-winning author, best known for his work *A Heartbreaking Work of Staggering Genius* and for founding the literary magazine *McSweeney's*. Amid his work running nonprofits and churning out books, he's been touring the country in the last year, hitting up as many Trump-supporter rallies as he can. He's trying to get to the heart of . . . what's going on out there.

Stemming from this period in his career, Eggers has released a new new book called *The Captain and the Glory: An Entertainment*. It's the tale of a ship's foul captain who has no knowledge of how to command a ship but takes on the job out of a mixture of spite and a need to shake things up. The ship, named the *Glory*, embarks on a dangerous journey wherein the only people who seem to profit are the Captain's incompetent and corrupt cronies.

This book may not be just about maritime life. Who's to say?

We sat down with Dave Eggers for a discussion about the place of literature in the modern age, the dream of moving his business to KC, and where to find optimism when it is in perilously short supply.

Dave Eggers: How are things in Kansas City? Are you a Chiefs fan?
Brock Wilbur: If I wasn't, they'd run me out of town.
Eggers: Yeah, I have a good friend who is the biggest Chiefs fan. He's in New York these days, so I have to hear about it every time you win. But my 49ers are going to be meeting you guys very soon, I think. I think it's a colli-

sion course. Nothing standing in the way. They would be drastically different offenses, but to see our defense against Mahomes would be fascinating.

Wilbur: Well, speaking of people leading a team . . . *The Captain and the Glory*. I think that you must be tired, at this point, of answering people's jokes about "Is there a metaphor here?" Why did you choose to tell the story this way, and why did you think now was the time to tell it?

Eggers: If you're anybody in the arts at all, you're trying to figure out how to respond to this time. Ever since the campaign of 2016, I was so shocked and bewildered and disappointed and confused by what was going on, and what I saw as a real radical shift in the level of public discourse, civility, and decency in politics—not that politics has been this bastion of decency since the birth of the republic, but I think that we expect some higher level of discourse. We had that for eight years.

No matter where you stand on the political spectrum, I think we can all agree that Barack Obama was a very decent human, and I think he showed our children that this is how a decent adult behaves. When that changed radically, you wonder how to respond, what an appropriate way to talk about the era is.

I've done a lot of journalism since the campaign of 2016, and covered Trump rallies and the effect of his policies on immigrants in particular. During all of that, I felt like I was getting a sober and reasonable set of truths from the era. None of that necessarily reflected the absurd, heightened bizarreness of the time. So I went to fiction and I went back to satire, and I thought that maybe this is a way to get near the cartoonish level of crazy that we live in.

Using allegory, setting everything on a cruise ship—which is sort of inherently comical—and reducing the cast of characters a bit, having a smaller world with its own set of rules, it trained me to get at some deeper truths and put things in starker relief. I found some of the more essential takeaways of the time. Setting a satire in contemporary DC with characters that are closer to the ones we know in real life would be harder and less interesting or even funny.

Reality is outstripping the power of satire every day. But changing the venue and changing the rules of the universe a little bit sort of was cathartic for me to write, and I think it will be cathartic for people to read and laugh a bit, and I think the biggest catharsis or comfort is that this book has an ending. That's the beauty of fiction or storytelling in general: you can contain the chaos of life within two covers. Here's the beginning, here's the middle, here's the end. Whether that's false comfort or not, at least for a moment, it gives us a way out. It finishes this chapter in American history.

Wilbur: Before I cracked the book, just in reading the description, there was a part of me that worried—this is tethered to a very specific time and I wonder about how it will age. By the time I finished the book, I shared your belief that this was the best manner in which to capture the absurdity of our time. This is the closest thing I've read to George Orwell's *Animal Farm*. That's a period I obviously didn't live through, but I can live through the absurdity via that text, and that's what carries on. And unfortunately finds new meaning later. That's why your book is an important book. It feels like it will both always be anchored in this era, but that it explains our national disconnect in a way that no textbook ever could.

Eggers: I reread *Animal Farm*, maybe once a year, and that was of his time, in a time when communism and capitalism were battling for the souls of humanity in a way that's not really at play as much right now. If it read in its time, I think it had a different meaning. I think readers then would've read different things into it, would've read different parallels to their time. And now, we can see it with a cold analytical eye, as more of a timeless allegory. But I don't know if you ever read *It Can't Happen Here*, the Sinclair Lewis book. When Trump was elected, *It Can't Happen Here* and *1984* went back on the bestseller list. I hadn't read it, but he had gone and interviewed dozens of people who were living through the rise of fascism in the 1930s in Europe. He sort of, as the title implies, he's trying to apply what happened in Europe to the West, and how easily it can occur. That book, again—you'd think that it's so specific to a time and a place, but the book is phenomenally readable, applicable, entertaining, and terrifying, with a few twists. It could all happen now, too.

You see the blueprint. Some of the best fiction has a specificity of time and place, but also a timelessness that we all search for. You can't try to write a timeless book, you know? It won't have any teeth; the specificity is the key. But ideally, there's lessons for all of time. I think, with what we're living through, we're seeing that success, charisma, and disruption is all very inclined toward self-harm. We think of elections as a protest or as an act of vandalism, or an act of gleeful disruption, sticking it to the establishment.

It's a very strange impulse that we have.

Again and again, you don't take our vote all that seriously, and you don't take our president all that seriously, and we again and again elect people who we would not hire in our companies or our businesses. We hire stable, steady, honest, stalwart, true fellow humans to work with us and handle our finances and unclog our toilets. But when it comes to the presidency, we throw all of that reason to the wind, and we're willing to roll the dice on someone who—regardless of his policies—is very erratic, very disrespectful, unpredictable, crude, ungenerous, punitive, immature, and grammatically challenged.

So history, maybe it's always been this way, but certainly we will get to a place where we take elections more seriously. That was an odd time when the clowniest clown of all could be elected to lead a storied and, in so many ways, admirable, glorious nation. We'd elect what everybody would consider one of the strangest and most unreliable humans among them. That's a weird thing for a sociologist to study, you know? Very strange. In every ancient society back to the Neanderthals, I'm sure there's the wise elder who rules judiciously. With all of this experience, they go to this person because they are wise, cautious, thoughtful, and they draw on all of their experience and they quietly issue a ruling that is acceptable to all. They go to the most stable and wisdom-filled of society. But we've almost done the opposite here, which is just very interesting from an anthropological perspective.

Wilbur: Thinking of politics as self-harm, that strikes a big chord in me because I know I would be much happier if I didn't spend all day every day with a phone in my hand, switching between news apps and social media and then watching news in front of me on the TV at the same time. I probably am not affecting anything except making myself miserable for the last three years.

Eggers: I try to get my politics in gulps. I think we all have to find ways to live in this time because you know, yesterday, the president, a man who is—I think he's seventy? He retweeted a doctored photo of two of his political opponents wearing traditional Muslim clothing in an effort to somehow shame or insult them with this association that he considers undesirable. Also, he somehow tries to conflate them—there's no way to even explain what he did in a way that makes sense or is acceptable or isn't outrageous and completely unprecedented.

We spent so long waiting for an impeachable crime, when I think something as even comparatively minor as that—if we do take ourselves seriously, and we do have a sense of decency, and we have respect for the office of the presidency and the honor of the White House, or we attach honor to it—that act alone of insulting and trying to slander one's political enemies through association with a military leader of Iran, that itself is an impeachable act. That is a misdemeanor and a high crime, too. That is completely beyond the pale.

But we've come to expect so little of Trump, and we have such low expectations for his behavior and thus the behavior of any president, that we've completely lost our way. We've lost the scale, the proportionality, we've lost the sense of decency, and what is decent, and who we are in relation to that. We can't recognize it anymore. That one act would have led to the downfall of any other sitting president; I really think so. But because we're the frogs, and we've been in this boiling water for so long, we don't know anymore the signs of our own boiling in a bubbling cauldron of insanity.

Wilbur: As the author of *The Circle*, you might have an opinion on this, but do you think that it's possible that social media is dividing us?

Eggers: There's so few places where everyone comes together to get one set of news. Social media has made it insanely easy to put oneself in an echo chamber where you only hear the same voices again and again, and they're heightened and they're outraged and they're hyperpartisan. If you look at the numbers for any one newscast, whether it's MSNBC or CNN or Fox News or whatever, they are so much smaller in terms of viewership than it used to be when you were watching Cronkite or you had a few other choices, and all of those newscasters were, I think, somewhat centrist and moderate and everybody was sharing one conversation.

I like the democratization of the media landscape. I like that I can create a blog or a social media venue that has potentially unlimited readership or listenership. I think it's a good thing. But at the same time, it had this unexpected consequence. People are no longer interested in a central, moderate conversation, but more feeding on—engorging on—the most extreme, self-replicating opinions. I think it does create a hyperpartisanship. If you only read one left-leaning news site every day, and that news site demonizes even the middle, where Biden is considered a Republican, etc., etc., then I think it's inevitable that you lose sight of the nuances of a political debate and the rationality.

You lose interest in the middle ground, you lose interest in the humanity of every part of the political spectrum, and you really stop listening to the other side. I don't know how many venues or opportunities there are just to meet and listen to people with different political beliefs.

It's one of the reasons I started going to Trump rallies. I could not understand why fellow rational adults could support this clearly unqualified person. Then, when I met the people, I almost invariably liked everyone I met, right when the articles of impeachment were handed down. I met so many people that I liked. We had all of these reasonable conversations and debates with people who were willing to listen. I listened, they listened, and it became almost invariable that we found ourselves inches away in terms of differences. I think that almost everybody I met would be convinceable that there may be a better way. I really do think—I've never met an unchangeable mind, actually. Maybe I just get lucky in the people I meet.

I do find everybody to be very reasonable and malleable. In the aggregate of these rallies, it can look mindless and sometimes scary. But individually, I think voters can be convinced. But we do have a lot of education to do, from kindergarten on I'd say, that democracy is serious and sober, governing matters, and people that occupy every office from the city council to the presidency should be the best among us. You know? We should be always electing not the flashiest, loudest person, but the most reasonable, most empathetic, and in some cases, not necessarily the most charismatic among us.

Wilbur: It ties into something that makes politics in the Midwest for us very tricky. It's difficult to be left-leaning here because, as difficult as the conversations are across the aisle, there's also a sort of dismissive tone about being a flyover state. Everyone out here in a state that went to Trump is therefore a Trump supporter. It creates a complicated box that trickles down to making the language of big ideas fall apart.

Eggers: You know, that blue-red designation is only, what, twenty years old? Wasn't it from 1998 election, I think? It's very new. It was done by one of the networks just to kind of indicate on the electoral map which way a state had voted. That quirk of one producer's idea on a network broadcast has further divided us.

I'm from Illinois, I grew up in a farm region of central Illinois. So my older brother was a Republican who worked for the George Bush Foundation, etc. So I've always been intimately aware of and in constant conversation with conservatives, and I'm always able to have productive conversations with them. The history of bipartisanship in this country when both sides are acting in the public interest . . . I love these bipartisan anecdotes and pieces of legislation. The McCain-Lieberman bill comes to mind. So many pieces of legislation that relied on a spirit of compromise.

In Congress, when you've been elected to do something, you've no choice but to get it done. This has changed quite a bit; there are so few examples. It's become difficult to compromise in the eyes of politicians, and voters, too. I don't think that they're aware necessarily of what it means to pass legislation, and how it's done, and that there are two sides.

So I'm obsessed with the educational part of all of this. We've got to do better with educating ourselves and our kids of the countless examples of bipartisan cooperation that led to every good thing that we have in this country. Neither side is going away. We're not going to be—one of the two parties is not going to disappear, so we have no choice but to cooperate with each other and stop villainizing each other. I think the blue, red, purple, all of these colors, they oversimplify all of these political beliefs. They make it seem intractable and unchangeable, how a state could vote.

I can't stand the term *flyover state*; it's just one of the most offensive things I've ever heard. The fact that it persists and you hear rational people say it—it's toweringly offensive. I grew up in what you would call a flyover state, but also grouping all of the complexities of any given state together because at the end of the day, the electoral votes went one way and not the other, is dangerously simplistic. Anything simplified becomes easier to pretend to understand in a few moments. All of that can become dehumanizing and leads to a dark path. If we just assume that we are all purple, that not only within the state you'll find every kind of voter, but in each human there's complexity and convinceability.

The last guy I interviewed at this Hershey rally was wearing a Trump Santa hat that said "Make America Great" on it, and he said every last thing that, normally, a Trump supporter would say about Biden, about the Clintons, but he also revealed that he had voted for Obama twice and even volunteered for him in 2008. That was shocking to me, because he seemed to fit into the stereotype of a Trump voter. But minds change. They can be drawn to one person or cause, and then be drawn to what would seem to be the polar opposite a few years later. I think that should give us all hope, especially in this election. I think Trump's bloc is going to flex and try to get to a vision of a better America.

Wilbur: In terms of changing minds, we've identified that this is a period of terrible data and instant news and flawed echo chambers and so on and so forth. Do you see that there's a purpose for literature in modern politics? What do you think that the role is of the books that you write right now? Do you think that somebody might pick up *The Captain and the Glory* and have their minds changed?

Eggers: There's a role for books. They can get to a level of complexity that the news can't necessarily get at. Books are so valuable to really get at the nuance of the country and tell complicated stories about individuals; we're all worthy of that. Even if we can't do that, we can at least give every human the benefit of the doubt and know that that complexity exists.

We can display all of these colors if we can allow for the fact that we do not know somebody by what they wear or anything like that. It would certainly work to lower the volume and lower the tension. I think that we are becoming more and more judgmental and quick to punish and dismiss in society. Inherently, we're a punitive society. We implicitly support the criminal justice system; that's part of our DNA. But maybe we can alter it to be more empathetic.

Wilbur: Your last book was a children's book called *The Lifters*, which was about finding hope. In the process of writing that, did you burn through all of your optimism for the year?

Eggers: [*laughter*] I think that *Lifters* was based, in part, on a town that I spent some time in, in rural Pennsylvania, a steel town. Pennsylvania's a state that I love and am fascinated by; it's so beautiful and so complex. It's got all of these beautiful little towns that have fallen on hard times, and I thought that that would be a good setting for a story that I already had in mind: kids being tasked with being the only ones who know how to hold up life in a collapsing town. I saw that as only vaguely timely or topical, but obviously there are parallels. I started it before the 2016 election, but it might have been published after and took on a new meaning, as everything does.

But I'm always optimistic, weirdly. Even though I'm outraged and despairing all the time, more than anything I'm bewildered because everyone I met at that rally were good people. I was in line at the parking lot, in the rain, it was about thirty degrees, for three and a half hours. I was just waiting in line, I wasn't sitting in the press pool or anything—

Wilbur: Well, who would sit in the press pool at a Trump rally? That's the splash zone.

Eggers: Yeah, that's a whole other story. So moving among people and chatting and sharing food under umbrellas, everything is calm and there's nobody—these are not rallies of racism and hate. They just aren't. Even though Trump blows a dog whistle and stirs up so much prejudice and hate himself, the people that come to the rallies are families and working people and farmers. People you could talk to, are decent and trustworthy. That's what's so confusing to me: Why would they put their faith in and vote for somebody who is not any of these things?

That's what I was trying to get at here (with *The Captain and the Glory*). You try and take all of these people who coexist on a ship for so long and have respect for each other despite their differences, and suddenly one half of them put control of their lives in the hands of somebody that previously had never been taken seriously, who had just been taking upskirt photos. That's how bizarre it is, and I think that's the sense of betrayal that has bewildered them. So many of us mix every day with everybody from every part of the political spectrum. I think that there's a weird sense that we just can't quite understand how reckless our fellow humans can be with democracy. I despair at that. I don't despair of the essential goodness of the country. We need to self-educate ourselves and our children. It's an incredibly heavy responsibility we have to choose the very best among us. That's the only thing I think we've gotta get right.

Wilbur: Finally, any big memories of your time in Kansas City you'd like to share?

Eggers: A good friend of mine who is the editor of *The Believer* had a great wedding in Kansas City, and we got to explore the city deeper. We had a moment when all of us at *The Believer* and *McSweeney's* came back to San Francisco and were like, "Why don't we move everything to Kansas City?" We'd get more space, there wouldn't be incredibly towering rents that we have living here, and we could start over and maybe occupy one of the beautiful buildings downtown. You still have views and sloping hills, you just have to deal with the snow. The whole staff, ten, fifteen years ago, everybody went to this wedding for a few days. It was too logistically complicated to do that, but I do think that it's a beautiful place. I'm an admirer of that era of downtown architecture that not all cities preserved. Cities like Albany and Buffalo, some towns have still preserved some of their best architecture from the twenties on. I haven't been there in a bit, so maybe I'll head over there.

Anyway, we'll see you guys at the Super Bowl.

Dave Eggers on Trump and the Perception of Truth in Unscripted Lies

Ashlie D. Stevens / 2020

"Any imbecile might decide on a certain Monday to become a captain, and by Tuesday, with no qualifications whatsoever, that imbecile could take charge of a 300,000-ton vessel and the thousands of lives contained within." This statement, one that is so reflective of this time in American history, is made in the opening pages of *The Captain and the Glory*, a new book by author Dave Eggers.

Eggers, who works in multiple genres, from nonfiction to screenplay, turns his gaze toward the Trump administration through this new satirical novel. He writes of a petulant Captain—a man who is quick to toss his opposition overboard, makes nonsensical morning announcements about spiders that typically slip into observations about his penis, and steers the ship and its passengers further and further out to sea.

I spoke with Eggers about his time on the campaign trail in 2016, his experience with Trump supporters and their understanding of truth, and catharsis.

Q: You began covering the Trump era as a journalist back in August 2016. When did you realize in your reporting process that there was an opportunity for a satirical novel like *The Captain and the Glory*?

A: From the beginning, I was sort of toggling between reporting and trying to think of whether there was a way to capture this year, the madness of the time. Because what I keep finding is when I do cover rallies and when I cover immigration issues and the individuals who have been affected adversely by those policies—that kind of work, I think, helps illuminate certain parts of this presidency and shine a light on people and families who have been struggling mightily due to his policies on immigration, asylum, and other related issues; there's something necessary about these individual stories, but they don't always get at the comical absurdity and the horror on a grand scale that I feel we've been going through.

So I just kept fiddling with ways to tell a larger story and capture the cartoonish madness and the loss of all moral compass and sanity. I think plenty of essays and columnists and late-night TV hosts have been doing a good job of reflecting on that every day, but I thought that there might be a spot for an allegory or some sort of parable that kind of put it in stark relief.

I think it was probably three, four months into his presidency when I started fiddling with this. I kept putting it away and then coming back to it, and then finally about maybe eight months ago, I came back to it again and found that it still felt relevant.

I'll continue to cover it as a journalist just because it helps me understand what's happening and it helps me understand the mindset of Trump supporters, but at the same time, I think that there's space for, not just this book, but dozens more that help us see the moment through different lenses—whether it's a horror story, a novel of grand scope, or a short satire. I see value in all those things because we've never quite lived though a moment where we were so confused by our compatriots.

Q: There is this line that has stuck with me: "Because he was unscripted when he told lies—he was the most honest captain they'd ever known." There seems to be this narrative in the media that Trump supporters have had the wool pulled over their eyes when it comes to the veracity of Trump's claims—but when you were speaking with them, were they aware that he was lying?

A: Yes. I really appreciate meeting Trump supporters, because every last one of them I've had a good time talking to, and I found a lot of common ground, and they have had surprisingly nuanced views.

They're very quick to acknowledge his flaws and frailties and fits, even. They don't care though. I think by and large, they're looking at the larger picture about judges on the Supreme Court and circuit courts. They're looking at tighter immigration laws. They're looking at winding down foreign wars. We're looking at economic effects, looking at somebody who is an outsider and isn't, you know, a perceived Washington sellout.

I think, to so many Trump supporters, is that this guy, who they see as a successful billionaire and occupies the White House, is still unvarnished, unscripted, telling it to them straight; and that means that it does not matter if he's telling the truth or a lie. It's telling it to them straight, which I know sounds like it's such a paradox.

If he says, "Iran is building a nuclear program and is threatening to attack four different embassies"—now, if he says that in an unscripted way, not from notes, but in some tough tone, profanity-laced, crude way—that seems more truthful than if he were making some official statement.

For them, candor is something apart from truth and far more important than truth.

Q: So, I've always been really captivated by stories that take place on boats—close quarters and kind of the liminality of being between two docking points. Why did you decide to set this weird, expansive story on a ship?

A: Well, I wanted to see all of the people to be more or less stuck with each other—and on a cruise ship in the middle of the ocean, you really have nowhere to go. You have chosen to be on that ship, living cheek by jowl with all kinds of people, some of whom they have a lot in common with and some of whom they have less in common with, but many have made their peace with their neighbors because they can't just hop out and row away.

And with a parable or an allegory, or even any short story, limiting the cast of characters and limiting the setting, you can sort of get at the core truth of the matter without too much noise or distraction.

I also like the idea of a cruise ship because it's so inherently silly; the thing about a cruise ship is that it's dorky. When you go on a cruise, you are buying into just the incredibly heightened dorkiness of every aspect—the uniforms and the shuffleboard and the pool and the badminton and the Disney characters.

But then because they are in the middle of the sea, you know, what I perceived to be the Pacific Ocean, if someone is thrown overboard, there is kind of a heightened horror. There is no one else to turn to; they're very vulnerable. So, I like that paradox of the silliness and the vulnerability that a cruise ship arrived at, and sometimes if you come across the right setting, the right moment in time, a lot of the writing is done for you.

Q: I'm guessing the subtitle of the book, *An Entertainment*, is a nod to Graham Greene. If so, why did you want to reference his work?

A: The first impetus was I just happen to buy old books at library sales; I just bought six more outside the San Francisco Main Library the other day. I just like old unusual editions and strange covers, and I'll buy books just for the title, and I'll buy them for their craft. I found this old edition of Graham Greene's *The Comedian* that had an interesting cover.

It's not one of his best, but I noticed the subtitle, *An Entertainment*. He had done that in some of his books, but it's hard to tell which books he would apply that to, because it wasn't that they were just the lighter books or the books that would become movies. It could be hard to parse why one would get the designation, but I just happened to read that in the two weeks before *The Captain and the Glory* went to press, and it just seemed right. Obviously the last third of the novel is full of horror and unimaginable suffering and cruelty and it gets very dark, and so with that in mind, giving it this sort of lighthearted subtitle seemed appropriate.

Q: In reading *The Captain and the Glory*, I was carried between all these emotions—humor, horror, sadness. Was that indicative of how you felt during your writing process as you digested some of the real-world events that inspired this novel?

A: Yeah, I think it is. You know, this book definitely comes more from the subconscious, as a lot of fiction does. Journalism, there's just no involvement of the subconscious there, really, because you're doing a service to what you saw, and you're trying to get right the experiences of people that you meet.

I honestly did not outline it. I didn't know what would happen next. I really was just like, letting that sort of natural subconscious storytelling mechanism that we all have take over. And that's why the writing was really cathartic for me, and it wasn't until I finished that I sort of was able to look back, and kind of like you would analyze your dreams look back like, "Hmm, why did I do that?"

And, you know, the other part of the catharsis is being able to finish a narrative, I guess, living in this time where we don't know where it'll end—but being able to write an ending was so therapeutic, even if, you know, falsely comforting for a moment. We do have to write a better story. That was what Obama said as he was leaving office: "We should tell a better story."

A Conversation with Dave Eggers

Scott F. Parker / 2020

Previously unpublished. Printed by permission.

Scott F. Parker: We're conducting this interview over email as the COVID-19 pandemic rages on, and across the country, even the world, people are protesting in response to the killing of George Floyd. I'm curious how you're doing, what you're doing, what you're thinking about during all this.

Dave Eggers: This is my second day out of bed. I'm reasonably sure I had COVID-19 last week, but I'm still waiting on the test results. I woke up last Saturday just feeling wrecked. I went back to bed, and that night my fever hit 102. For the next four days I had fever, chills, migraines, and crippling fatigue. I think I was out of bed about an hour each day; nothing more was possible. But I'm feeling better now, and still curious if it was actually coronavirus. I didn't have the chest pain, loss of smell, or many of the cold/flu symptoms, so it was just as confusing to me as it's been to so many millions. In any case, I feel grateful to be up and about. It's startling how useless your flesh can feel.

The strange thing is that if I got it, I didn't get it when I thought I would. I went to four protests after George Floyd's murder, and in all cases I was in close proximity to thousands of people, all of us yelling for hours. It was astonishing to go from months of total isolation to these explosions of grief and rage, but everyone was very careful, and every single person had a mask on. So it's been incredible to find that tracers have found no real evidence that any protests have spread the virus. The difference was the masks.

Overall, this period has been one of bottomless pain with glimmers of hope. The US is having this essential reckoning on race and police violence, and I have some optimism that it will bring about real change—at least in some states, in some police departments. But we are perhaps chipping away at 5 percent of the problem right now. We next have to address mass incarceration, wrongful incarceration, the lunacy of the death penalty, our collective gun madness, and our generally hyperviolent and hyperpunitive society. It will take years of concerted and focused effort.

SFP: A book for you is not just its text. I think that's safe to say. You take design, layout, material, size, so many things into account. When you make an art object, whether it's a book or something else, what are you trying to do? This question is prompted by the nature of your work, but of course turns pretty abstract: What is art for? What is the meaning, the purpose, the magic? Or maybe it can be narrower this way: How do you think about these things?

DE: I was an art student in college, and have been a graphic designer since high school, so I consider the whole book as an object that needs care and attention—to every page, every stitch. That's been the mission of McSweeney's since the beginning—to make each book a beautiful object almost as a means of survival. There have been so many times in the last twenty years when we were assured that physical books would soon be extinct, so at McSweeney's we thought one way to ensure the survival of the physical would be to make that tactile experience of owning and keeping the book-as-object so pleasurable and superior to the sterile ugliness of e-readers that people would fight to keep physical books alive. It's been nice to see that the e-reader market has hit a (fairly low) ceiling. People do like the look and feel of a real book in their hands.

But to get to your question, What is art for? I had this answered for me yesterday, when I finished reading Emerson Whitney's memoir, *Heaven*. McSweeney's published this book, so it will seem like logrolling to mention it, but I'll say this. The book was acquired and published without any of my say-so—the staff at McSweeney's can publish whatever they wish—so I came to Emerson's book as a regular reader. And the book, to me, was a force of pure light. I read it in two mornings and felt awakened, enlightened, moved profoundly, and inspired to be a better writer, too. The book is about Emerson's childhood, and their troubled but loving mother, and Emerson's journey through gender and trans-ness, but even trying to describe it is reductive and insufficient. In terms of my own reading, there hasn't been a more powerful evocation of childhood since Dorothy Allison's *Bastard Out of Carolina*. As a work of art, *Heaven* is a perfect thing, with no word out of place and with a highly delicate balance of the personal and the political, the private and the universal. Art justifies itself when it's perfect and truthful and alters the chemistry of the reader's mind.

SFP: What is a writer's job these days? Is it something different in this era than it has been in the past?

DE: No, it hasn't changed. Some feel their job is to envision an improved world. Some hope to entertain and thus brighten what can be an existence rife with pain. Some are committed to creating perfect things for their own sake. All are equally valid. Any attempt to say what any artist *should* do is inherently anti-artist. The artist just can't be constrained or compelled—that begins a very dangerous line of thinking that has produced terrifying results in autocracies. I don't mean to go from your innocuous question to Soviet gulags, but we have to always remember that the artist's freedom must be absolute, because art itself must be absolutely free. Otherwise it's not art.

SFP: I guess what I really want to know is, in terms of both your writing and your many other endeavors, what motivates you to do the work you do?

DE: Sometimes it's outrage. A lot of the nonfiction I've written comes from a place of outrage—a profound disappointment in humanity when we fall short of our best selves. But at the same time, the nonfiction is also an attempt to understand something that's been opaque to me (and likely others, too), to illuminate an unseen corner of history or ourselves.

A lot of the work humans do, I think, comes from a need to feel useful. I can live two weeks feeling relatively useless, but if I help someone change a tire, that's the highlight of those two weeks. It's just a fundamental element of human nature—engagement justifies itself and validates our use of the world's oxygen.

Writing fiction can often feel indulgent; sometimes I feel selfish for taking eight hours in the garage to write, say, a funny picture book. But even though that picture book might not feed someone or change legislation, it has its place, too. Emerson Whitney's book, *Heaven*, is educational, but it's also, at the root of it, a personal story. Why tell a personal story? Why create beauty for its own sake? There's no easy answer, but the joy I felt, the awakening I felt, while reading her book, made me very sure about the necessity of art.

SFP: Does that account, at least in part, for how prolific you are?

DE: I really don't consider myself prolific. Most of the things I start I don't finish, and the number of days when I do nothing are too many to count. But at age fifty, you do get a bit closer to knowing how to do whatever you do, so as lazy as I am, there's slightly more likelihood that I'll finish something I begin.

SFP: To what degree do your many other commitments come at the expense of your writing?

DE: It's rare, but it happens. Every so often I'll be on a good streak with a book, and I know I need to continue that streak lest I lose the momentum—but then I have to spend a day in a board meeting. That's a tough day for me.

I can get frustrated, and I think of that Delmore Schwartz title, "In Dreams Begin Responsibilities." But generally I can get the time away when I need it. More than anything, the obstacle is simple procrastination. I should be writing fiction right now, but I'm answering your questions instead. Thank you for the excuse to not-write, and also goddamn you.

SFP: And, to flip that around, how do your other commitments enhance your writing?

DE: There's no direct relationship to my fiction, for example, and the nonprofit work. The wall between them is fairly impenetrable. In a way, they're havens from each other. Working on real solutions in the real world solves some of the uselessness and solitude felt when writing alone in a garage for eight hours a day. And sometimes, after a three-hour board meeting conference call, all I want is to be alone again in that garage.

SFP: How do you allocate your time between writing and other projects?

DE: A writing day is a writing day. No phone, no email, no meetings, no lunches. I need a full eight to twelve hours of nothing time to get any real work done. Even one meeting ruins the day for me, so I try to stack all the outside-world stuff into certain days, so I can leave the writing days alone. Then, during those writing days, when I sit alone in a garage for the better part of ten hours, I get about forty-five minutes of work done. It is a terrible system.

SFP: One of the defining characteristics of your writing is its global concern. How do you think about this aspect of your work in terms of the traditions you belong to as a writer?

DE: I don't know of any traditions I belong to—but am happy to have some suggested to me. I'm from the Midwest, and didn't have a passport until I was twenty-six, so that previous life, lived in a bubble, informs a lot of what I've done since. And when you write a memoir as your first book, for me at least, it's a literary colonic—it gets most or all of your own life out of your system, all at once. So it freed me to look beyond myself.

SFP: What can you say about the role of collaboration in your writing?

DE: The main place where that figures in is with picture books, and the collaborations are wildly fun and full of actual, catapulting delight. When an illustrator like Angel Chang sends me artwork she created in response to my words, it just sends me skyward. There's no better feeling. It's the best kind of call and response.

SFP: Early in your career, you said that writing fiction feels "like driving a car in a clown suit." I assume that is no longer the case. How did it change? What does it feel like now?

DE: I guess I got used to the clown suit. Again, having just read Emerson Whitney's *Heaven*, the blinding power of the first-person memoir is tough to equal. That directness is very powerful and appeals to us because we feel we're being told an unguarded truth without any obfuscation.

That said, fiction can achieve the same thing, though I think it's sometimes more challenging to achieve that emotional power. The hurdle is higher. I have to remind myself of that every day.

SFP: On the whole, your style is much plainer than it was early in your career. What do you attribute this to? What are your ambitions as a stylist?

DE: I would argue that my style has always varied according to the needs of the story. After a few books with more minimal prose, *Heroes of the Frontier* was a return to a denser, more lyrical style—or I thought so, at least. But that book was not read as widely as some of the more stripped-down books . . . *The Circle* is somewhere in between, I think. But in any case, it's funny, because many of the writers I love best are inimitable prose stylists whose every sentence could only be theirs. But to my own surprise, really, I turned out to be less devoted to one style. I have no idea, to be honest, if this is a good thing or not, but I remember noticing the same restlessness, and shapeshifting, in Ishiguro, and that gave me some comfort.

SFP: You often mention reading or rereading *Herzog*. Who/what else do you reread?

DE: Willa Cather's *Shadows on the Rock*. Joan Didion's *Slouching Towards Bethlehem* and *The White Album*. Joseph Heller's *Catch-22*. Ralph Ellison's *Invisible Man*. *Anna Karenina*. I read passages of Camus's notebooks every day—every page has something shatteringly right. Vonnegut's *Slaughterhouse-Five*. Achebe's *Things Fall Apart*. Ishiguro's *The Remains of the Day*. This is just a list off the top of my head that I'll want to amend and correct tomorrow.

SFP: What were the origins of your book *Understanding the Sky*?

DE: I've been interested in flight for a long time, and I've been a bit amazed at how much we take it for granted. For thousands of years, humans have yearned to fly, and now we can fly in myriad small-scale ways, and we don't bother. It's remarkable. We get in planes, sure, and then we close the blinds and watch TV. We're over it. We are a lunatic species.

Anyway, when I was a kid, ultralight flyers became moderately popular, and I always meant to try one. It wasn't until I was about forty when I looked up a place in Petaluma, California, that gives rides on these ultralights—now called trikes. They're a weird hybrid of motorcycle and hang glider. I was so floored by the experience that I tried to recreate it in a book—thus *Understanding the Sky*. I'm pretty sure at least eleven people read it, which in a way sort of proves the point about flight. We've lost our interest in it utterly. But I do recommend it.

SFP: One of the things I appreciate about the conversation you had with Ezra Klein on his podcast is how directly, yet gently, you described the dangers of our constant connectivity. Do you notice our mass addiction to devices affecting writing?

DE: I actually don't know if it's affected anyone's writing lately. Years ago, I had a few friends say they had to choose between tweeting and writing, for example, but I think those people are perhaps anomalous. It seems, to some extent at least, people find a balance. Or they try to. I do know that whenever I ask a roomful of people, "How many of you have a perfect balance between life and technology?" no one—ever—raises their hand. This surely is unprecedented in human history, that there are devices that everyone has, that everyone feels they can't do without, but with which they have an uneasy, unsure, unsettled, and even untrusting relationship. But we keep them on our person at all times.

That said, I think the younger people are dealing with the balance better in many cases. As a kid, I did my homework in front of the TV, which was on eighteen hours a day in my house. Somehow I managed a balance. Young people are like that today—they still manage to write brilliantly, create new things, read four thousand pages of the Harry Potter series, and more books are written every month than used to be written in a decade. I feel we will be okay.

Index

About the Editor

Credit: Alyssa Henry

Scott F. Parker is the author of *Being on the Oregon Coast* and *A Way Home: Oregon Essays,* as well as the editor of *Conversations with Joan Didion* and *Conversations with Ken Kesey,* among other books. He teaches writing at Montana State University.

Printed in the United States
by Baker & Taylor Publisher Services